Along
the Way

Along the Way

CONVERSATIONS ABOUT CHILDREN AND FAITH

RON BRUNER &
DANA KENNAMER PEMBERTON,

Editors

Abilene Christian University Press

ALONG THE WAY

Conversations About Children and Faith

ACU
PRESS

Cover design by Greg Jackson, Thinkpen Design, LLC
Interior text design by Sandy Armstrong

For information contact:

Abilene Christian University Press
ACU Box 29138
Abilene, Texas 79699

1-877-816-4455
www.acupressbooks.com

Table of Contents

Section One
Catching up with the Conversation

1 *An Invitation to a Conversation* 9
Ron Bruner and Dana Kennamer Pemberton

2 *The Story of Why We Believe What We Believe
About Children and Faith* 17
Ron Bruner

3 *Understanding Childhood Spirituality* 31
Steven Bonner

Section Two
Children at Home

4 *Living Deuteronomy 6: Parenting as a Spiritual Discipline* 47
Ron Bruner

5 *Reading and Living the Bible with Children* 61
Samjung Kang-Hamilton

6 *Praying Alongside Our Children* 77
Samjung Kang-Hamilton

Section Three
Children and the Faith Community

7 *Reshaping the Church into an Intergenerational Body* 95
Holly Catterton Allen

8 *Communion: A Table without Boundaries* 111
Nathan Pickard

9 *Baptism and Children: Finding Good Instincts* 125
Jeff W. Childers

10 *Baptism and Children: Finding Sound Practices* 141
Jeff W. Childers

Section Four
Our Children's Ministries

11 *Ministry with Children: Partnerships with Purpose* 159
    Ryan Maloney

12 *Respect the Text and Respect the Children:*
    Reconsidering Our Approaches to Bible School 175
    Dana Kennamer Pemberton

13 *Practicing Spiritual Disciplines with Children* 191
    Suzetta Nutt

14 *Children Serving and Proclaiming Christ:*
    Joining the Mission of the Church 207
    Shannon Rains

15 *Holy Hospitality: Following the Call of Jesus to*
    Welcome ALL Children 219
    Dana Kennamer Pemberton

Contributor Biographies 235
For Further Reading 239
Endnotes 243

Section One

Catching up with the Conversation

Chapter 1

An Invitation to a Conversation

From Ron Bruner and Dana Pemberton

*Good communication is as stimulating as
black coffee and just as hard to sleep after.*

Anne Morrow Lindbergh

What is reading, but silent conversation.

Charles Lamb

Dana: Please accept our invitation to join a conversation. We wish that we could just get a cup of coffee and sit down to chat with you! Perhaps someday we will sit together, talk and breathe the same air, but for now words on a page will have to suffice. There are discussions about countless issues going on in this world, including person-to-person dialogues in coffee shops and living rooms as well as exchanges through media like blogs and Facebook. Although we enjoy some of those conversations ourselves, we believe that some of these interactions are more important and inherently life changing than others.

    Ron: When the conversation turns to children, and especially to children and faith, we're all in. We don't know of a topic more vital to families, to churches, or to humanity itself, than that of children and their relationship with God. We've found that there are many open questions about children and their faith, sometimes because existing answers are totally inadequate for our current context and at times because no one has ever seriously addressed those questions in print. So there are two driving forces behind the dialogue about children and faith in this book: first, the belief that the faith of children is of central importance and second, the concern that we still have substantial work to do to adequately answer many important questions connecting children and faith.

Dana: Ron and I have been enjoying conversations about children and faith for many years now. We have dialogued about this subject with a growing network of friends in places as diverse as teacher's workrooms, church building foyers, and college classrooms. We have talked with groups at varied events including workshops, seminars, graduate classes, and conferences for scholars. Those discussions have covered a broad range of topics connected with children and faith: resources for teachers, recruiting volunteers, developmental realities, special needs, spiritual formation, and the theology of children. Over the years we have learned much from our friends in these passionate conversations about children and their faith.

Ron: Because that dialogue has been so helpful to our lives and in our work with children, we've decided to share the fruit of that discussion. We've invited eight of our friends—Holly, Jeff, Nathan, Ryan, Samjung, Shannon, Steven, and Suzetta—to join us in a more public conversation that takes shape in this book. In these pages we share what we have learned in our dialogues, consider the possibilities for many questions that are still open, and invite you, our readers, into a conversation where you can work with us to find answers that are suited for your children and your community. After all, we believe that each child is unique and each family and church are distinctive contexts; there is no one right answer for all children in all places. However, we believe that Christians should be more knowledgeable about children and more motivated to seek their best interests than any other people on the planet.

Dana: It's important that you, our readers, understand that we've invited friends into this conversation who are experienced in ministering with children and youth. They have served in classrooms, homes, church camps, and church vans to work alongside children in the formation of their faith. All of our friends share the concerns that other parents have about their own kids; each has enjoyed the blessings that come from working alongside the children of those in their church family. Some of us are grandparents and well understand that a godly love for children and concern about their spiritual formation remains a serious life-long interest.

Ron: Though grounded in years of rich experience, this book is also rooted in careful scholarship and research. The friends joining us in this conversation often have significant scholarly credentials to go with their years of practice. They've done their homework, and many of them have spoken or written in scholarly environments about children and faith. Though each page is informed by serious scholarship, we promise to keep the conversation in this book in clear and practical language that we hope all Christians will find useful.

Dana: For those from other faith traditions, please understand that I know that many of us are exploring the same questions and facing the same challenges as we work within our churches to share God's story so that it will be formed in the next generation. I have had many opportunities to share in conversations with children's pastors and volunteers across the country from many different traditions. You have challenged me, taught me, and affirmed me. We have laughed together, learned together, cried together and prayed together. So I am so glad that you have joined us in the pages of this book. Welcome!

Ron: Everyone is invited to this conversation, yet we want those who join in to understand that our dialogue is rooted in the perspective of a particular faith group: churches that have emerged from the Stone-Campbell Restoration Movement (SCM), specifically: Churches of Christ (*a cappella*), the Christian Church (independent), and the Disciples of Christ. The discussion in this book comes from a group of friends all of whom have come from and worship with the Churches of Christ, but we expect that it will be very accessible to others, particularly those in the SCM.

Dana: This book was written by a group of practitioners and scholars from the Churches of Christ who care deeply about the spiritual formation of children in our faith tradition. We share a rich history—with its own strengths and struggles—that has shaped our personal faith and our communal practices. So this book is, in some ways, a family conversation. "We" wanted to have a talk with those who share our particular heritage within the larger community of faith.

Ron: We have compelling reasons for inviting people with differing perspectives into this dialogue. We celebrate the fact that so many congregations among the Churches of Christ have begun to devote significant effort and resources to children's ministry. We think it wise that so many churches have called ministers to full-time work with children. One of our concerns is that we've begun to practice children's ministry before we've clearly defined *what* it is that a children's minister is to do and *how* they ought to do it. God has provided the opportunity for us to pursue those questions from multiple perspectives. Some children's ministers come to their work with ministry and theological savvy, others come from an educational background. Instead of differing viewpoints representing an inherently hopeless conflict, this is an opportunity for healthy dialogue and learning. As someone interested in practical theology, I am sometimes concerned that my "excellent" theological ideas might actually fly in the face of what any teacher knows to be good educational practice. Friends like Dana who have a different background and perspective can redirect my thinking and my practice if I misstep.

Dana: I come to the conversation with a blend of perspectives. As a professor in teacher preparation and former schoolteacher, my practices with children are informed by what I know about development, learning, differentiation and positive behavior support. Even in the context of the college classroom, as a Christian educator I evaluate my practices through a theological lens. I believe that our practices with children—in schools or churches—should be chosen not because they "work," but because they are consistent with what we believe. Our practices are not neutral. Within every educational approach is embedded a theory. In our churches, this means that we must ask the question of theology as well. Do our practices and our theology align?

Ron: Theology, education, psychology, and sociology are all vibrant disciplines; human beings are making new discoveries in these fields every day. Since it's challenging enough to keep up with one discipline, the idea of being multi-lingual in all of these areas of study is unrealistic. That's why it is essential to have friendly conversations between those who know these disciplines well—they can tell us where our perspectives ring true to their study or where our ideas are dissonant. For example, as theologians work on a theology of children, they are wise if they listen to the voices of others. A developmental psychologist can speak to the ability of a child to understand certain concepts. An educator can describe the ways that children learn through social processes.

Dana: We bring these and other disciplines together in conversation in four sections of this book (1) Catching up with the Conversation, (2) Children at Home, (3) Children and the Faith Community, (4) Our Children's Ministries

Ron: Parents, ministry volunteers, and church leaders confront many important questions about children. Let's take a look at some of these questions and see how this book approaches them.

Historically, how have those in Churches of Christ ministered to children? What is the relationship of children to the church? What are our historical theological commitments? These are questions that Ron Bruner takes up in Chapter Two. He revisits the Stone-Campbell story to discover how our unique history has shaped our theology of children.

Are all children spiritual, or do they have to learn how to be spiritual? Are they born with a connection to God, or do we have to provide that connection for them? In Chapter Three Steven Bonner helps us understand the inherent spiritual nature of children and the role of parents in nurturing that spirituality.

What are my responsibilities for the spiritual care of my own children? How can parents help children shape a faith that remains resilient in this world? Ron picks up his pen again to pursue these questions in Chapter Four. Using Deuteronomy 6 as a framework, he explores ways that parenting for faith is a spiritual discipline.

How do I share God's word with my children and teach them to pray in meaningful ways? Samjung Kang-Hamilton offers practical insights in Chapters Five and Six as a parent who has raised children in faith, intentionally teaching them the biblical story and engaging as a family in meaningful prayer.

If children are truly a part of the Body of Christ, how do we include them in the congregational life of the church? In Chapter Seven, Holly Catterton Allen challenges us to reconsider our common age-segregated practices. From her experience in an intergenerational congregation, Holly gives us clues for how we might truly welcome children as full participants in the faith community.

What do we do when a child wants to take communion? Is the Lord's Supper only for those who have been baptized? What does this practice say about our church? Nathan Pickard struggled with these questions on a personal level, studied the question deeply, and proposes new perspectives for us to consider in Chapter Eight.

In the Churches of Christ, we believe in the essentiality of baptism. But do we know what we really believe? Do our instincts guide us well when our children approach us with questions about baptism? In Chapter Nine, Jeff Childers guides us through Scripture to discover a richer understanding of the meaning of baptism. In Chapter Ten, he continues the conversation, offering suggestions for sound practices that flow out of a more coherent view of salvation and children raised in the church.

Do we always minister to children or, as they grow, do they move toward an ability to minister with us? How does ministry alongside the church form children spiritually? In Chapter Eleven, Ryan Maloney describes the move from ministry *to* and *for* children toward ministry *with* children. He reminds us that the church ministers better when children minister with us.

What do we want to accomplish in our Bible classes for children? What can children understand? Are we really teaching them what we think we are teaching them? What do our curriculum approaches say we believe about children and the word? In Chapter Twelve, Dana Pemberton challenges us to reconsider our approaches to Bible school, evaluating whether our methods are consistent with our beliefs.

Can children learn to be still before the Lord? Can they meaningfully practice the spiritual disciplines of silence, prayer and contemplation? In Chapter Thirteen, Suzetta Nutt takes us on her journey with children as they learned to practice spiritual disciplines together.

What is the role of children in serving a hurting world? Should they be protected from pain in the world, or should they join God's people in compassionate service for those who are hurting? In Chapter Fourteen, Shannon Rains explores ways the mentoring of children in compassionate service is essential to their spiritual formation. She reminds us that children can also lead us to reach out to others in ways adults might have missed.

What do we do with children who do not fit—who might make us uncomfortable or even frighten us? Do our beliefs about children place barriers in our way when confronted by these children? How should we change our perspectives and find ways to offer true hospitality to all children? In Chapter Fifteen, Dana Pemberton challenges us to consider practices and perspectives that are unwelcoming to children whose differences challenge us. She provides guiding principles to extend the hospitality of Jesus to all children.

We do not assume to have all the answers. In fact, we often discovered new questions as we explored these topics together and in our individual work. Our hope is that this book will start conversations in your faith community and in our fellowship as a whole. These dialogues will require careful listening and godly grace. You may not agree with all you read here. In fact, the authors hold diverse opinions about some of the topics in this book. Still, it is time to think seriously about the call to welcome children—to engage in serious communal discernment as we seek to nurture them in faith. We cannot let our personal discomfort keep us from asking hard questions and seeking the path God would have us take, whether that involves change or renewed commitment to long-held beliefs and practices. Remember that we are people of the Restoration Movement and restoration is always ongoing. Thank you for joining us along the way.

Chapter 2

The Story of Why We Believe What We Believe About Children and Faith

Ron Bruner

There's an old saying about those who forget history.
I don't remember it, but it's good.

Stephen Colbert

Saying what we think gives us a wider conversational range
than saying what we know.

Cullen Hightower

The true spirit of conversation consists in building on
another [person's] observation, not overturning it.

Edward G. Bulwer-Lytton

Our conversation about children and faith begins by taking our bearings. We are actually joining a conversation that has been going on for quite some time now. Before speaking up, we need to understand where we are in the dialogue, and find out how we got here. Fortunately, the conversation about children within the Churches of Christ is a unique story that is well documented. So, for those of us who are a part of the Churches of Christ and for our friends who are listening in on our conversation, we will retell that narrative.[1]

Every faith family converses with a unique view of the universe in mind; each has a distinctive theology that shapes its practice and history. They shape their theology—their view of God and spiritual things—by bringing different kinds of authority into dialogue: interpretations of the biblical text, the writing and practice of Christians who have gone before, their own human experience, and logic. Different faith groups value varying sources of authority to differing degrees. Conversations in the Churches of Christ have long tended to stress the overwhelming authority of Scripture and the use of logic in reading it. That has become part of our spiritual DNA. The purpose behind these choices was noble: the restoration of a unified church.

A cappella Churches of Christ are one strand of what has come to be known as the Stone-Campbell Restoration Movement (SCM). Early leaders of the SCM believed that reestablishing unity among all those who called themselves Christians was a goal of the highest importance. In order to do this, they believed that a restoration of the first-century church, a church that *was* essentially united, would empower modern Christians to reestablish unity. They believed that this restoration could be accomplished by a careful, common sense reading of the biblical text. Knowledge of history was also useful; one might peel back the layers of history and tradition to discern where the church had departed from the biblical standard. For several generations, those in the SCM were somewhat successful in uniting people of differing backgrounds. Eventually, though, the SCM itself became three separate faith groups: the Disciples of Christ, the Christian Church/ Churches of Christ, and *a cappella* Churches of Christ.

The Search for a First-Century Perspective of Children

The Campbells and Baptism

Alexander Campbell and his father, Thomas, became a part of the SCM as it emerged and were key figures in shaping it. While serving a congregation in Washington, Pennsylvania, in 1809, denominational authorities censured Thomas for his open fellowship of believers with a different doctrinal perspective. Thomas felt that this ruling supported human creeds in place of divinely inspired Scripture. As a result, Thomas wrote the *Declaration and Address* as a plea for religious unity. Modeled after the *Declaration of Independence*, the *Declaration and Address* called Christians to read Scripture in a particular way and to prefer Scripture over creedal statements. Thomas hoped this approach would unify conflicting factions of Christians by restoring a primitive, first-century form of Christianity, a hope that became one of the core beliefs of Churches of Christ.

Not long after writing the *Declaration and Address*, the Campbells discovered that this document would indeed require them to re-examine their faith. At Abraham Altar's farm in 1809, Thomas observed that "where the Scriptures speak, we speak; and where the Scriptures are silent, we are silent." After some silence, Andrew Munro replied, "Mr. Campbell, if we adopt *that* as a basis, then there is an end of infant baptism." This upset several. Thomas, though, was in no hurry to stop a practice that these families had followed for generations. He felt that each family should decide whether they would practice infant baptism.[2] Gradually, though, his son Alexander found no biblical support for infant baptism and decided to treat it as he believed the early church dealt with circumcision:

> We look at baptism now in nearly the same point of view in
> which the primitive Church looked at circumcision, and con-
> sider the cases, if not altogether yet nearly parallel; so far so, that
> we must either forbear or otherwise reject a great number of
> God's dear children without his special warrant, if not in express
> violation of his Divine commands: "Him that is weak in the faith
> receive ye."[3]

In subsequent weeks, though, other matters occupied the Campbells' attention.

In 1811 Alexander married Margaret Brown. Together they served the Brush Run church near Bethany, West Virginia.[4] A year later their first child, Jane, was born. Jane proved to be a significant disruption in the spiritual story of the Campbell clan.[5]

Though the Brown and Campbell families had Presbyterian roots and followed the tradition of baptizing their infant children, Alexander questioned whether he ought to do this. He searched his Bible and scholarship for answers: "Who should be baptized, and why?" After three months of study, Alexander had peeled back layers of history to find his answer: only those old enough to sustain their own belief in God should be baptized. He understood that Scripture neither authorized infant baptism nor reported the apostles baptizing babies. Though baptized as an infant, Alexander now believed that baptism to be incorrect; he was baptized again as an adult believer.[6] On June 12, 1812, Matthias Luce immersed the adult Campbells in the deep pool at Buffalo Creek,[7] despite Thomas's concern that emphasis on baptism would disrupt hopes for Christian union.[8] Years would pass before Jane would grow up and choose baptism for herself.

Campbell's reading of Scripture continued to shift. When he wrote the book *Christian Baptism* in 1851, Campbell believed that infant baptism was more than mistaken; he found it, in the unrestrained language of his day, a "profane tenet"[9] and a "manifold evil."[10]

Royal Humbert explains why Alexander rejected infant baptism: (1) historically, it had made every child an involuntary member of a state church, (2) infant baptism brought persecution to those who didn't practice it, (3) it robbed children of responsibility and choice in their spiritual life, (4) infant baptism was not the New Testament equivalent of circumcision, but (5) it was what Campbell called "a post-apostolic and Roman Catholic rite."[11] For Campbell this meant that infant baptism was neither a practice of the primitive church nor one with biblical precedent.

Election

Alexander faulted the theology of children in other groups as well. He considered the Calvinistic doctrine of election to misunderstand the biblical text, keeping parents from appreciating the spiritual status of their children. In an attempt to uphold the absolute sovereignty of God, Calvinists claimed that God had chosen from eternity the fate, saved or condemned, of every human being. This doctrine caused grief for the parents of children dying in childhood that can hardly be overstated. Parents worried; could God have chosen their dying child to be among the lost, and once dead, would that child be lost to them forever? This doctrine, together with the high childhood mortality rate in the 1800s, led to tragedies that remain heartbreaking.

In 1814, "Raccoon" John Smith moved with his wife, their four children, and his young brother-in-law to a cabin in Hickory Flats, Kentucky, where he preached for several neighboring Baptist congregations.[12] The following January, Smith left to preach at a congregation about 20 miles away, leaving his wife, Anna, in charge of the farm. That evening a dying neighbor called Anna to her bedside, so she left her brother Hiram to watch her sleeping children. At about 10 o'clock, fire engulfed their home and burned it to the ground. Hiram and the two younger children escaped, but the Smiths' older boy and girl died in the flames. Messengers raced to bring Smith home. On the way home, his Calvinist perspective darkened his thoughts:

> He tried to borrow support from religion, and to find, in the promises of Scripture, solace for his wife. But the thought that, perhaps, his children had passed through the flames of their burning home only to writhe forever in the still fiercer flames of another world, sent a keen agony through his soul . . . "I can give her no consolation . . . If I tell her that our babies are glorified, the thought that possibly they were of the non-elect will only aggravate her woe." His own faith was bewildered by this thought, which haunted him like an evil specter as he rode along. He tried to persuade himself that non-elect persons do not die in infancy; but his mind would not accept the subterfuge. He dreaded, therefore, to meet his wife's look of anguish, and to hear her ask the question, "Are our children among the elect of God?"[13]

Smith's fears were the logical result of the Calvinist doctrine of election. His concerns about Anna's feelings didn't last long; shortly after rebuilding their home, she died and was buried next to her two children.[14]

As Smith passed his thirtieth birthday, he continued to study the doctrine of election through Scripture and the written work of Alexander Campbell. Campbell rejected the doctrine of election because "it is no gospel to proclaim, that 'God from all eternity elected a few individuals to everlasting life . . . "'[15] Even though he was raised to believe this, he was "from the apostolic writings alone, convinced, that to teach, preach, or proclaim such a system, is not to teach, preach, or proclaim the gospel I find in the New Testament."[16] What did Campbell offer instead? "God . . . has in sincerity called men to look to his Son and be saved, and given the fullest assurance that whosoever will, may, can and ought to come to him and be saved; and that all that disobey this call have no excuse for their sin."[17] After careful study and consideration of Campbell's writing, Smith changed his thinking. He came to see that Calvinism was wrong its assertion that the fall of Adam, the "moral death" of humanity, had resulted in the loss of human free will. A completely sovereign God created human free will and has not taken it away. A Christian, supposedly dead to sin, can still choose to sin; a sinner, dead to righteousness, can still do right. Therefore, God does not elect a limited number of individuals to salvation but elects a chosen people, of which humans can choose to be a part.[18]

Original Sin

Most of Campbell's contemporaries believed that the guilt of the first sin, original sin, passed from Adam and Eve through parents to every child at birth. The two most common responses to the idea of original sin were that: (1) all infants should be baptized at once to remove that stain, or (2) all children stood in spiritual jeopardy until such a time as they experienced conversion. Neither was acceptable to Campbell. He also might have defended the innocence of children, but instead chose a more complex solution.

Campbell did sometimes use the word "innocence," but not as a term for a spiritual condition. Children too young to have a knowledge of good and evil could be innocent of "actual and personal transgression," yet still be counted a "sinner by Him who inflicts upon them the peculiar and appropriate wages of sin."[19]

> There is, therefore, a sin of our nature as well as personal
> transgression. Some inappositely call the sin of our nature our

'original sin,' as if the sin of Adam was the personal offence of
all his children. True, indeed it is; our nature was corrupted by
the fall of Adam before it was transmitted to us; and hence that
hereditary imbecility to do good and that proneness to do evil,
so universally apparent in all human beings.[20]

Despite this struggle with a sinful nature, Campbell didn't believe that
children were in spiritual danger. Instead, he: (1) distinguished between
sin inherited from Adam and personally committed sin, and (2) suggested
that the action of the second Adam, Jesus Christ, protected children.
Campbell argued,

Because of the interposition of the second Adam, none are pun-
ished with everlasting destruction from the presence of the Lord
but those who actually and voluntarily sin against a dispensation
of mercy under which they are placed: for this is the "condemnation of the world, that light has come into the world, and men
choose darkness rather than the light, because their deeds are evil."[21]

This doctrine, based on Romans 5, became a part of the American religious
climate through the Puritans.[22] Exactly how this "interposition" works,
though, Campbell never made clear.

Conversion

These shifts in thinking resulted in a conversion process affecting generations of children growing up in SCM churches. At first, belief and baptism
were the requirements.[23] Later, in dialogue with the Campbells, Walter
Scott constructed the "five-finger exercise," a tool designed to teach children how to obey God.[24] The five-finger exercise actually had six points:
"belief, repentance, immersion, forgiveness, the gift of the Holy Spirit, and
eternal life;" the sixth point being held in the palm of the hand.[25] This
eventually became the five step "plan of salvation" practiced by Churches
of Christ: hear, believe, repent, confess, and be baptized.[26] The shift from
the subjective camp meeting conversion experience to a definite, visible

process signaled a dramatic shift in the SCM understanding of children and salvation.

The work of the Campbells established a basic, yet incomplete theology of children. Children are viewed through the twin paradox of being innocent but yet still sinners, and no guidance is given about an appropriate age at which a child might embrace baptism. Their contribution to the conversation, though, brings promising ideas on which to build: believers baptism, the election of all to salvation (with the possibility of disobedience by many), and the rejection of original sin.

J. W. McGarvey

In 1864 near the end of Alexander Campbell's life, J. W. McGarvey wrote an article for Campbell's paper, the *Millennial Harbinger,* that delineated how God saves children. Entitled "Religious Duties of Children" McGarvey asserted: "it is now well understood in the religious world, that before infants arrive at years of moral accountability, their eternal welfare is not endangered." [27] At some later point in time, it becomes necessary for children to yield "positive obedience" to the gospel. That age, warns McGarvey, "is somewhat difficult to determine, and the question is a very perplexing one to conscientious parents." There is no precise age for obedience; children must display not just a knowledge of the facts, but also sufficient moral development. He proposed three tests by which the careful Christian parent can discern a child's readiness for baptism: (1) an understanding of the design of both the Lord's Supper and baptism, (2) an understanding of the "obligations imposed" by both of these rites, and (3) "a strength of purpose sufficient to maintain a religious course of conduct with some consistency." [28]

The problem, McGarvey noted, is that even though born innocent, children appear to engage in sinful conduct before becoming old enough to meet these three tests and receive baptism as a means of forgiveness. How are they to deal with their sin until then? McGarvey suggests that there are three essential "conditions of pardon in the gospel scheme." They are: faith, repentance, and immersion. Although some children are not yet ready for baptism because they do not meet the three tests mentioned above, they can still believe in the power of God to forgive their sins and choose to repent of them. "If, then, the child can believe with all its little heart, and repent of all its known sins, who shall say that this is not its duty?"

Parents should, he cautioned, teach children to do their spiritual duty, lest they send any child "into the presence of a God it has not learned to love, defiled with little sins of which it has not repented." McGarvey spoke from experience:

> It has been my lot to have one such little one torn from the very
> centre of my heart, and borne to the silent land; but her dying
> lips bore witness that she loved the Savior; and for years before,
> her nightly prayers and the tear of penitence which sometimes
> glistened in her eye, bore witness that she was being brought
> up in the instruction and discipline of the Lord. I have had no
> higher honor, though I have had no deeper sorrow, such is the
> weakness of my soul, than to commit such a child to the keeping
> of him whom she knew and loved so well.

McGarvey didn't question God's acceptance of his child. Repentance and prayers for forgiveness kept childish sins from disrupting this girl's relationship with God. McGarvey clearly expected to see her again in heaven.

McGarvey enters the conversation by responding to some gaps left in Campbell's theology of children: (1) how do we know when a child is ready for baptism, and (2) how do parents cope with the wrong-doing of their children? His suggestions about readiness for baptism are grounded in common sense. Although his concept of faith and confession for childhood misbehavior are commendable, McGarvey leaves the conversation, as did Campbell, without rooting this aspect of his beliefs in any authoritative texts.

T. W. Brents

As the SCM progressed, certain doctrines became more fixed. Milligan's 1868 *Scheme of Redemption*, for example, faithfully echoed Campbell's teaching about children.[29] Another important book defining doctrinal boundaries was T. W. Brents' 1874 *The Gospel Plan of Salvation*.[30] Brents describes conversion as a four-step process: faith, repentance, confession, and baptism.[31] In the chapter "Who Should Be Baptized?" Brents addresses infant baptism and describes a way of reading Scripture (familiar to many in Churches of Christ) to evaluate it:

> We know of but three ways by which the practice of infant baptism could be taught in the Divine Volume, First: By the express command of the Lord, or some one speaking by inspiration. Second: By example; i.e., where the Lord or some inspired man, baptized infants, or where it was done in his presence, by his consent or approval. Third: By a passage of Scripture from which the baptism of infants is a *necessary inference*. A merely *possible* inference is not sufficient, for while a thing is only *possibly true*, it is still *possible* for it to be *false*.[32]

Consistent with Campbell, Brents neither believed infant baptism to be biblical, nor children to be members of the church.[33] In his view, children carried neither the burden of original sin nor the guilt of any sin themselves; Brents abbreviated the spiritual status of children to a simpler concept: innocence.[34] At the same time, he didn't consider children to be a part of the church.[35] How did Brents advise parents to see to their children's salvation? "Be baptized yourself; you cannot obey God for your children; but you can bring them up in the nurture and admonition of the Lord, and when they are old enough to understand the Lord's will, you will have the consolation of seeing them obey it for themselves."[36] After Brents, there was no significant development in thinking about the theology of children in the Churches of Christ until over a century later.

Moving from the Twentieth to the Twenty-first Century

Everett Ferguson

A scholar with a distinguished career in the study of the ancient world, Everett Ferguson's contribution to the conversation was to give the church an accurate view of its first-century self. He entered the centuries-old discussion on infant baptism with articles and sections of his books.[37] In his 1996 book, *The Church of Christ*, he discusses the theology of children. Ferguson concisely defends the classic position of Churches of Christ: (1) infant baptism finds no support in Scripture or early church history, (2) the practice of infant baptism preceded the emergence of the doctrine of original sin, (3) consequently, original sin provides no "theological support" for infant baptism, (4) children are innocent, (5) the child of a Christian "grows up in holiness," which brings a believers' child into a relationship with God not experienced by children of unbelievers.[38] Ferguson acknowledges, though, that his view, and that of the Churches of Christ, is incomplete because "the theology of the child is little developed in churches that practice believers' baptism."[39]

Jerry and Becky Gross

After several generations, some began to question the theology of children within the Churches of Christ. Jerry and Becky Gross challenged the concept of the "age of accountability." Unable to locate the concept's origin, they assert that it is not a biblical term, but a Protestant idea predating the SCM, a theological term with no precise definition.[40] As a "controlling concept," they argue that it focuses on baptism and a narrow period of life: from ten to thirteen years of age. Also, they suggest that designating an age for spiritual accountability confuses the relationship between the church and children who have yet to reach that age—are they participants or observers? The concept of accountability also minimizes the wrongdoing of children and exaggerates their innocence. By asserting that children are not yet accountable agents in this world, they are prohibited from positive participation in the life of the community as persons with gifts and responsibilities. Additionally, this concept prioritizes rules of the community over relationships among the community, unfortunately marking baptism as the legally mandated completion of individual spiritual transformation and not as an irreplaceable rite of passage on a path of spiritual growth within a community.

For the Grosses, the better question is not, "When are children accountable," but, "How do parents and the church nurture faith throughout life?"

From a "faith development" perspective, baptism happens in the natural course of events. Because spiritual growth is a life-long process, all ages are important. Faith development focuses more on relationship skills than external rules and facts. After all, if Christianity requires an exclusively Christian environment for Christians to behave appropriately, what kind of faith is it? Instead, faith ought to empower truth to serve people, instead of valuing truth more than souls.

Tommy King

Tommy King attended to some gaps in the theology of children among Churches of Christ in his 1994 Doctor of Ministry thesis, *Faith Decisions: Christian Initiation for Children of the Glenwood Church of Christ*.[41] King's reading of scripture on the spiritual condition of children is similar to that of a Mennonite theologian, Marlin Jeschke.[42] Neither believes that children born "in the church" must ever be separated from it. Children are part of the kingdom and need to be treated as such. Even children not "born into the church" are adopted as a part of the spiritual family. Noting the historical tendency in Churches of Christ to exclude unbaptized children from the kingdom, King asserts that:

> The reluctance to assign kingdom status to children could lie in a tendency to identify the kingdom with the church. If the church is synonymous with the kingdom, then all members of the kingdom would be members of the church as well. Such a view limits the boundaries of the kingdom of God. Rather than simply stating that the church is the kingdom, it is more accurate to describe the church as existing within the kingdom of God. Certainly the kingdom is larger than the earthly church. The boundaries of the kingdom encompass the heavenly beings known as angels, cherubim, and seraphim as well as the great cloud of witnesses who have gone before (Heb. 12). The boundaries of the kingdom also encompass the church, which is composed of those who are justified, cleansed from sins,

participators in Christ and the Spirit. The boundaries of the kingdom encompass children.[43]

King agrees with McGarvey that the kingdom has larger borders than those of the church—he also brings children within those borders.

King questions whether children growing up within the church can really experience a "crisis conversion" like that associated with revivalist preaching.[44] Since they do not appear to have grievous sin in their lives and meet with the church family or their youth group regularly, from what evil lifestyle are they converting? King asserts that it is not only possible, but *preferable*, that children in the church avoid a crisis conversion. Those youth will experience a gradual transformation as they choose to have a faith of their own.

Where Do We Go from Here?

In each of the chapters that follow, our conversation partners will seek to move this conversation forward. Many of us will find statements in these pages that we can wholly endorse; we may possibly find others with which we would disagree. We should remember, though, that we cannot have a conversation without diverse perspectives and differing opinions. Someone has to start the conversation. Those who follow should respect their courage in speaking first. The early church was able to maintain unity despite the differences in how they understood faith, not because everyone agreed. Communal discernment is a Christian spiritual practice precisely because Christians in the real world will read life situations differently and propose different plans of action to deal with those situations. It should be a part of our character as Christians to be able to work through these disagreements in a godly and peaceable way.

Questions about children and faith often raise emotional issues; the precious souls of children are at stake, after all. Those natural feelings have spurred leaders in Churches of Christ to seek biblical and practical solutions to the spiritual needs of children. After an initial flurry of development, that theology remained static for nearly a century and a half. However, since the

1990s, parents, ministers, and scholars within our faith family have begun to re-evaluate the matrix of beliefs that make up our incomplete theology of children. This book will seek to continue the dialogue by answering some of the questions about children and faith that remain open. The conversations in the book are not meant to be the final answer, though; instead we intend to start vital conversations about our beliefs that we hope will lead to an ongoing dialogue and a theology of children that is biblical, sensible, broad, flexible, and durable.

Chapter 3

Understanding Childhood Spirituality

Steven Bonner

I am the proud father of three children, the youngest of whom just turned eleven. Recently we received news that one of our dear elderly friends from church had been transported to the local heart hospital. At that point, we didn't really know the extent of his condition. As my wife and I got ready to visit him in the hospital, I asked my eleven-year old daughter to get her brother. We shared the news with our kids and then suggested we gather for prayer. I asked my daughter to lead us, which she was eager to do. Standing there, eyes closed and hands clasped, my daughter offered the most beautiful and heartfelt prayer. Tears came quickly as concern for our elderly friend was lifted to God.

As I reflected on this simple yet thoughtful event, I have been reminded of the spiritual insight of children. Through her simple prayer, my daughter demonstrated with words and emotions not only care for her elderly friend, but a deep and meaningful connection to God. Through child-like faith she asked for protection and recovery of health. She boldly called upon God to take care of her friend. There was no hesitation. There was no doubt, just bold unadulterated faith. With her petition voiced, she closed the prayer *"in Jesus' name"* and we all said, "Amen." She voiced a hope that her family and extended church family have modeled for her. She demonstrated for me what has become a foundational reality as I grow in my understanding of children's spiritual formation: children are spiritual meaning makers from birth. They have the capacity to know God and sense God's very presence and as such, ought to be active participants in the community of faith.

Coming to terms with the spiritual capabilities of children has taken some time. Through my own children, ministry, and reading, I have come to see, like others, that spirituality is an inherent aspect of the human condition—all are born with spiritual capacities.[1] Created in the image of God, children are not merely wet cement into which adults impress the mark of *their* lives lived in Christ. Children, too, are disciples in God's kingdom. Jesus, who holds children up as models of kingdom greatness, has much to say about the place of children in his kingdom. If then children are created in the image of God and Jesus makes a special place for them in his kingdom, then those two realities alone must shape and inform the spiritual environments of children. The home and the church must become interlocking systems that invite children deeper into the life of the Spirit. For all disciples, young and old, are on the Way. We journey as co-pilgrims *with* children, side-by-side teaching, enriching, inviting, and inspiring all who have been called to participate. The kingdom pilgrimage is an amazing journey that is simply incomplete without the beauty and wonder of children.

Created in the Image of God

Theologically, the spiritual formation of children is a *creation* reality. Endowed with the *imago Dei* (the image of God), children are from birth spiritual beings in relationship with God. As such children are not merely blank slates, they are whole persons who are born in connection with God.

Genesis 1:26–27

In Genesis 1:26–7 God said, "Let us make humankind in our image, after our likeness . . . God created humankind in his own image, in the image of God he created them, male and female he created them" (NET).[2] In their ancient near-eastern context, these two verses make unique claims about God and humanity. In two verses, the Genesis account affirms that all humanity is related to God, not just the king. All humanity carries the status of royalty. All human beings bear the divine image, reflecting the form and function of God. This gives all humanity inherent value. That is, our value is not in our performance or what others say about us, but in our status as children of God. Human beings have the privilege of relating to God through the God-given mental and spiritual capacities bestowed in the *imago Dei*.[3]

Dallas Willard states, "'Spiritual' is not something we *ought* to be. It is something we *are* and cannot escape, regardless of how we may think or feel about it. It is our nature and our destiny."[4] Children, created in the *imago Dei*, have value in and of themselves and are inherently spiritual. It is their nature, our nature. As such, children construct their image of God and their personhood with which they will relate to God. Similarly, Catherine Stonehouse asserts, "If we truly are created in the image of God, we must know God in order to fully know ourselves and who we can be."[5] A child's active formation of this image is shaped and molded in the context of the family and the congregation among which the child develops. In these environments, children actively construct their image of God. This is the beginning of getting to know God.

Active Makers of Meaning

As those created in the image of God, children are not merely blank slates, sponges, or empty vessels that come to us ready to be filled as passive recipients of spiritual information. Children are born to us as active makers of spiritual meaning. They make meaning in unique and personalized ways.[6] When we engage children as passive recipients, we deny their agency as those created in the image of God. We *de*personalize them and make them into something less than what they were created to be.

Childhood has historically been understood through *production line* and *greenhouse* analogies. Adults have treated children as raw materials to be shaped and molded or seeds to be nurtured by adults. These analogies rob children of their agency, as they require adults to do things *to* or *for* them.[7] In these paradigms, children are dependent on adults for their spiritual formation, development, and growth. It makes a profound difference if we envision our children as active, growing, relational beings rather than passive inanimate blanks slates. Children, rather, ought to be engaged as active participants in the journey of faith. They have genuine experiences of God and are active agents who along *with* adults think theologically and interpret God's work in the world. As I will explain below, we ought to consider children as pilgrims on the spiritual journey as they walk alongside adults. This perspective recognizes that children, created in the image of God, have inherent value and are active participants *with* adults in the kingdom of God. I echo the sentiment of Scottie May and her coworkers, "Children matter! They matter to God. They matter to the church of Jesus Christ. They matter because of who they are: children are complete human beings made in the image of God."[8]

Whole Persons

As those endowed with the image of God, children enter the world blessed with the immeasurable gift of the capacity to know God. Children are, therefore, learners and teachers. They are whole persons born with a spiritual capacity and have as much to teach adults about life in the kingdom as we adults have to teach them.[9] In our churches, we often value children for their future contributions. We affirm on the one hand that they are part of the church, but our practices teach something altogether different. Our practices tend to convey that their value lies in their future potential instead of who they are in the present as children of the King. From the perspective of spiritual formation we affirm that children are whole spiritual beings. As Csinos and Beckwith remind us,

[They] don't need to learn certain things or reach a certain developmental stage to be spiritual. They *are* spiritual. And, like people of all ages, their spiritual lives can be formed, nurtured and shaped. Spiritual formation is based on views of children that see them as inherently spiritual beings who are already in relationship with God.[10]

Therefore, children *are* disciples. They are members of the kingdom of God *as* children. They are active agents who creatively construct meaning and significantly shape their own spiritual lives as well as the lives of others.[11] They routinely experience the transcendence of God and are able to live faithfully out of that relationship. As whole beings created in the image of God, we must affirm that children's spirituality is an integral part of their development. If this is so, do we risk hindering their spiritual development by overlooking or altogether rejecting their experiences and journey with God? My prayer is that we would not impede their journey.

Jesus' View of Children

Catherine Stonehouse reminds us, "Hindering children on their spiritual journey would be a serious offense."[12] Jesus speaks directly to this reality. In fact, Jesus communicated rather persuasively that kingdom values turn the values of the world upside down. It was true then and it is true now. Although the world still tends to marginalize children, they *are not* marginalized members of the kingdom. They are real members, now. In fact, as Jesus teaches, children are models for adults who look to enter the kingdom. Further, when we continue to overlook and marginalize children, we live inconsistently with the teaching of Jesus.[13]

Turn Around, Welcome, and Do Not Cause Little Ones to Sin

Severe punishment awaits those who hinder children from coming to Jesus. In Matthew 18:1–9, the disciples are arguing about who will be the greatest.[14] In response to their ambitious spirit, Jesus brings a child into their midst and stands him among them. He then said,

> I tell you the truth, unless you *turn around* and *become* like little
> children, you will never enter the kingdom of heaven! Whoever
> then *humbles* himself like this little child is the greatest in the
> kingdom of heaven. And whoever *welcomes* a child like this in
> my name welcomes me (NET).

The words of Jesus are powerful. First, he turns his disciples' perspective of children on its head. While Jewish children were understood to be blessings from God, children were still marginalized; they had no status. Jesus realigns their conceptions about greatness and status with kingdom values. Second, Jesus uses strong, unambiguous language about what it *looks* like to enter the kingdom of heaven. One must *turn around*. That is, Jesus told his disciples that if they want to enter into the kingdom of heaven they must undergo a transformation, and in effect, undergo a change of position! Additionally, they must *become*, that is, undergo a change. Taken together, Jesus unravels their preconceived notions of status, rank, and position. They must transform and undergo a change– they must resemble children or they will never enter the kingdom. By humbling oneself to the status of a child, they become the greatest. Third, those who *welcome* children, in fact, welcome Jesus. Welcoming those who are unimportant and **statusless** with open arms is a sign of the kingdom now come.

In the next verse, Jesus illuminates the danger awaiting those who would cause division between Jesus and little children, "But if anyone causes one of these little ones who *believe in me* to sin, it would be better for him to have a huge millstone hung around his neck and to be drowned in open sea."[15] Here we see that Jesus took children and their faith quite seriously. What happens to these little ones is a matter of great consequence.[16] In Jesus's words, their worth cannot be overstated. Coming between Jesus and them has dire consequences.

It Is a Matter of Justice

In other passages, we see the disciples struggling to grasp and live out the values of the kingdom Jesus was teaching them. In Mark 10:13–16, we read of the disciples actively scolding those who brought their children for Jesus to touch and bless.[17]

> When Jesus saw this, he was *indignant* and said to them, 'Let the little children come to me and do not try to stop them, for the kingdom of God belongs to such as these. I tell you the truth, whoever does not receive the kingdom of God like a child will never enter it.' After he took the children in his arms, he placed his hands on them and blessed them (NET).

Only Mark records that Jesus was *indignant*. The word here carries the sense of being angry at something seemingly unjust. For Jesus, prohibiting these children from coming to him to receive his blessing was a matter of justice. The disciples were acting out of the norms of their cultural milieu; Jesus was an important rabbi who was not to be disturbed by "insignificant" children. Jesus gives them new eyes with which to see. These little ones belong in the kingdom. In truth, the disciples learn that if they do not receive the kingdom of God *like a child*, they will not enter into it.

The placement of these verses in the gospel accounts strengthens these statements. In Matthew and Mark, this passage appears between the discussion of divorce and the rich man. In Luke, this passage is between the parable of the Pharisee and the Tax Collector and the story of the wealthy ruler. Certainly this placement is no accident; all three authors appear to want their readers to compare and contrast the spiritual status of children with the adults mentioned in the texts that come before and after this one. Children who are humble, innocent, and self-less come to Jesus with empty-hands. Adults, however, who exalt themselves, marginalize the innocent, and live selfish lives come to Jesus seeking justification. How then will we adults enter the kingdom of heaven? When we come like children, hands empty and relying on the grace of God.[18]

Parental Faith and Compassion

In a world where children lived on the margins of society, treated as unworthy and often forgotten, Jesus repeatedly responded with compassion. In

Matthew 9:18ff and Mark 5:21ff, Jesus responds with compassion to the faithful request of a grieving father. Jairus, a ruler of a local synagogue and a man of wealth and status, prostrates himself before Jesus. His burden as the father of a critically ill daughter is all that matters. Prestige and dignity are no longer important. Demonstrating unparalleled compassion Jesus heals in response to his faith. Through his tender touch, Jesus arrests the power of death and demonstrates the power present in the kingdom of God.

In John 4:46–54, Jesus heals the sick son of a royal official who responds in faith. In Matthew 15:21–28 and Mark 7:24–30, Jesus casts an unclean spirit out of a Canaanite woman's daughter. Matthew records Jesus as saying, "Woman, your faith is great!" In both of these narratives, the parents were Gentiles who through their faith secured healing for their children. First, Jesus' response to these parents demonstrates that Jesus loves and has compassion for all children. Second, these passages demonstrate that parental faith is important. It is no exaggeration to say that a parent's faith has direct bearing on the physical and spiritual health of their children. [19]

Implications

From these passages we learn that Jesus loves children and that they belong in the kingdom. Children, "are not marginal members of the kingdom, just tagging along with their parents, waiting to grow up to be real members. No, children are models in the kingdom of God, showing adults how to enter."[20] We learn also that Jesus holds up children as examples of kingdom values. According to Stonehouse and May,

> By doing so, Jesus reveals the great difference between the king-
> doms of the world and the kingdom of God. The Greeks and
> Romans viewed children as raw material to be formed, or unin-
> formed beings to be educated. Jews believed children needed
> teaching and discipline so that they would learn to live like their
> ancestors and the adults in the faith community. However, Jesus
> holds up children as teachers for adults. Within the kingdom

of God, adults are challenged to be open to learn from children and others who are the least.[21]

Further, we dare not hold children back in their relationship with Jesus. For Jesus this is a matter of justice. Those who hinder the faith of children or cause them to sin will answer for their transgression. In God's kingdom, children are examples of discipleship and are vital participants in kingdom life. As such, children share in the provisions of God and the life of the community of faith.

These conclusions from biblical texts lead me to one final implication for churches today. Our children, nurtured in the context of the body of Christ, ought to understand themselves to be disciples in relationship with Christ. Jeff Childers argues that "*disciple, discipleship,* and *following Jesus* are expressions that capture the image of a person in pursuit of Christ."[22] Further, as active disciples of Christ with child-like faith, our children are understood to be saved.[23] My eleven-year old daughter, whose prayer for an elderly friend so touched her mother and I, has her own vibrant relationship with God.[24] She has grown up a believer, enjoying fellowship within the faith community, and continuing to appreciate a relationship with God. Instead of hindering her growth by treating her as an outsider, Jesus calls me to treat her as a peer in the Kingdom of God. Even more than that, careful attention to her spiritual growth can empower growth in my life as well.

Spiritual Ecologies

In the passages above, Jesus teaches us about the spiritual lives of children and how one is to relate to them. The most straightforward approach to do this is to be child-like ourselves. We best learn to do this when we are with children. When we are with children, we learn they are very sensitive and responsive to God's presence.[25] We also come to understand that adults provide important pieces for their developing picture of God. This does not occur in a vacuum; it happens as we share life together in the home and in the church.

Spiritual Formation in the Home

We usually don't need to convince our children that they are a part of the family. From the moment they are born, they are included. There is no "rite of passage" that makes them full members of the family.[26] They are family. Of all their microsystems, or immediate settings, the spiritual formation that takes place in the home is the most foundational. [27] Within the ecology of the home, it is important that we nurture children to see their part in a much larger story, that we immerse them in spiritual relationships, and that we practice rituals that ground and develop their faith.[28] Healthy childhood spiritual formation takes place when parents invite their children to share their experiences of faith that occur in the day-in and day-out of life. This has the effect of infusing and embedding spirituality in the lives of both children and parents.[29] Parents actively draw attention to the spiritual and live out of that reality by inviting their children to explore and stretch their spiritual muscles in conversations and shared experiences that invite the presence of the Spirit.

Historically, parents were encouraged to *pass on* their image of God to their children. *Passing* language, however, effectively ignores the agency of the child. If our children only receive faith from their parents, we are not fully welcoming them, nor are we expecting them to participate and contribute. Further, passing language tends to mislead our children and ourselves with the notion that God is static—merely a commodity to be consumed. Children become consumers and parents become faith distribution managers. We should confess instead that we serve a living God who is active and participates in and directs our lives, not a static God whom we can pass down from one generation to the next. Parents ought not simply *pass on* their faith; rather, they should seek to cultivate the unique faith of their children as they invite their children to merge their story with God's story.[30] Nurturing the God-given faith of children helps them develop their own identity as followers of Jesus, and it calls upon us to nurture in them the loving way of Jesus.[31] Alongside parents, God informs and nurtures young disciples in the home with the goal that, one day, the young disciple will step out and own their faith.

Formation in the Church

The other forming microsystem for childhood faith is the local church. As we have seen, God designed children and adults to share life together. Each help the other grow spiritually. Therefore, the spiritual formation of children in the church is not about programming, but about reciprocal formation, "ministry *with* children, ministry that involves serving children, being served by children and serving the world with children," as Csinos and Beckwith remind us.[32] As we incorporate children into the life of the church through service and worship, their sense of belonging grows. The congregation loves them, and they can reciprocate that love, as they become active contributors. This perspective affirms that children have unique gifts to offer the faith community. The authors of *Children Matter* remind us, "Along with adults, children grow spiritually through expressing their faith and love for God in service, when as members of the church—not just *future* members—they do the work of the people of God."[33] Since our children are children of God, we should *so* weave them into the life of the church that they cannot ever recall life without Christ. Theologically, when full incorporation of children occurs within the context of the faith community, the kingdom of God is most truly realized.

On the Way

Throughout this chapter, I have argued that spiritual formation of children does not occur *to* or *for* children but *with* children. This *with* language encourages language of journey, of pilgrimage. I believe that children are disciples on a journey of spiritual formation. As adults, we are our children's co-pilgrims.

Spiritual Pedagogues

This journey of faith formation is a shared journey. The language of formation moves away from education, instruction, and training and towards participation in a particular way of life. As John Westerhoff III has said, "Jesus' way is the way of being *with*."[34] I refer to this **withness** as spiritual pedagogy and those who are inclusive of children on this journey as *spiritual pedagogues*. In modern English the word "pedagogue" refers to a teacher. In ancient Mediterranean cultures, though, the word referred to one who was a "child-tender," that is, someone who served as a custodian for the young.[35] The role of the pedagogue with a particular child might span a decade or more. The pedagogue was to be a constant companion to the child: escorting the child to school, overseeing meals, supervising social engagements, and protecting the child from harm. Additionally, and important for our use of the word, the pedagogue was responsible for the moral development of the child through discipline and protection. The pedagogue served as the moral guide.

I believe the concept of the *spiritual* pedagogue is useful for our understanding of children's spiritual formation. The spiritual pedagogue journeys with the child, shares life with the child, helps mold them and shape them into the image of Christ. The spiritual pedagogue invites the child into active participation in the kingdom and together; they serve others and live out God's love. God inspires the faith of the child along the way. As the child matures, they come to understand:

- their faith is beautiful and alive in God
- they have value and are valued
- their presence matters
- they are active contributors to life of the community
- they are beloved of God.

The spiritual pedagogue is a traveling companion who ignites faith and inspires transformation even as they themselves are influenced and transformed in relationship with the child. This is a spiritual journey of companionship that would have each and every participant come to more fully realize who they are in Christ as they actively step into each other's lives. A child's faith, while a gift from God, must be inspired. This happens best when children are in relationships with adults who too, are growing in Christ.

Conclusion

This chapter has asserted that children, welcomed into the kingdom by Christ, are active participants in the community of faith. As those created in the image of God, children are whole persons who have agency, and they interact with the world as active meaning makers. As faithful young disciples, Jesus holds children up as examples of faith and what one must become to enter into the kingdom of God. For the church, this means that our children are not only safe, but saved since they, ideally, have never known life without Christ. They live in continual connection and relationship with God and when they come to baptism, they do so as believers who own their faith and the baptized way of life. Children's spiritual formation occurs most notably in the home where parents nurture the growing faith of their children. This, in partnership with the church, creates a spiritual ecology that is God-ordained and ideal for holistic spiritual growth. Children, like adults are pilgrims on the Way. With spiritual pedagogues to assist in and ignite their faith, children will never know life apart from Christ. Through the power of the Spirit, the sacrificial love of faithful parents, and the active incorporation into the body of Christ alongside loving and authentic adults, God forms children spiritually into the image of Christ.

Section Two

Children at Home

Living Deuteronomy 6
Parenting as a Spiritual Discipline

Ron Bruner

Parenting is about more than raising children in the faith. It has the potential to foster religious transformation in the one who attempts such care. Engaging in the practice of parenting gives rise to new knowledge and a new way of being, not in sacred time and space but in the very concrete minutiae of life in all its messiness.

Bonnie Miller-McLemore[1]

Kids already do a lot of learning from adults, and we have a lot to share. I think that adults should start learning from kids. . . . Learning between grown-ups and kids should be reciprocal. The reality, unfortunately, is a little different, and it has a lot to do with trust, or a lack of it.

Adora Svitak, 12 year-old author[2]

Just weeks before the birth of their second child, my daughter and son-in-law invited us to come help prepare their home for Jack's arrival. Lauren and Andrew's first child, Lily, had been using the "baby's room" for two years; now she needed a "big girl's room" so that Jack could have the baby's room. The mission for Nina (Ann) and Granpa (Ron) was to convert the guest bedroom into Lily's room. Nina organized closets and decorated the room. Granpa assembled a trundle bed only slightly less complicated than the Space Shuttle. As we were finishing, Nina noticed the darkness of the room when the lights were off; she decided to place luminescent stars on the ceiling so that the room wouldn't seem scary for Lily.

Later, I found Nina on a stepladder holding a star to the ceiling while two-year old Lily carefully supervised. "No, not there," Lily said, "over there!" Ann moved the star over a few inches; "Yes!" Lily exclaimed. One by one, Nina and Lily arranged a canopy of constellations into a calming night sky. With stars in place, we returned home, glad of God's gift of life shared among three generations.

The story, though, wasn't finished; two weeks later Lauren called Ann with the epilogue. As was their habit, Lauren had been telling Lily her Bible story before saying prayers and going to sleep. It was time for the story of creation: "In the beginning, God made the heavens and the earth . . ." Lauren started.

"And Nina helped with the stars!" Lily responded.

"Yes, and Nina helped with the stars." Lauren answered. When Lauren repeated this story to us, Ann and I laughed for a long while.

Before questioning the thinking of this young theologian, we should remember that her Nina did indeed place the stars that she sees at night. Those stars imitate the Creator's work and remind Lily of our larger universe. Lily is connecting her memories and story with the larger story of God; at the same time, she reminds us that we participate in the ongoing creative work of God ourselves. That's good theology. Children like Lily come to a healthy understanding of God and their spirituality when they are immersed in environments where every generation is constantly and intentionally attentive to the spiritual. Spiritual parents, and spiritual grandparents, form spiritual children and are shaped spiritually by those children.

Raising Children is a Spiritual Discipline

For Christians, parenting is more than education or socialization; it is a spiritual discipline. Beyond dipping into the shared practice of a few disciplines like prayer, Scripture reading, or family devotions—the spiritual discipline of parenting is the complete immersion of our life with children into the holy. Practicing spiritual disciplines for an hour or more daily is praiseworthy, but to think that we should confine our spirituality to one or two parts of the day is to miss the point of Deuteronomy 6:

> Hear, O Israel: The Lord is our God, the Lord alone. You shall love the Lord your God with all your heart, and with all your soul, and with all your might. Keep these words that I am commanding you today in your heart. Recite them to your children and talk about them when you are at home and when you are away, when you lie down and when you rise. Bind them as a sign on your hand, fix them as an emblem on your forehead, and write them on the doorposts of your house and on your gates (Deut. 6:4–9, NRSV).

When we say, "from A to Z," we don't just mean A and Z; we're talking about the entire alphabet. As Israel heard the words from Deuteronomy, and as we hear them as the people of God ourselves, we need to hear "when you are home and when you are away" as meaning *everywhere*. We should understand "when you lie down and when you rise" as *all of the time*.[3] Awareness of God's presence, attentiveness to conversation about God, and consciousness of the action of God in our world, are woven throughout the life of faith. All space and time hold the potential for holiness to those who are alert. To keep God perpetually present in our lives and those of our children is a spiritual discipline.[4]

The spiritual discipline of parenting is important for a host of reasons. As believing parents, we want our children to enjoy a relationship with God and with a faith community, a relationship that transforms them into godly adults. The transformation of our children ought to deepen our own spirituality because growth in faith is co-developmental and comes more from experience than the "language of instruction."[5] Shared spiritually formative practices prepare children and parents to cope with a challenging world, and to stay connected with God and one another.

Parent and Child Engaged in Spiritual Formation

Human beings are souls, a combination of body and spirit so intertwined that only God can separate them. Children are souls, not blank slates (see Chapter three), nor do they depend upon the prompting of adults to become spiritual; children are naturally spiritual beings. Rebecca Nye observes that:

> Children's spirituality is an *initially natural capacity* for aware-ness of the sacred quality to life experiences. This awareness can be *conscious or unconscious*, and sometimes fluctuates between both, but in both cases can affect actions, feelings and thoughts. In childhood, spirituality is especially about being attracted towards "being in relation", *responding to a call to relate* to more than "just me"—i.e. to others, to God, to creation or to a deeper inner sense of Self.[6]

Although children are inherently spiritual and attuned to the spiritual, day-to-day interaction with family, friends, and a local congregation—in part-nership with the Spirit of God—*forms* the shape of their spirituality. My definition of *spiritual formation* builds on that of Evan Howard: "Spiritual formation is the ongoing intentional and semi-intentional process by which God, the community, family, and the individual bring a believing individual or community more fully into a resemblance of the image of Christ, an awareness of the Spirit, and unity with God."[7]

God created us, after all, in the image of God (Gen. 1:26). Theologians disagree as to precisely what the "image of God" refers, but it appears to mean several things at once. Like God, humans are spiritual beings, capable of making free choices, equipped with spiritual perception, skillful in moral thinking, gifted with creative ability.[8] Unfortunately humans make choices that cause them to distort that image; incautious communities and families can raise children in ways that misshape that image as well.

Spiritual formation occurs as our image comes to more closely resemble the image of God, as we learn how to believe, behave, belong, and become.[9] Let's work with these terms to see how living out Deuteronomy 6, sharing a life of faith in spiritually formative ways, takes shape in our world.

Believe

Children instinctively believe in the divine; spiritual formation shapes their faith into a specific belief in and love for the God of Abraham, Isaac, and Jacob: "You shall love the Lord your God with all your heart, and with all your soul, and with all your might" (Deut. 6:5–6, NRSV). Even though children instinctively believe, that doesn't mean that they won't ever have any questions. The voice of Deuteronomy anticipates the faith questions of childhood. "When your children ask you in time to come, 'What is the meaning of the decrees and the statutes and the ordinances that the Lord our God has commanded you?' then you shall say to your children, 'We were Pharaoh's slaves in Egypt, but the Lord brought us out of Egypt with a mighty hand'" (Deut. 6:20–22, NRSV). Remembering the bigger story of God is most often the way to our answer. When we avoid simplistic and unrealistic answers to the surprisingly deep questions of our young theologians and instead find peace in the truth that God is mysterious and greater than our best understandings, we can have challenging conversations with our children and remain believable. It is permissible to say, "God only knows." In any case, we must take the faith questions of our children seriously; together we must work for a deeper understanding.[10]

Belief deepens over time. Childhood faith can be very simple and yet children can cope with faith-challenging events because they handle mystery and ambiguity better than many of us who are older. Children are used to inexplicable things happening in their universe; a mysterious God whose full identity, actions, and motives are not clearly known can remain believable to them. As children grow older, their understanding grows more complex; the old, easy answers are not always acceptable. As we will see later, this questioning is a necessary and normal part of building one's own faith.[11] Maturing children should, over time, shape a more complicated, sophisticated version of their faith. Mystery, though, will always be a part of the relationship between God and humans. Our God is bigger than human knowing.

Behave

When it comes to behavior, every community has boundaries as to what is and isn't appropriate. Behavioral expectations change depending upon a person's age, context, or community. Gordon Allport describes children's efforts to internalize behavioral boundaries as the passage from "fear" to "ought" to "self-control."[12] For example, young children often obey rules because they fear the consequences: they may not get Dad's approval, they might upset their Mom, or they might even have to go to timeout. As they mature, they begin to do the right things because they have a feeling of "ought"—even though they may not want to act correctly, it seems the right thing to do. The most mature form of behavior is that of self-control, action not requiring external control or social justification. When children are very young, they tend to behave because an outside power controls them (an external locus of control); as they mature an internal locus of control marks their behavior. God and parents help empower this transition. Parents must create opportunities for children to learn to control their own actions and, occasionally, suffer the natural consequences of failing to do so. Self control is a fruit of the Spirit (Gal. 5:22–23) and is, therefore the result of persistent human effort provoked and empowered by the Holy Spirit.

Christians have a wealth of ethical material to guide their behavior. Is there a way to teach young children an ethical code that will grow as their understanding does? The Ten Commandments and the surrounding law set ethical boundaries in five unique areas: with God, with others, with self, with property, and with nature. The wording of these boundaries is sometimes complex and hard to remember. For the very young, we can simplify this with the word "respect." Respect is one of the few virtues that any member of society might expect, even from strangers. Respect is the primary motivation Jean Piaget finds for the developing moral judgment of children[13] and Thomas Lickona locates respect "at the very center of moral development."[14] This virtue—connected with the five areas listed above—produces a set of principles that will grow to guide children. These five ethical principles are imperatives that govern the behavior of adults and children.

- Respect God.
- Respect others.
- Respect self.
- Respect property.
- Respect nature.

Since respect is the thin version of several virtues, these virtue-principles can deepen as children are better able to enact them. For example: respect for God deepens into wonder and awe, respect for others becomes "love your neighbor," respect for self develops into self-control and humility, respect for property expands into stewardship, and respect for nature grows into nurture of life.[15] Godly behavior is not so much rule-keeping as it is relationship-keeping. In real life, rules sometimes conflict with other rules. Good behavior goes beyond rules to maintain a right relationship with God, others, self, things, and nature.

Even though we believe that God will graciously forgive childhood wrongdoing, it is a mistake to avoid accountability in the moment. For example, if a child calls a friend an ugly name we should hold them responsible. The child is guilty, the behavior must change, and consequences must follow. Expressing regret, taking responsibility, making things right, true repentance, and asking forgiveness are shapes that apology can take.[16] Merely saying "I'm sorry," is rarely enough, especially since childhood apologies are so often insincere. Other proportional and related consequences are appropriate. It is impossible to discipline a child without first disciplining ourselves; we must choose to take the time to walk through the consequences with the child. We should invest time in a conversation that brings a spiritual awareness of the reasons why such misbehavior is wrong; misconduct damages relationships and makes those relationships "not right," which displeases God. Only behavior that maintains or builds relationships is righteous. So, even though some things we humans do can't be undone, can we help our children imagine ways that they might try to make things right again?

It is a mistake to think that humans, and especially children, ought always to choose behaviors logically. Humans use a number of God-given tools to make decisions: logic, emotion, habit, identity, Scripture, social influence, and communal discernment. Unfortunately adults, and especially men, tend to discount emotions as important decision-making input. Emotions are good, after all—God made them. They shouldn't be ignored or discounted because emotions provide access to the collected lifetime experiences in our unconscious mind. The unconscious mental process is something like this: "My situation reminds of me another situation, which turned out well/horribly. Therefore, I ought to act like I am excited/worried." Parents should work alongside their children to help them become emotionally aware. Instead of denying their emotions, children can learn to slow down and carefully "read" their situation: "What is really happening here?" "Why does this bother me?" "How can I cope with these feelings when I know that being in these circumstances tends to make me feel this way?" These conversations can teach young and old the wisdom of communal discernment.

Parents can discern from these conversations the concerns of the child, visualize the perspective such concerns produce, and empathetically imagine the emotions at their root.[17] The ability of the child to identify and value the emotions that they experience can empower them to make better decisions. Often, emotional responses have a positive or protective purpose. For example, emotions may bring a child to feel compassion for others. Parents should affirm such feelings in their children. In cases where emotions provoke other than righteous behaviors, parents may choose to help the child discover a healthier and more godly reading of the situation. Together, they can approach God in prayer from that mended point of view. Prayer is a specific spiritual discipline with the power to reform our values, the relationships and things about which we are concerned,[18] and to reshape our interpretation of our experience (see Chapter six).

Belong

The spirituality of children is inherently relational; Christians should encourage their children to understand that they belong to an enduring community: the people of God. Jesus said, "Let the little children come to me, and do not stop them; for it is to such as these that the kingdom of heaven belongs" (Matt. 19:14–15, NRSV; cf. Mark 10:13–16; Luke 18:15–17). By the definition of Jesus Christ, children are within the reign of God, among the people of God. Like the children who walked among the people of Israel as they wandered through the wilderness, children have a special place in the grace and providence of God. Children need never walk away from God or the people of God, but they can. They have a choice. Just as the children of Israel reached a time when they had to accept of their own will their place among their people (their *Bar Mitzvah* or *Bat Mitzvah*), so children in the reign of Jesus must eventually choose either to remain within that reign, or to leave to find another people.

In Churches of Christ, maturing youth choosing to remain within the church as adult believers must claim their identity as a follower of Jesus through baptism (see Chapter nine). However, baptism isn't the final destination of spiritual growth; instead, it's a necessary landmark in the ongoing life of transformation. This makes the journey for a child raised in the church more of a process of *confession* than a process of *conversion*. We should hope that our children, instead of taking a life detour and needing to convert from some ungodly lifestyle, will move forward with their spiritual formation, having chosen to claim as their own the walk that their parents and faith family have shared with them over the years.[19]

The logical result of the imperative of Jesus to "let the little children come" is that children have a full place in the life and the ministry of the church. The ability of children to participate in a real ways in corporate worship should receive our careful attention (see Chapters seven and eight). Their ability to participate in the ministry of the church can strengthen our ministry and our children (see Chapters eleven and fourteen).

Become

Spiritual formation through becoming happens when we understand that taking on the image of God is a lifelong process. Human spirituality was never intended to be static. Becoming takes place through the day-to-day putting off of vices—like complaining, lying, and disobedience—and putting on instead certain virtues—such as patience, truthfulness, and obedience. We do this through practicing spiritual disciplines until we acquire virtuosity in doing them (Col. 3:5–14).

In the process, we must respect the uniqueness of each child's spirituality. Some will prefer to seek God with their head, like Paul—intellectually. Others will lead with their heart as did Peter. Some, like David, will prefer to lift God up to the heavens with song and speech; others, like Elijah and Elisha, will find more meaning in serving the powerless as they work to enact God's kingdom in this world.[20] Parents need to be alert to the spiritual activities that are life giving to their children and make space for more of those activities. Living in a household that is inattentive to a child's need for spiritual formation, or the particular shape of their spirituality can misshape or starve their spirit. Living among a toxic congregation, one that denies a diversity of gifts or the importance of children, can have a similarly negative effect.[21] Consequently, the careful spiritual formation of a child requires parents to be intentional and to construct individualized practices for them.

Social scientists and theologians have constructed a number of models describing spiritual formation.[22] The model that remains the most useful is the four-stage model of John Westerhoff III.[23] The first stage is that of early childhood (preschool): **experienced** faith. "The child explores and tests, imagines and creates, observes and copies, experiences and reacts," according to Westerhoff. "Children's actions influence those with whom they interact, and the actions of others influence them."[24] Experienced faith shapes how they *behave*. The second stage, **affiliative** faith, occurs as children move into elementary school or early adolescence. "During this period persons seek to act with others in an accepting community with a clear sense of identity," Westerhoff observes. "All of us need to feel that we *belong* to a self-conscious community and that through our active participation can make a contribution to its life."[25] Some people, as early as late adolescence, enter into a **searching** faith. Those experiencing this stage undergo three processes at once: critical judgment or doubt, experimentation, and commitment.[26] Armed with their growing critical capabilities, they ask difficult questions; they experiment with different answers, perhaps even those of other faith groups; they commit to these answers one at a time until they can find one that works. They seek to understand what they personally *believe*. Those moving past a searching faith, usually not sooner than early adulthood, find themselves with an **owned** faith.[27] By this point, faith is totally integrated into all aspects of a person's life and mission, with faith calling them to *become* a coherent imager of God in all aspects of their lives. As we commit to walk with our children through a lifetime of faith, this is the place for which we aim: lives launched with maturing faith in and relationship with God, empowered by the Holy Spirit, faithfully serving as a part of the body of Christ.

Spiritual Disciplines Shape Us

The most potent tools to accomplish spiritual formation are spiritual disciplines. Spiritual disciplines are regular, methodical, historic Christian practices: prayer, Bible study, meditation, silence, and simplicity, for example.[28] This book gives detailed attention to prayer and Bible study in the family (see Chapters five and six) and other spiritual disciplines among the church (see Chapter thirteen). Disciplined, repetitive work on a practice, like prayer, becomes habit, habit pursued with increasing excellence becomes virtue, the accumulation of virtue becomes character, and the ongoing process empowers a transformation of character toward a more accurate image of God (spiritual formation). Thus, prayer might serve to transform those who pray into humans who better live lives of thankfulness before God. Acquiring virtues, and setting aside vices, are fundamental moves in spiritual formation and transformation.[29] When we fail to work on building virtues, the human tendency is to enlarge our vices instead.

The practice of spiritual disciplines works like the discipline that forms musicians. Through the practice of necessary skills—reading music, hearing pitch, maintaining tempo, and playing their instrument—they move from ear-splitting noise to excellent performance. Students learn new techniques from masters who teach them; they practice scales repeatedly until they are flawless; they accompany other musicians and find their place in the larger piece of music. Some will surpass their teachers. Some will become virtuosos. Our musical analogy highlights several realities about spiritual disciplines: (1) they can be difficult, some more than others; (2) the early stages of practice can be uncomfortable; (3) growth takes time; and (4) our children may excel in disciplines in ways that surpass us (and that may be a good thing).

As parents come to value spiritual formation, some efforts may produce more parental guilt than growth for the child. The desire to have home devotionals, for example, shows high aspirations. Some families find this practice frustrating in the complexities of contemporary life, and especially, single-parent families.[30] Perhaps these families, instead of sanctifying one time and place within the family's routine and residence, could choose instead to sanctify all of its time and space? There is evidence that this type of practice shaped ancient Celtic Christian life.[31] Joyce Denham describes how a Celtic child might have experienced such a day:

> The boy opened his eyes: it must be morning. . . . He said a dressing prayer as he wriggled into his tunic. He whispered a hasty bathing prayer. . . . He set out with his father for a day's work on the hills, and they said the journey blessing and prayed for the protection of their home. From the day's dawning to its ending they spoke the herding blessings for their cattle, uttered prayers for the seeds, and gave thanksgivings for family and shelter and food. At dusk, the boy stretched out his arm and recited an encircling prayer to the great and powerful God of heaven and earth. He called on God as Three-in-One: a Trinity of God the Father, God the Son and God the Holy Spirit, who is greater than all of the forces of darkness and evil.[32]

This description echoes Deuteronomy 6:7, "when you are at home and when you are away, when you lie down and when you rise" (NRSV). Is it possible that we, as parents, might imagine how this could look in our home, with our children?

Living a Life of Discernment

Finally, let's consider a spiritual discipline that can empower parents to imagine a way to pursue the day-to-day spiritual formation of children alongside their own. That discipline is spiritual discernment. God values discernment (1 Kings 3:9–12), discernment marks us as the people of God (Deut. 4:9), and we ought to see discernment's value in leading us closer to God (Rom. 12:2). Parents can use discernment to build a plan for spiritual formation, but discernment also empowers ongoing adjustments. So how can we learn to do this? We'll build a method of spiritual discernment based on the work of Elaine Heath.[33] Here are the steps: (1) show up, (2) pay attention, (3) read the story, (4) cooperate, and (5) release the outcome. Prayer should bathe each step.

For your child's sake, and your own, **show up**. We need to witness their lives; they need to know their importance to us. Share frequent meals around the table together, participate in children's ministry, sponsor youth trips—your children want you there.[34] When you're doing things you're passionate about, invite them along to see if they're interested.

When we're with our children, we need to **pay attention**. Who and what are important to them? What do they struggle with? What are their dreams? Where does God appear to be acting in their lives?

How would we **read the story** of their lives? What can we celebrate? How can a look at the bigger story bring hope? Are there biblical stories or other Scripture that this situation brings to mind? How does conflict in their lives reveal God's power in their narrative? How can linking their story with God's give them peace? Can we let their story be their story, not ours? It's not our children's burden to fix the flaws in our saga, after all, but to find their own story.

In what ways can we **cooperate**, both with the dreams of our child and the action of God? Can we facilitate a connection with a mentor whose career is our child's dream? Ought we to fund the tools that develop their gift, or help them to earn those tools? How can we work alongside God in this situation?

Finally, we need to **release the outcome**. If we have properly allowed the Holy Spirit to guide us this far, then we must be content, even if our answer is not what we would have originally imagined. God didn't design the world to conform to our expectations. Trust God. Trust your children.

My prayer is that God will guide your spiritual discernment and be with you and your children as you learn side-by-side what it means to walk with God, to make holy all places and all times. My hope is that "you and your children and your children's children may fear the Lord your God all the days of your life, and keep all his decrees and his commandments" (Deut. 6:2, NRSV).

Chapter 5

Reading and Living the Bible with Children

Samjung Kang-Hamilton

One night, my daughter and I were reading from a Bible paraphrase aimed at mothers and daughters. Hannah, who was five years old, asked the question, "Who closed the door of Noah's ark? One Bible said that God did, and the other Bible said Noah did. Which Bible is right?" I was surprised by how carefully she had been listening, though I should not have been, for in reading with my children, I discovered that they were silent observers, careful listeners, and natural theologians. Children have much to teach us, just as they have much to learn from us. After that conversation, I listened for more insightful questions from her. Our times of reading the Bible together became meaningful rituals for us as family. Although bedtime rituals became less appropriate as our children entered their early teenage years, the creation of other rituals, formats, events, and occasions for reading the Bible continued. These times with our children taught us how God's grace enriches our spiritual journey together.

This is why the phrase "reading and living the Bible with children" aptly captures the layers of meaning uncovered by Bible reading with children. Consider each word in the phrase. First, there is the matter of reading. Some speak of America as a post-literate culture, for many people receive information primarily through oral or written media in sound bites biased toward the sensational, the lurid, and the superficial. On the other hand, Christianity, which emphasizes serving God with all our being, requires some degree of reflection. For this reason, Christians have historically emphasized reading. Reading the Bible is, of course, a special case. Both children and adults respond to it in ways that bring about Christian nurture and spiritual growth.

Second, parents and other adults read the Bible *with* children, because the encounter with Scripture is at its heart a shared activity sustained by a community. In reading the Bible with children, adults can see its words with fresh eyes. We ask new or long-forgotten questions, and we recapture the invigorating freshness of the Bible itself, not just as the inspired word, but as the inspiring and nurturing word.

This recapturing happens in the church and the family. For better or worse, both family and church mold our character, values, and beliefs. In particular, how the Christian adults in a family structure their lives provides modeling, guidance, and meaningful experiences. The home can celebrate faith and bring it to life. Admittedly, given today's lifestyles, committing time for Bible reading challenges many families. Some parents say, "I know it is important to make time to read the Bible and pray with our children, but it is hard to find the time." Other parents think, "Isn't it the job of our church to teach the Bible to my children?" Many simply do not know where to begin because family Bible reading was not in their childhood experience.

Some data support these claims. According to a Gallup poll, only 59 percent of Americans read the Bible occasionally, though 88 percent of households own a Bible. A Tyndale House survey showed that 64 percent of Americans said they are too busy to read the Bible. The same survey revealed that 80 percent of Americans find the Bible too confusing and hard to understand.

By the time most Americans reach their early teens, they believe that they understand the Bible well, in spite of the evidence to the contrary. About half of churched children leave the faith on entering adulthood. In short, there is a gap between what we think we know and what we do, in fact, know.

Third, the life-giving nature of Scripture becomes clear to adults when we relearn how to live it out *alongside* children. As we help our children live as spiritual beings in the world, we introduce them to the true human nature that God has made available. As part of that introduction, we learn to read the Bible not as a book of rigid rules or curious stories, but as a discourse about life with God and each other. Adults join children as fellow travelers, all of us seeking a deeper relationship with God.

The next few pages will explore these aspects of reading the Bible in the context of homes and other child-friendly environments. My hope is to offer directions for further discussion and reflection. I recognize that some children and their adult caregivers face challenges that others do not, but hope that the principles discussed here can be adapted to many situations.

The Bible and Children

To begin, the Old Testament instructed Israelite adults to tell children about the story of God's redeeming work in the exodus and, indeed, their whole history (Exod. 13; Deut. 6; Ps. 78). The Bible's emphasis on adult instruction of children has continued in Judaism and Christianity to the present, growing ever more important. For centuries, part of that instruction has centered on teaching and learning the Bible as a book that sustains the life of prayer and spirituality, of relationships, and of communities in profound ways. The Bible shapes people into the image of Jesus Christ. In reading the Bible, the church's children become apprentices in the ways of Jesus Christ, a role that includes learning Scripture. But the question is, how does this happen?

What Is the Bible, and How Do We Encounter It?

To answer that question, we should begin by reconsidering what the Bible is and is not. As N. T. Wright has often said, the Christian message is not advice or theory but good news. As the surest expression of that message, the Bible collects poems, laws, stories, prophecies, wise sayings, dialogues, apocalypses, letters, sermons, and other sorts of texts. Passing on these texts from generation to generation nurtures human beings as creatures capable of forming healthy communities with each other and standing together before their creator in joy and gratitude.

A classic biblical text espousing such a vision is the book of Deuteronomy, which envisions parents and communities passing on the stories and rituals of the faith. Some scholars have spoken of the book's "commemorative culture," i.e., its emphasis on Israel's collective memory of God's gracious acts lived out in the present for the sake of the next generation. In this context, Deuteronomy 6 enjoins parents to tell their children about the faith at every transition point of the day because every member of the community, not just special people, must know the story of God.

Or to put it very briefly, the Bible is the one book that speaks to our faith in an authoritative, yet liberating way. The Bible is the most reliable and comprehensive source of God's self-revelation to humankind. Through its pages, we learn who God is, and therefore who we are as God's creatures, companions, subjects, disciples, and children. We learn models for living with God, for the Bible teems with both positive and negative human exemplars and frames the most important moral questions for our deliberation.

Some may ask whether children can, in fact, understand the Bible. The answer is both yes and no. Yes, even the very young can understand parts of the Bible and, at a certain level, its key messages. As Dorothy Jean Furnish says, the Bible is an event in the environment of Christian children.[1] That is, exposure to the Bible over time allows children to hone their skills of interpreting it and thus making meaning in their own lives. True, many aspects of the Bible require study beyond the abilities of children, but they may encounter it at levels appropriate to their intellectual and emotional development and can continue to re-encounter the same texts repeatedly with profit.

Reading the Bible can occur in ways that appeal to children through play, drawing, retelling, song, dramatic reenactment, journaling, discussion, friendly competition, chanting, memorization, and other activities that appeal to several learning styles at once. Regular practice combined with spontaneity and creativity can lay a foundation in Scripture that remains with children throughout their lives.

If reading the Bible involves both adults and children, then it becomes important to ask how adults (parents and others) relate to children, the interconnections between family and church, and how all those layers of association and community influence how we understand the Bible. Together, adults and children can feel the emotions that characters in the Bible might have felt, and thus learn to respond to Scripture at multiple levels. They can, in short, learn to live the Bible with each other.

Exploring the Bible at Various Ages

First, many of us have learned to think of human development in terms of stages. Individuals differ, but human beings develop in fairly consistent ways through the life cycle. We take for granted developmental theories, but often do not recognize aspects of spiritual development. How children think, make decisions, reply to questions, use language, and relate to other persons grow over time. Adults interacting with them should expect these changes and should help children engage the Bible (and all spiritual matters) in ways suitable to their stage of development. Moreover, since children have different experiences, abilities, opportunities, and limitations, adults should attend to their words and actions in order to understand their thoughts. Our goal is not merely to provide answers, but to foster an attitude of curiosity. How we answer children's questions matters because it sets the tone for their approach to faith going forward.

As J. J. Dillon has put it, children are "deep thinkers and feelers who wrestle with life's mysteries and hunger for meaning and value by which to live their lives."[2] They can imagine themselves in a caring, instructive, gentle, and life-giving relationship with God. Adults strengthen children's capacity to receive spiritual knowledge from God by helping them value their inner lives—imagination, awe, and wonder. We help them articulate this inner life in spoken and (later) written language, in art, and in music. Adults can help children develop early in life attitudes of simplicity, generosity, and empathy that will serve them throughout their lives.

Similarly, Kathy Coffey has noted that adults can help cultivate the inner lives of children by knowing that children wonder at the world. Accordingly, she counsels adults to recognize that children long deeply for God and ask spiritually significant questions in concrete (not abstract) forms. She then counsels adults to engage in wonder alongside children and help them dream about their own lives as Christian persons, an act she calls "the most productive approach" to their formation.[3]

The sort of approach to children's spiritual formation that I am arguing for also appears in the Synoptic Gospels, which portray Jesus welcoming children into God's Kingdom. In the Gospels, children become touchstones for discipleship because they trust God's protection and mercy. They are citizens of God's merciful Kingdom, models of how to enter God's reign, and examples of humility and service. To welcome them is to welcome Jesus. Along with many other biblical texts, the Gospels portray them as sources of hope and bearers of the future.

Second, as every adult knows, the relationship between them and children changes over time. For example, a newborn infant needs a level of physical care that a third grader ordinarily does not. In general terms, children develop spiritually in the following ways. *Young children* encounter the world through their relationships with their caregivers and through their senses. With allowance for their short attention spans, they need to learn to trust the Bible, which they do by handling it, looking at pictures related to biblical stories, and singing simple songs appropriate to their age. Adults can hold them in their laps and read to them.

Meanwhile, *lower elementary school aged children* are still concrete thinkers, but they begin to seek cause-and-effect relationships in their experiences, to memorize bodies of knowledge from which they draw inferences, and to develop learning styles distinctive to them. Children in this age group willingly explore issues of faith and morality related to the Bible, even if they tend to see things in black-and-white ways. They ask good questions, which adults are tempted to over-answer. Keep the answers simple, but respectful. By engaging a range of reading strategies, children can learn the Bible more deeply.

Upper elementary aged children, because their brains are developing new capacities for abstract thought, begin to see inconsistencies in the world around them. In thinking about their own faith development, they can employ many of the Bible reading strategies discussed below. If we remember that children in this age group must form an identity separate from their parents if they are to flourish as adults, we can be a (relatively!) non-anxious presence in their lives.

Third, if we speak of "adults' life with children," it is important to think broadly. Healthy families do not live as self-contained units. The role of the family has evolved a number of times over the past few centuries. In the West, family size has shrunk since the early nineteenth century, and most of us no longer count children as significant contributors to family income or status. An increasing number of children live with only one parent and experience strained family relationships. So it makes no sense to take the "ideal" family, whatever that is, as the central reference point for healthy spiritual nurture. Rather, we should recognize that all children need spiritual adults in their lives, and that we must strengthen families and friendships for this to happen.

The model I am offering here assumes an ongoing relationship involving children and adults. It also assumes that these adults embrace spiritual growth as a lifelong commitment, a process that requires critical thinking, imagination, and grace. Children who enter such a relationship fashioned by the adults around them will learn to see the Bible as the living word of God that bears witness to God's redemptive work in the world.

Choosing a Bible for Children

If all of this is true, then adults must work to teach the Bible to the children around them. Yet finding a Bible or Bible storybook appropriate for children is a difficult challenge. Such book needs to be (1) responsible to the biblical text (accurate, balanced, free of sectarian bias, etc.); (2) understandable by children; and (3) attractive and inviting. The adults who create such works try to meet these standards, though not always successfully. It helps to know a few things of relevance.

To begin, although the Bible has been translated into several thousand languages and dialects, in most languages it exists in only one version, often one made long ago. Readers of those languages may face difficulties in procuring the right Bible for children, though the proliferation of easy-to-read versions in many languages is remedying this problem. For English-speakers, the situation is different. There are arguably too many translations and paraphrases. Owing to this diversity, English-speaking children may use four or five different translations before reaching adulthood.

One way of choosing a Bible is allowing children to help in the selection. Choose one they will enjoy reading and looking through. For example, the New International Readers Version, based on the New International Version, addresses beginning readers and is less literal than the NIV. The Children's Easy-to-Read Bible from the World Bible Translation Center is appropriate for both children and adults who are less facile readers. For late preteens, the NIV, Contemporary English Version, or New Living Translation (actually a paraphrase) may be helpful. Teens may prefer the Common English Bible or, if they are superior readers, the New Revised Standard Version. The translations do often have theological associations. The NIV, NLT, and related translations come from conservative evangelicals, and the CEB and NRSV from a combination of mainline Protestants, Catholics, and Jews.

This chart illustrates the reading level of some popular translations:

Translation	Reading Level by Grade
International Children's Version (ICV)	3.9
New International Version (NIV)	7.8
Common English Bible (CEB)	7.8
The Message	8.5
New King James Version (NKJV)	9.1
New Revised Standard Version (RSV)	10.4
New American Standard Version (NASV)	11.3
King James Version (KJV)	12.0[4]

In addition to Bibles, children's Bibles and Bible storybooks can be helpful. A children's Bible is a volume that excerpts texts from the Bible itself, often in abbreviated form, while a Bible storybook retells the biblical story in whole or in part. A few popular books in these categories include *The Beginner's Bible* (ages 3–5), *Read with Me Bible* and *First Bible Stories* (ages 4–5), *The Big Picture Story Bible* (ages 4–8), *The Jesus Storybook Bible* (ages 5–10), *The Gospel Story Bible* (ages 6–12), *The Lion Bible for Children*, *A Family Treasury of Bible Stories*, *The Children's Illustrated Bible,* and the *DK Illustrated Children's Bible.*

In choosing such books, it might be helpful to ask the following questions:

- Does the story accurately reflect the biblical text it presents?
- Does the book as a whole present the Gospel accurately? For example, does it portray Jesus as a nice guy who helps people, or as the Savior who reveals God?
- Does this book prepare children appropriately for the time when their faith will outgrow it?
- Does the text avoid difficult issues altogether, or does it face them in ways appropriate to children?
- Do the illustrations fitly represent the text, or do they take on a life of their own?

Unfortunately, many Bible storybooks merely teach simple moral lessons and turn biblical characters into morally uncomplicated people. Thus, the richness of the Bible itself gets lost, and the power of God's redemption of real people (not idealized people) also vanishes. A good example of this phenomenon is the way in which the story of Noah's flood is told: a horrifying story of the consequences of sin and the precariousness of biological existence becomes a cute little tale of animals floating about in a boat. An epic of divine justice and mercy degenerates into a simplistic moral lesson. I am not suggesting that parents should be petty or literal-minded about such things, only that we need to make informed decisions.

In summary, whether we read our children the Bible itself or a book based on it, we want to honor God's presence in their lives and foster in them the joy that characterizes the faithful follower of Jesus Christ. By beginning or ending our reading time with prayer or singing or conversing together about the day, we can help our children do so. In these ways, we can cultivate in our children an attitude of wonder and expectation as they encounter the God of Scripture.

Select Ways of Reading

This brings us to another set of practical concerns. What do we mean by "reading" when we speak of "reading the Bible"? Certainly the familiar practice of the adults reading the biblical text to children is valuable. But there are other ways of achieving the same goals, depending on the rhythms of a given family, the age and interests of the children, time available, and so on. Remember that children do not read, as adults often do, simply for the right answers to the question or the solution to the problem at hand. They also read for enjoyment, for empathy, and for expansion of imagination, all goals suitable for the reading of Scripture. Children experience the theology of the Bible at many levels and can read it in many different ways. Let us explore several of these together.

Role-Playing

A fine form of recreating biblical texts is through role-play. Children can imagine themselves as characters in the biblical text, think about how a story might have happened or explore what a psalm might look like in the lives of real people. Dramatizing the biblical story helps the children feel a part of it.

Music

A related form is singing, putting Scripture to music. Children are often good at inventing songs related to a given biblical text. Alternatively, one may use a song related to the Bible that already exists. Of course many biblical texts (especially, but not limited to, the Psalms) have already been set to music. Singing the word together aids in memory and connects us with each other.

Prayerful Reading and Meditation

And then there is a centuries-old practice called prayerful reading or *lectio divina*, which is a Latin term meaning "sacred reading." In this style of group reading one person reads the text, perhaps repeating it several times, and then invites the hearers to comment on it however he or she wishes. For many children, drawing while listening to the biblical text is an effective way of learning as well.

Lectio divina has four major components: reading with a heart that seeks God, meditation on the Scripture itself, prayer rooted in Scripture, and contemplation of God in ways shaped by the Bible. Readers should ask questions such as, what does this text say about God? What does it say about me? Naturally, the ways of phrasing such questions depend on the age and maturity of the children involved, but the overall approach is useful for all but the smallest children. This method allows children and adults to enter the text wherever they can.

Alexander Campbell engaged in a similar practice with his family, dedicating two hours each day to spiritual matters. He argued that parents should approach Bible study as a child would, with an open heart and mind, and that they should meditate on God's word day and night, sit in God's presence, and listen for God's instruction. Such an approach to spiritual reading of Scripture profoundly influences a family's outlook on life.[5]

A companion behavior that early Christians learned for enriching prayerful reading of the Bible was deliberate silence. It is necessary for their spiritual well-being to teach children how to be silent, not in a nagging or restrictive way, but in order to help them settle their minds and become open to God in their lives. Parents and other adults can help by allowing time between their reading for children to close their eyes, think about what they've heard or read, and visualize themselves as part of the story. In a technology-saturated world, silence creates space for healthy mental processes.

Storytelling

Storytelling is the most familiar, but too often Christians are suspicious of the power of story, in spite of the fact that much of the Bible takes that form. Yet in telling stories, adults can be creative and encourage children to use their imaginations, entering the biblical text with passion. Storytelling allows children to develop emotionally rich relationships with the story-teller and the characters in the text.

How might thinking about storytelling aid children's engagement with Scripture? As the Old Testament scholar Walter Brueggemann argued in his book, *Belonging and Growing in the Christian Community*, nurturing children's spirituality requires focusing on five aspects of storytelling:

1. Children need to be *receiving* the spiritual story of love and redemption through the compassionate care of their parents and their faith community.
2. Children should be *hearing* the story of their spiritual tradition regularly in connection with the stories that make up their daily lives.
3. Children must be *celebrating* their stories of faith and personal spirituality stories through rituals such as special holidays and recognition of acts of charity and compassion.
4. Children need opportunities for *telling* spiritual stories in their own words, both to others and to God in prayer.
5. Children need ways of *becoming* "history-makers," people whose words and actions contribute to a more just and compassionate society and encourage others to do the same.[6]

Slow, deliberate, but pleasurable reading allows children and adults to grow together in these ways, to enter into the story of God's work in Israel and the church as full participants.

If Brueggemann is right that children (and the rest of us) need to hear and celebrate and experience the Bible, then we must ask what it means to live out, and not just read, the Bible. I think this means two different things: (1) Bible reading is part of a holistic set of spiritual practices that include prayer, fasting, hospitality, and service, all of which adults can help children learn and experience; and (2) Bible reading must lead to action. So, for example, if our family reads about Jesus feeding the 5000 hungry people, we can then discuss how our family can serve other people and act upon that discussion in prayerful, loving, generous, and serving ways.

Living Out the Bible with Children

Attentive adults also know that children seek to make meaning out of their experiences. They draw connections among the things in their mental worlds, often in surprising ways.

Adults and children make meaning together in several concrete ways, all of which relate to reading the Bible together. First, in *family faith conversations*, children enjoy discussing many things, from stories that adults invent to stories of our lives at an earlier time to broader issues in the world. Open-ended discussions on relevant and controversial issues create an atmosphere for dialogue and growth. At bedtime and mealtime, in the car or on the athletic field, we share our lives together. Being open with our children about our successes and failures helps us model honesty and generosity, accountability and forgiveness. The Bible becomes part of this larger conversation.

A few years ago, as part of our faith conversations, my husband and I wrote, in consultation with our children, a short list we called "Ten Touchstones for Life." We told them that we were praying for them in connection with this list because we wanted them to be people who experience daily God's love as lived out in spiritual disciplines that reflect their status as persons created in God's image. The list said

1. God loves you and all other human beings and works for your redemption. Despite appearances, God is faithful and trustworthy.
2. You are a spiritual being, capable of continuing growth through diligent prayer, disciplined study of God's word, creative service, humble sacrifice, and thoughtful reflection.

3. You are part of a community to which you can make a significant contribution. You have both an obligation and opportunity to better the world around you.
4. Words count. Choose your language well to reflect your own dignity and that of others.
5. Honor your own body, mind, and spirit with appropriate exercise and self-discipline.
6. Remember that love builds up. Do not sacrifice your dignity for the sake of winning the so-called love of someone else. Do not demand that of someone else.
7. Remember that anger, fear, and hatred diminish you as a human being, as well those who are recipients of your negative behavior.
8. Remember that you are more than what you have. The relentless pursuit of more things diminishes you as a spiritual being, as a human being.
9. Remember to work tirelessly for peace. This will often be difficult and will require you to confront those who abuse their power. But in the end it will enhance the world you have entered.
10. Remember that this world is not the end. While it has great importance in its own right, it part of the larger continuum of eternity, which you should keep in mind as you live here.

The list is imperfect, but it offers some guidance for life, not just for teens, but also for adults and the children in their care. It also reminds us that reading the Bible as a spiritual practice takes place in a context of overall attention to spiritual health.

The second mode of life together is *family ritual and devotion.* Families need rituals for their own well-being and cohesion. Without rituals, life degenerates into chaos. Times of shared celebration or mourning reduce conflict and promote family cooperation and integration. Ritual is a way of organizing time, space, matter, and relationships so as to make us aware of God and our place in God's transcendent plan. It is important that we have regular times of praying, singing, reading Scripture, discussing our lives together. Both adults and children need such times. When our children lived at home, we prayed together at mealtime and celebrated the anniversaries of their baptisms in order to foster a spiritual awareness in them and ourselves. Such rituals need to be intentional and thoughtful, but they do not need to be "churchy."

As an avenue of meaning making, rituals help orient children to spiritual practices. For example, when our children were in elementary school, we asked them to plan our weekly family devotional. At first, they imitated what they had seen at church, complete with a worship bulletin, songs from a hymnal, readings of the Bible, and a short sermon. (And the sermons of second graders are always interesting!) But over time, they began to innovate, to draw new connections, so there was always a time in the service they called FLAP, an acronym for "faith, love, and praise." Though aware of the humorous nature of the name, they were serious about translating love and faith into concrete practice. In short, they were meaning-makers.

The third way in which adults and children grow together spiritually, and thus make the Bible come alive, is through *outreach and service.* In the country of my childhood, we valued family solidarity, unity, harmony, and commitment to each other. Since my husband and I married, we have tried to pass on to our children those values, which coincide with Christian principles. We live together and serve together. To be sure, many families struggle to serve others because they face too many problems of their own. Yet often, acts of selfless mercy can transform woes into healing as well as bring help to those in greater need.

A fourth way of connecting the Bible to life is through *hospitality.* Obviously, hospitality is a valued practice in Scripture, from Abraham and Sarah receiving the angelic guests to Jesus preparing a final meal for his disciples on the Thursday before his death. As Diana Butler Bass puts it, "Through hospitality, Christians imitate God's welcome. Therefore, hospitality is not a program, not a single hour of ministry in the life of a congregation. It stands at the heart of Christian way of life, a living icon of wholeness in God."[7] Christian hospitality does not extend only to our friends—a practice that Jesus forbids—but to all we encounter. By practicing biblical hospitality together, welcoming those who are different than us or with whom we may disagree, we live out the true meaning of the Bible and translate its words into actions.

Conclusion

Reading the Bible is part of a web of multigenerational spiritual practices. We do not read the Bible simply for information or answers to key spiritual questions. We read the Bible because doing so leads to spiritual maturity, and we want our children to grow up to be just, generous, honorable, loving, and forgiving people.

By attending to Bible reading as a sustained, meaningful, and life-giving practice, adults can help children grow in faith, moving through the life cycle from literal, concrete thinking to abstract thinking in appropriate ways. We can equip "God's minors," to quote a phrase from Alexander Campbell, for a lifelong pursuit of spiritual maturity. Along the way, we adults can also grow, for the best way to learn is to teach, and the best way to be loved is to love.

Chapter 6

Praying Alongside Our Children

Samjung Kang-Hamilton

In his children's book, *The Story of Ruby Bridges,* Robert Coles tells the story of the little first grader who was the first black child in her all white elementary school. Facing the howling mob and the scorn of fellow children, Ruby persevered. At one point, her teacher noticed that she had turned to the crowd and seemed to say something. She asked Ruby why she had faced them. "I didn't stop and talk with them," she said. "Ruby I saw you talking," Miss Hurley said. "I saw your lips moving." "I wasn't talking, I was praying. I was praying for them."[1]

I believe that prayer is the most important Christian spiritual practice learned in a family. Yet prayer does not come easily. It is a discipline that we learn through constant practice and reflection. When we were children, parents and other adults modeled for us how to position our bodies for prayer and how to speak words that come from our hearts. Hopefully, they taught us that prayer is not an activity for special occasions, but one that shapes who we are as human beings all the time. This is why the Apostle Paul urged his converts to "pray without ceasing" (1 Thess. 5:17), which does not mean ceaseless talking but ceaseless attention to our dependence on God.

According to a 2013 survey by Pew Research, more than half (55 percent) of Americans claim to pray daily, while another 23 percent do so weekly or monthly, and only 21 percent seldom or never. Even among the religiously unaffiliated, 21 percent said they pray daily. A 2012 survey by the same organization found that 76 percent of Americans agreed with the statement "prayer is an important part of my daily life," a percentage that has remained relatively consistent over the last twenty-five years.[2]

Since many of us live busy, hurried lives (whether by choice or not), how can we teach our children to pray? Without prayer just being one more thing on the to-do list, how can we proceed? Perhaps we simply begin by praying alongside children regularly, consistently, and with attention to all aspects of life. The conscious, daily, personal prayer of families and other influential adults nurtures the spiritual health of children because it connects us with each other and with God. Prayer speaks to the true nature of our existence as creatures beloved by and dependent on God. It also orients us to the desires of God for humanity, challenging our complacency and tendency to serve Mammon. Authentic prayer changes us because the encounter with God is always transformative. Prayer reminds us that we are not the world's judges but humble servants charged with offering cold water to the thirsty and clothes to the naked. Children raised in an environment in which prayer is a living reality are different from those who are not.

In my family, we have tried to take seriously the old adage, "The family that prays together stays together," while being aware of the many exceptions to this so-called rule. When our children lived at home, we had a family devotional on Fridays in which we all knelt down and held hands together as family. No matter how difficult our week had been, or how frustrated we were with each other, we tried to carry on this practice at home or at the local park.

During his turn to pray, my husband always prayed for me, thanking God for what I do for our family and asking for my spiritual and physical well-being. Children are blessed by hearing those who care for them praying for each other. This provides a model for how to treat those closest to them. Family members sincerely praying for one another can forge deep connections.

If prayer is a learned approach to life, a discipline or practice that touches all aspects of our existence in ways that can make us more loving, generous, and grace-filled, we should ask what resources for prayer exist for us. Although we often speak about prayer in Bible classes and other church settings, many of us still struggle once the doors are closed. The following will discuss biblical understandings of prayer and ways of praying that believers have long found valuable.

Prayer in Scripture

An obvious feature of the Bible is that it contains hundreds of prayers. These include not just the 150 psalms and the book of Lamentations but scores of others scattered throughout every literary genre. Ignoring this aspect of Scripture would create serious misunderstandings of its nature and purpose and reduce it to a mere book of laws and stories. More to the point, the diversity of these texts cautions us against thinking about prayer too narrowly. We do not pray simply to get what we want, even important things like physical health or family happiness. No, we pray to become who we need to be, people who live in close harmony with God. Without getting this point right, our prayers become too predictable, self-centered, and sterile to do much good.

For Christians, the touchstone prayer is the "Our Father" or "Lord's Prayer," which appears twice in Scripture. In Luke 11, Jesus teaches it to his disciples on their request that he "teach us how to pray, as John taught his disciples" (Luke 11:1). In Matthew 6, however, the prayer features as part of the Sermon on the Mount (in fact near its center) in the context of a long discussion of acts of piety that honor God. Though the wording of the two versions differs slightly, they are essentially identical. The "Our Father," which became part of Christian communal worship near the very beginning of the church's life, encourages those praying to invite God into the world of human experience. It expresses our deepest longing for the just and peaceable kingdom of God to be present on this earth, and it calls upon us to reduce our demands on life to their essentials so that we may be free to be with God. As the German theologian Dietrich Bonhoeffer once put it, the Kingdom for which we pray is "God's miracle, of breaking through death to life, and it is the miracle that supports our faith and our prayer for the kingdom. . . . If God is truly God—then God is God, then God's kingdom is miraculous, the epitome of miracles."[3]

However, the disciples' request to learn how to pray should not be taken too literally. As observant Jews, they already knew how to pray. They had learned from childhood the words of Psalms and countless other prayers. Yet their request does make sense because they wanted to learn from Jesus how to pray more deeply and thus how to enter into the Kingdom. So the language of the "Our Father" is performative: saying these words helps us enter into the reality they describe (just as "I now pronounce you husband and wife" creates a marriage or "strike three" compels a batter to return to the dugout). Those who pray the prayer, unless they are amazingly resistant to the words they utter, take on new desires, relationships to material possessions, and ways of interacting with other people. And this is the essence of Christian prayer.

The tradition behind the Our Father includes numerous forms of prayer:

- Praise and thanksgiving
- Lament based on trust
- Confession based on hope for forgiveness
- Intercession based on belief in God's providential care
- Request for basic needs
- Fixed hours or repetition

Since Christians from earliest times have prayed this prayer both in private and in community, the words have trained us to think of prayer in particular ways.

These broader-based understandings of prayer point us to its deepest goal, which is communion with God in whatever way God grants us. Prayer is thus not primarily our activity, our achievement, our work, but the work of God in us as we listen for divine guidance and belonging. Prayer, as Bonhoeffer might say, affirms the miracle of God's Kingdom.

Since prayer is a comprehensive activity, it involves every aspect of our being, mind, spirit, and body. Thus, we read in the Bible of faithful people using their body to stand in acknowledgment of God's majesty (Gen. 18:22; Mark 11:25), raising their hands to reach out to God (Ps. 63:4; 77:2; 141: 2; 1 Tim. 2:8), lifting their eyes to heaven for God's help (John 17:1), kneeling to indicate their humble reverence before God (Dan. 6:10; Acts 9:40; 20:36), and bowing down for the same reasons (Gen. 17:3; Neh. 8:6; Pss. 66:4; 72:11; 138:1–3; Luke 5:12). Since we can only encounter God in the context of our own reality as embodied creatures limited in time and space, we discipline the body and the mind for prayer in these ways.

Therefore, if we are to model for our children the full richness of Christian prayer, we must share with them different practices of prayer. By varying the time and place of prayer, we allow each occasion to be a joyful exploration of life in God's Kingdom. Sometimes it is helpful to give children words to say, perhaps in the form of a "prayer starter" such as "God, sometimes I think . . ." or "Jesus, I want to be like you when . . ." Such orienting phrases teach children to be thankful for concrete things and to talk to God when they feel alone or afraid. They should be free to employ words, gestures, or movements that feel comfortable for them. What might seem odd in adults can make sense for children.

We do need to remember, however, that children can be very literal-minded. For example, my husband tells the story of when he was five years old and just learning to pray. He had been told in church that God gives us whatever we ask for, and so he asked God for a pet rabbit on the assumption that the adults had correctly stated how prayer work. Unfortunately, he didn't realize that in the matter of rabbits, God ordinarily works through parental intermediaries, who in his case either didn't know of his desire for a bunny or decided to veto it. An unanswered prayer created a brief faith crisis still remembered decades later. Parents and other adults praying with children do well to listen to their children very carefully in order to discern what the children understand.

"Lord, teach us to pray, as John taught his disciples." What, then, are ways in which the church has prayed through the centuries? What might we learn from their experiences?

Models for Praying alongside Children

To answer these questions, I propose that we consider twelve methods of praying. There are many ways to pray, but these twelve models provide useful starting points. Readers may differ in which of these they find useful or meaningful, but the discovery of new ways to pray benefits all people of faith. Some of these will be unfamiliar to some, but they all have centuries-long precedent behind them, usually from the New Testament itself. The first several forms offer young children good entry points into the life of prayer, while the later forms may be more appropriate for older children. Once children become comfortable with different ways to pray, they can gravitate toward those that best fit their relationship with God.

Prayer Walking and Watching

Among the most active ways of praying is prayer walking, which means strolling about your neighborhood or town and praying for whomever or whatever you see. This practice can release pent-up energy and orient children to their wider environment. Such a practice also helps children to observe their world closely, noting both the good and the evil all about them. Good locations for prayer walking include schools, parks and wilderness, historic sites, and sites of ministry. Children can thank God for the flowers and trees, their neighbors and friends, and whatever else they see. Another form of prayer walking happens while walking through a labyrinth, a sort of maze with stops marked by words or symbols that focus on particular virtues or concerns. On my university campus, there is a stone labyrinth constructed on the ground and modeled on the one at Chartres Cathedral in France. One can walk through it slowly and meditatively, looking at the words and praying about aspects of one's life. Such a practice is also very accessible to children. You might even draw your own labyrinth together with sidewalk chalk. As you walk and pray with children, gently answer their questions and listen to their thoughts as you experience God's presence together.

A closely related practice is prayer watching, which involves choosing a space not usually frequented by the participants and engaging in prayer activity (including Bible reading, silence, perhaps sharing refreshments). All but the youngest children can participate actively in this form of praying as well.

Combining physical activity, observation of the environment, and prayer in these ways teaches us to widen our circle of concern and to think of prayer as an activity we can do throughout the day. Children who have such an experience early in life can begin to think of prayer as more than just a series of requests for their personal needs. They see prayer as ongoing conversation with and awareness of God.

Praying with Poetry and Song

Another long-established form of prayer is the use of poetry and song, a practice that goes back to the book of Psalms. Children often enjoy hearing poetry in many forms, and as they get older, can write their own. For example, when our son was ten years old, he wrote an acrostic poem for a church group, aiming at the prompt "Image of God":

I am in the image of God,
My image really matters.
And I was created equally,
Good, and productively.
Especially I am his image!
On God's path we go,
For he has loved me so.
God's image is so great
Only he gets to choose our fate.
Do respect the Image of God!

The poem hung on the wall in his room for years. Such an affirmation of faith shapes into prayer and allows an upper elementary age child to create an imaginative artifact in his or her own spiritual journey.

For younger children not yet able to write their own poems, reading the poems of others–rhymed or unrhymed–offers an orienting way to pray. In her children's book, *This Is What I Pray Today: Divine Hours Prayers For Children*, Phyllis Tickle offers a Sunday waking prayer based on Psalm 116:

> God hears me when I pray
> I know that this is so
> And I am going to speak to God today
> In all the places where I go.[4]

A smaller child can find in such a poem a sense of well-being and comfort.

Similarly, songs offer appropriate words for prayer. Children can profit from hearing and singing such simple prayers as "Father, We Thank for the Night" or "Jesus Loves Me" (the last verse of which says, "Jesus take this heart of mine, / Make it pure and wholly thine, / Thou hast bled and died for me, / I will henceforth live for thee"). When our children were in elementary school, every morning in the car, we sang the song "This is the Day That the Lord Has Made" in English, Spanish, and Korean as our group prayer for the day. As children grow older, they can reflect on the ideas of such songs and incorporate them into their own understanding of prayer.

Conversational Prayer

Yet another form of prayer involves ordinary conversation with an extraordinary partner, i.e., God. The prayers of Jesus take this form, as in John 17, which has the intimate feel of one person talking with a close friend. Family or church groups involving adults and children can pray this way together, simply including God as a member of their group as they seek God's guidance, protection, instruction, and blessing. Such prayer uses simple, straightforward, and spontaneous, language for everyday experiences.

Five ingredients make this form of prayer meaningful. (1) There is no need to take prayer requests, since the conversation involves everyone, though it is appropriate to interrupt a prayer and ask what someone means by whatever he or she has said. (2) Do not put anyone on the spot by demanding that he or she pray. Let good will and spontaneity be the order of the day. (3) Address one topic at a time, and make space for affirmation ("Amen," "that's right"). (4) Let the group leader pray first, at least early in the group's life, but otherwise let the movement be free flowing. And (5) let utterances be brief. Anyone can pray more than once, but it is important not to monopolize the time. Children participating in this form of prayer learn to respect other people and their needs and desires, and most of all to respect God as the One who cares for every aspect of our lives but calls us to prioritize the most important.

Prayer in Solitude and Silence

All prayer requires focus and the removal of distractions. Prayer in solitude and silence emphasizes freedom from the pressures of the outside world. This is why Jesus often left the company of other people to attend to his primary work, communication with God. Silence and solitude create the space in the soul for us to be able to hear God.

Many families find that designating a space in the house as a spot for silence helps children learn to respect each other's need for quietness and disconnection from excessive media stimulation. Other families mark not space, but time. Young children can learn that quiet time each day is part of the rhythm of a healthy person, a source of well-being rather than a punishment. By honoring our in-born need for regular solitude, silence, and prayer, we can create adequate space for a spiritual life to develop. Unplug the technology for five or ten minutes for younger children (longer for older ones) and allow them to spend quiet time drawing, reading the Bible, journaling, and so on.

Why is silence so important? In reflecting on this question, Mother Teresa wrote,

> God is the friend of silence. In that silence he will listen to us: there he will speak to our soul, and there we will hear his voice.

> The fruit of silence is faith. The fruit of faith is prayer, the fruit of
> prayer is love, the fruit of love is service, and the fruit of service
> silence. In the silence of the heart God speaks. If you face God
> in prayer and silence, God will speak to you. God is the friend of
> silence. His language is silence.[5]

This sense of the interconnection of silence with all the primary Christian commitments (faith, hope, and love) offers an important insight into the nature of prayer. Silence is essential in prayer because it allows us to still our heart, to become free of distractions and excessive stimulation, so that we may hear God speak.

Breath/Jesus Prayer

One important form of prayer occurs during both moments of solitude and silence and times of intense outside pressure is the breath prayer. This is a prayer that a person can say in one breath; famous examples include: the Eastern Christian prayer, "Lord Jesus Christ, son of God, have mercy on me"; Francis of Assisi's "My God and my all!"; and, arguably, Jesus' words from the cross, "Forgive them, for they know not what they do" and "Into your hands I commit my spirit." Children, as well as adults, can learn to say such prayers throughout the day, in times of peace and security, and in times of crisis and conflict. Some breath prayers come from well-known songs such as "Be With Me Lord, I Cannot Live Without Thee," "Be Still My soul," or "Be Still and Know I am God." In my own life, these breath prayer songs gave me peace when I immigrated to this country, and they are still my daily prayers in various situations. An eight-year-old who prays, "the Lord is my shepherd" may have greater capacity to face bullies at school or to make good ethical decisions than he would otherwise. A child who reminds herself that "God loves me and cares for me" has a resource for life that others do not.

To learn such prayers, adults can help children find a comfortable, understandable way of praying. Let children sit straight but comfortably, pay attention to their breathing so that it is restful and not labored. Wait awhile and then pray with the rhythm of their breathing, inhaling and exhaling to the words. For more advanced practitioners, this sort of prayer offers occasion for reflection on individual words and phrases. So, for example, one might think about what it means to say that Jesus has mercy "on me"—why do I need mercy? How do I extend it to others?

Some parents might wonder if this sort of prayer comes under the category of "vain repetition," which Jesus forbids, or some sort of New Age gimmick. The answer is no. The breath prayer is an ancient Christian practice that responds to our need to focus in prayer. Since focus is one of the hardest things to learn in life, especially for children, breath prayers meet a real need. Because they are simple and meaningful, they help us attune our souls to God.

Prayer Journaling

Another form of praying that helps focus is prayer journaling. This is not the same thing as keeping a diary, though it resembles that long-celebrated practice. For children who have learned to read and write (say, by third grade), prayer journaling is a tool for reflecting on God's presence, nurture, and guidance in everyday life. An inexpensive notebook can provide just the right opportunity for them to write their thoughts, draw pictures of their environment as they understand it, and work out their spiritual reflections in a comfortable way. Over time, these journals become cherished keepsakes for their family.

The prayers in the journal can be the child's free composition (in any of the forms we are discussing), or a prayer they found in the Bible or elsewhere. Some children enjoy copying Psalms and then drawing pictures related to them. Such an activity allows them to express thankfulness and peace, as well as any anxieties they may feel.

Inner-Healing Prayer

Another type of prayer is that for inner healing, also called the centering prayer. In the church, because we are heavily influenced by the secular culture, we have come to believe that our job is to attend to the ordinary affairs of life while God's job is to attend to our souls. In the Bible, however, the exact opposite view dominates. God will give us food and clothes, while we must attend to our inner beings (with God's providential care present, of course). In her book *Spiritual Disciplines Handbook,* Adele Ahlberg Calhoun notes that prayer for inner healing invites those with emotional wounds to enter the safe and healing presence of Jesus.[6] In this safe place, those seeking wholeness and freedom open themselves to listen to Jesus and his word to them. Children also carry about pain and anxiety (for example: actual or potential death of loved ones, transitions beyond their control, and divorce), and inner-healing prayer can help them cope with the anxiety they face daily. Adults can help children in simple ways by reading stories of Jesus healing the sick, talking through these stories of God's mercy and love, and then praying about the suffering in their own lives. Childhood may be idyllic for some, but not for all. We do well to bring prayer to bear amid the challenges of children's lives.

Contemplative Prayer

Since the aim of prayer is to be in communion with God, an indispensable aspect of it is contemplation. Such prayer meditates upon God's goodness, might, justice, faithfulness, and waits for God's presence. It is both a way of being in relationship with God and a means for deepening that relationship.

For children, contemplative prayer is a difficult challenge because they are concrete thinkers. Yet it is possible to talk through such prayers with them. Ask them, "What do you think God is like? Do you know that you can trust God all the time? What do you think it means to say that God is everywhere?"

More generally, contemplative prayer makes sense as part of a conversation about spiritual matters, rather than as a freestanding way of praying. When our children were small, we used to go to the park, sit on a bench and pray in order to help them develop an awareness of the inner life, cultivate patience, and discover that there is more to life than consumption. This sort awareness can be the best gift we give our children.

Intercessory Prayer

Even more basic is intercessory prayer—asking God's attention to other people. If adults help children broaden their focus of concern so that they understand that God is not a lottery in the sky (rabbits don't always come for the asking!), we can help them pray intercessory prayers. Through these prayers we invite divine blessing, healing, or protection for others. We can teach children to pray for their friends and families, for other adults they know, and even for those they do not like or respect. Such prayers not only make us more compassionate, but they also orient us to God's concerns for the world.

Several aspects of intercessory prayer are important. It

- Expresses concern for God's intentions for the world, as Abraham and Moses found when praying for wicked people;
- Changes us as we encounter God, as Joseph found in Egypt;
- Voices our desires to God and seeks God's response, as Job found in his raging;
- Joins us in love with the love of Christ, as we seek to trust God's intentions for us;
- Makes us aware of the presence of the Holy Spirit in us, as Paul says to the Romans;
- Aids us in cooperating with God's actions on behalf of humankind.

While we make a mistake when we think of intercessory prayer as the main form of prayer, its importance is still great.

Praying Scripture

Intercessory and contemplative prayer merge when we take up the form of praying Scripture. This ancient practice appears in the Bible itself. For example, early Christians prayed Psalm 2 and applied it to their own lives (Acts 4:23–27; 13:32–34). Begin by reading a passage of Scripture, meditate on its meaning, and then pray into the text. For example, if the text is Psalm 23, then one begins to remember how God has cared for him or her, provided for needs, removed serious obstacles to spiritual growth, and so on. Thanksgiving and expressions of trust can characterize a prayer from such a text.

A special form of praying Scripture is *slow reading*, or *lectio divina*. (See also my discussion of this practice in the chapter on the Bible and children.) In praying this way, one should concentrate on a word or phrase in the biblical text and consider its implications for life. Read the text, meditate on its significance, pray about it, and wait for the gift of insight that God gives. By teaching this form of prayer to children, adults can model for them a contemplative life that is no longer controlled by our own egotism and will to power, but by a view of God as the One who is far above us.

Fixed Hour Prayer

Another ancient form of prayer is the fixed hour prayer. Ancient Jews such as the prophet Daniel or the apostles in Acts 3 prayed three times a day (dawn, noon, dusk) in order to organize the entire day around prayer. This practice later became the basis of the Muslim practice of praying five times per day. Children and families engaging in this practice can similarly reorient their lives by rethinking how they understand time. Time becomes less a commodity to be managed than a gift to be received.

In *This Is What I Pray Today: Divine Hours Prayers For Children*, Phyllis Tickle offers a beautifully illustrated book of prayers for children based on selected Psalms, each for a fixed time of day. Adopting the same principles underlying her books on divine (fixed) hours, in this book she offers prayers for each day, beginning with Sunday, that help readers pray at each transition point of the day (waking, resting, and going to sleep). The book helps families take the spiritual journey together.

Reflection Prayer/Examen

Finally, the prayer of examen is based on personal introspection. It is a prayer for discerning the voice and activity of God within the flow of the day and is an important vehicle that creates deep relationship or self-awareness. One begins this prayer by recounting the episodes of the day, its successes and failures, and then brings those experiences to God. A family or mixed-generational group may take turns praying about other's experiences. This practice models for children concern for others, attentiveness to the spiritual dimensions of everyday life, and honesty and openness with trusted companions. Leading questions (such as "What part of today am I most thankful for?" or "What is something I did today that I need forgiveness for?" or "In what ways did I notice God in my day?") can support the cultivation of these virtues. By reflecting on our day, week, month, or year, we can learn to see what God has done and so acquire a new perspective on our Christian walk with God and our family and friends. At the dinner table or other settings for family conversation, we can teach our children this practice of finding God in their daily life.

Conclusions

Like adults, children can engage in a range of prayer practices suitable to their age and maturity. Modeling for them a range of practices helps them think deeply and broadly about prayer, find the mode of prayer most meaningful to them, and develop a spiritual maturity that is frankly unobtainable in any other way.

Adults may listen sensitively to children to direct their natural desire for a relationship with God into constructive channels. By encouraging creativity and imagination and by creating regular rhythms of life that include set times of prayer and that balance silence and solitude with good communication in the group, adults can make prayer an organic part of the child's experience so that it becomes simply a normal part of life.

When our daughter was ten years old, she wrote a song to God:

Lord, you are holy and worthy.
You are the creator of the world and of your holy realm.
Your kingdom lasts forever. You made everyone equal on
 the earth.
You sent Jesus here for us to save our sins.
Everyone praise the Lord!

The lamb of God who is our savior and king!
The Lord be with you.

She wrote the words on paper that she affixed to an old bit of wooden paneling which has hung at the entryway of our house ever since. The poem marks our front door as a transition point between family and public space and states quietly that both are the realm of God's concern, which we acknowledge in our prayers. Just as Ruby Bridges learned that prayer invites God to change the world, so may other children learn that today we must choose which experiences define the future. Cultivating a life of prayer helps children experience God's peaceable kingdom all their days on earth.

Section Three

Children and the Faith Community

Reshaping the Church into an Intergenerational Body

Holly Catterton Allen

The small church plant that we have been part of for seven years meets in intergenerational small groups every Sunday evening with babies, children, teens, and emerging adults, young adults, middle adults, and senior adults all together. Recently during a discussion about persecution, Kelsey, a seventh grader, asked the group for some advice. She told us that her classmates had been harassing her about her beliefs, and that recently she had pushed back at them, saying, "I can believe what I want." Kelsey then asked the group how she *should* answer those around her who challenge her faith. The response of the group was multi-layered and supportive. One of the high school students in our group offered encouraging words; two ninth grade boys listened with keen interest; two elementary boys, sitting on the floor also followed the conversation closely; a grandmother in the group offered support and insight, one of the parents in the group did also. The two preschoolers were playing with toys in the middle of our circle, but eyes and ears were attuned.

Later when the group gathered in a standing circle, holding hands, Kelsey's dilemma was lifted in prayer; I was watching during the prayer to take in the response of the group. I noticed that a couple of the teens nodded during that part of the prayer; three-year-old Matthew had placed his hand in his grandfather's hand, but had not offered his other hand to Kelsey (who was standing next to him). During the prayer, Matthew peered intently at each person in the group, working his way around the entire circle. When Kelsey's name was brought up in the prayer, Matthew peeked up at Kelsey, touched her arm, and, as she opened her fingers, he slipped his small hand into hers as they shared a small, shy smile.

This type of *intergenerational* ministry is common in our small group settings—though admittedly it doesn't happen every week. But in general, this type of informal intergenerational interpersonal ministry is rare in contemporary American Christianity—for the simple and obvious reason that the generations are rarely together in order for intergenerational ministry to occur.

During the last hundred years, our society has begun to systematically separate families and segregate generations. Age-graded public education, the movement from extended to nuclear family, the prevalence of retirement and nursing homes for older persons, and the growth of preschools for the young have contributed to a pervasive segregation of young and old.

Churches have been among the few places where families, singles, couples, children, teens, grandparents—all generations—come together on a regular interactive basis. Yet, the societal trend toward age segregation has moved into churches also. Age-based classes for children (as well as adults), youth ministry, and separate worship services for adults and children tend to separate families and age groups from each other, so that children could experience Christian community as age-segregated throughout their lives.

Why Have Churches Tended to Separate the Generations in Recent Decades?

Several factors have contributed to the age segregation so prevalent today when Christians gather for worship, service, ministry, or simply for fellowship. Four of these factors are cultural influences, the recommendation of church growth strategists, the dominant ideology of individualism, and the influence of developmental psychology.

Cultural Influence

The move toward age segregation in society *in general* is one factor that has contributed to age segregation in American churches. Throughout the ages, Christians have tended to emulate—often unintentionally or unthinkingly—the culture around them, and as American culture has become more and more age segregated in the last hundred years, churches have followed that same trend. Mary Pipher, an American clinical psychologist who speaks and writes about culture says: "A great deal of America's social sickness comes from age segregation. If ten 14-year-olds are grouped together, they will form a *Lord of the Flies* culture with its competitiveness and meanness. But if ten people ages 2 to 80 are grouped together, they will fall into a natural age hierarchy that nurtures and teaches them all. For our own mental and societal health, we need to reconnect the age groups."[1]

Church Growth Strategists

Building on the missional principle that people want to become Christians with others like themselves,[2] some church growth specialists in the 1970s and 1980s began to promote homogeneity (around ages or stage of life) at the small group level and even at the macrochurch level.[3] Though age– or stage-defined small groups can provide empathy and social comfort, ultimately they have had the effect of sorting faith communities by generation.[4]

Individualism

Another factor that promotes age segregation in church life is the dominant cultural ideology of individualism, evidence of which is seen in worship wars between generations. Much could be said, but put simply we have arrived at a time when our own individual (or group's) happiness and relational satisfaction takes priority over the needs of the whole faith community. Evangelical churches in particular tend to "emphasize *individual* spiritual empowerment," and, according to William Dinges, are growing because of their consumer-friendly attention to individual needs.[5] And when individual needs are considered paramount, churches tend to offer special programs for children, teens, young, middle, and older adults, so that individual age/stage needs can be met more conveniently.

Influence of Developmental Psychology

From my perspective, the principal reason age and/or stage segregation is so pervasive in faith communities is that we have allowed educational, developmental, and cognitive psychology models to supersede theological models of spiritual formation. Since mid-twentieth century, church leaders have become increasingly aware of the importance of cognitive developmental differences between children and others, the unique psychosocial developmental issues of teens, and the differing life stage needs among adults.[6]

Piaget's work in cognitive development—the way persons of various ages *think*—revolutionized preschool and elementary education in public schools in the 1960s and 1970s—and eventually Sunday schools as well. Christian educators began to implement teaching-learning approaches that were more age appropriate for children such as the use of the five senses, body movement, visual aids, active involvement—all excellent ideas. Eventually, developmental concerns were applied to the worship hour, and some faith communities began to offer "children's church" options in the late 1960s and early 1970s.[7] Youth ministry was (and is), in part, a response to the unique psychological/emotional/social needs of teens such as differentiation issues, identity development, and distinctive doubt/faith concerns. And with adults, ministry leaders have become keenly aware that single twenty-somethings adjusting to the adult work world, coping with financial responsibility, and navigating a sexually charged environment face vastly different concerns than Boomers who are adjusting to retirement, coping with health worries, and navigating a world where they are marginalized and far less powerful than in their prime. A sensitive leadership deeply aware of the broad spectrum of these cognitive, social, and life stage needs would understandably perceive dividing by age or generational cohort as a sensible, even laudable, means of meeting those needs.

Given the power of the factors outlined above—the general societal acceptance of age segregation in American culture, recommendations of church growth experts, entrenched individualism, and diverse developmental and life stage needs, why should church leaders even consider moving toward a more intergenerational approach to Christian spiritual formation? The simple yet profound answer to this question is that intergenerational Christian experiences uniquely and especially nurture spiritual formation for *all* ages. This is not to say that spiritual formation doesn't also happen in age-segregated settings. However, the pendulum has currently swung predominantly toward age segregation, and this chapter is a call to balance, because the unique spiritual blessings that abound in cross-generational Christian settings are missed when the generations are never together.

Why Bring the Generations Back Together?

The unique spiritual benefits of all ages worshiping, praying, learning, working together are lost when segmented populations do them exclusively together. What are these unique spiritual benefits intergenerational faith communities engender? Among the many benefits for both adults and children are

- A sense of belonging: "College-aged people don't cut themselves, suffer from eating disorders, change majors seven times, change churches ten times or abandon church altogether because they're flighty. They do so because they don't know where they belong."[8]
- Support for troubled families: All faith communities have families who are facing severe difficulties. How does bringing the generations together uniquely benefit these families? Sharon Koh, senior associate pastor of Evergreen Baptist Church-Los Angeles, Rosemead, California says: "When our church is intentional about cross-generational interactions, it expands the concept of family beyond the nuclear family alone. . . . Because of this new concept of family, many inadequacies in the nuclear family can be made up for, in Christ's name."[9]

- Better use of resources: Chad Hall remarks, "Both young and old have resources to share. Generational homogenization results in an overabundance of one type of resources in certain congregations. Many older generation churches have plenty of money and facilities, but lack the energy and fresh vision young congregations have aplenty."[10]
- Character growth: "Churches who value their young and their old will have to deal with clashing perspectives, which may slow things down, make decisions harder to come by, force compromise on difficult matters, and automatically elevate the value of relationship over that of task."[11] "But when generations collide, the ensuing conflict reminds everyone that Church is not about me. . . . Who knew that church could be the cure to narcissism?"[12]
- Opportunities for sharing one another's spiritual journeys.

Besides these general blessings for all ages, children, teens, emerging adults, young adults, middle adults, and older adults experience *particular* blessings when they journey with all ages. Children especially need cross-generational relationships; one study indicates that one important aspect of children's growth toward faith "is a loving, caring, close relationship with other Christians."[13] The author of the study concludes "in the nurturing process of our children, we must allow them to develop deep personal relationships with as many of the people of God as possible."[14] One reason these relationships are so crucial for children is that in a few years they will be seeking mentors to accompany them in their adolescent years, and recent studies indicate that these mentors are frequently met years earlier, when the mentees were children.[15]

For teens, intergenerational faith experiences offer:

- Extended faith family ("aunts," "uncles," "grandparents") when blood family is distant.
- Support as they negotiate Erikson's identity vs. role confusion crisis.
- Opportunities to mentor pre-adolescents.

- Opportunities to serve those outside their teen worlds.
- Wisdom and encouragement while negotiating transitions from childhood to adolescence.
- Physical, emotional, psychological, and spiritual support when life falls down: parental divorce, sibling illness or death, failure in school, being bullied, feelings of loneliness.
- Opportunity to find examples and mentors among emerging adults and older adults.

For emerging adults, intergenerational faith experiences offer:

- Much-needed community.
- Support for lingering issues regarding identity development.
- Opportunities to mentor teens.
- Opportunities to serve outside their bubble.
- Wisdom and encouragement while negotiating central life issues such as job/career choices and a marriage partner.
- Physical, emotional, psychological, and spiritual support when facing difficult situations: faith doubts, addictions, financial instability, poor choices, illness
- Opportunities to find examples and mentors among those further ahead on the journey.

For young, middle, and older adults:

- Support for transition into the next stage of life.
- Support for the stresses of marriage, or support for living strong as a single adult.
- Physical, emotional, psychological, and spiritual support for the stress and weight of parenting young children, teenage children, and young adult children.
- Opportunities to *find* examples and mentors among those further ahead on the journey.
- Opportunity to *be* examples and mentors for those following on the journey.

- Physical, emotional, psychological, and spiritual support when facing grief or loss: with children, in a divorce, job loss, chronic or terminal illness.
- Hope from those who have travelled the journey before.
- Opportunities to begin pouring into the generations who follow.

What support is there for these wonderful benefits of intergenerational settings? My book with Christine Ross *Intergenerational Christian Formation: Bringing the Generations Together for Ministry, Community, and Worship* (2012) outlines extensive biblical, theological, theoretical, empirical, developmental, and sociological support for benefits and blessings of cross-age Christian experiences. For the purposes of this chapter, I will highlight some key findings that support the idea that intergenerational Christian experiences are uniquely spiritually formative.

Biblical and Theological Support

In Scripture, coming to know God is typically presented as a family- and community-based process. God's directives for God's people in the Old Testament clearly identify the Israelites as a relational community where the children were to grow up participating in the culture they were becoming. In the religion of Israel, children were not just included, they were drawn in, assimilated, absorbed into the whole community with a deep sense of belonging. Emerging from its Jewish heritage, the early church was a multigenerational entity. All generations met together, worshiping, breaking bread, praying together, ministering to one another in the context of the home (Acts 2:46–47; 4:32–35; 16:31–34).

Though Scripture also certainly offers examples in which the generations were not together (e.g., the Israelite warriors fighting in the Promised Land, the leaders of the church meeting in Jerusalem about the Gentile question), there is a pervasive sense throughout Scripture that all generations were typically present when faith communities gathered for worship, for celebration, for feasting, for praise, for encouragement, for reading of Scripture, in times of danger (e.g., *all* were present when Jehoshaphat prayed for God's intervention to save Israel from the surrounding enemy 2 Chron. 20:13, 20), and for support and service.

Support from Current Research

Empirical research also exists regarding spiritual benefits of cross-generational Christian experiences. Comprehensive, extensive, recent research from three sources—Kara Powell, Christian Smith, and David Kinnaman—powerfully supports the importance of intergenerational experiences for spiritual growth and development.

Powell, author of *Sticky Faith,* conducted her research in response to the increasing number of youth who move away from their faith commitment when they graduate from high school and leave their youth group. [16] She suggests that she was looking for a silver bullet to pass on to youth ministers—something they could do in order to instill faithful perseverance in these youth. Powell reports that the closest thing she found to a silver bullet was this: involvement in all-church worship during high school is more consistently linked with mature faith in both high school and college than any other form of church participation. [17] In addition, Powell's research found that the more students serve and build relationships with younger children, the more likely it is that their faith will stick. [18] What these two findings have in common is that they both highlight integrally *intergenerational* activities.

For a couple of decades, David Kinnaman (with the Barna Group) has been conducting research with emerging adults (and others) about their faith, beliefs, and practices. In *You Lost Me,* he outlines factors that contribute to faithfulness from fifteen years of research. His first comprehensive, global takeaway from this research is that *intergenerational relationships in faith communities are crucial.* [19]

For over a decade, Christian Smith has been following thousands of participants who were 13–17 years old when he began interviewing and surveying them in 2003 about their spiritual and religious beliefs, practices, and insights. Smith's findings are complex and multi-layered, but for our purposes (the impact of intergenerational Christian experiences), Smith says that religious socialization in America takes places in two spheres, in individual family households and in *multigenerational religious congregations*, and he concludes: "If nothing else, what the findings of this book clearly show is that for better or worse, these are the two crucial contexts of . . . religious formation in the United States. If formation does not happen here, it will—with rare exceptions—not happen anywhere."[20]

Furthermore, Smith states:

> "The empirical evidence tells us that it does in fact matter for emerging adult religious outcomes whether or not [the participants] have had nonparental adults in their religious congregation to whom they could turn for help and support. . . . It matters whether or not [they] have participated in adult-taught religious education classes, such as Sunday school. *Adult engagement with, role modeling for, and formation of youth simply matters a great deal for how they turn out after they leave the teenage years.*"[21]

Of course, the problem is that adults can have no influence with youth if they don't know them and are never with them. That has been a serious problem for decades. However in the past few years, there has been a phenomenal rise in interest in bringing the generations back together; they are *not* asking whether it is a good idea; they are asking: How can we bring the generations back together?

How Can We Bring the Generations Back Together?

This, of course, is the key question: "How can we do this—how can we bring the generations back together so that they may bless one another and grow each other up in Christ?" The last third of this chapter will describe concrete ways to bring the generations together. Wherever I speak on this topic, I hear fresh intergenerational ideas from local churches:

- In New Hampshire a church has planted a "giving garden"; this church has brought together the expertise of seasoned gardeners with enthusiasm and energy of children, youth and young adults to create a beautiful garden whose produce they give away to supply local food kitchens.

- A church in the Northwest for many years has created fabulous 10' x 12' banners that record events of the year: births, deaths, baptisms, etc. These banners hang in the entry area and down the halls displaying milestones and spiritual markers in the life of the church and tributes to saints who have gone before.
- Every summer a church in my community offers an intergenerational learning opportunity for everyone in elementary school and up. Everyone gathers for ten weeks to learn together. University students who attended this church as children have recalled these intergenerational learning times as spiritual markers of their childhood.
- A church in Tennessee made up primarily of older members gathered every Wednesday for years for an evening potluck; a few years ago they began inviting children of the neighborhood to join them. What had been an insular weekly event became a cross-generational outreach opportunity that blessed the children and the faith community.

As you read through the following descriptions, you will realize that your faith community is already creating cross-generational opportunities; one key challenge is to parlay these opportunities into more intentionally spiritually nurturing events.

Intergenerational Worship

Families need to be worshiping together. Children in Old Testament times worshiped with their families on feast days, special celebrations, and on Sabbath. Children in the early church worshiped in house churches with their families. Eddie Prest recommends particularly including children in worship, saying, "The optimal spiritual impact upon children will take place in a warm, belonging, caring and concerned interaction with the gathered people of God, particularly in worship."[22] Most congregations send the children away for some of part of the worship gathering time. Some faith communities offer unique worship settings for children, middle schoolers, teens, and emerging adults as well as offering both a contemporary and traditional worship service; these many options essentially separate the church generationally. If we are to bring the generations back together for that unique worship hour, how can we do so in ways that spiritually bless all generations? I offer a few suggestions below:

Literally welcome the specific generation. For example:

- Children or teens: "We are so glad to have our children among us today; our newest member is here today, little Ryan; we are glad Remi is back among us from her illness; we are delighted our high school band members are back in town after their trip to the Rose Bowl." In larger churches where specific events would exclude too many, more generic welcomes can include: "We are glad to have our newly minted graduates among us (or our new middle schoolers, our new first graders, or our new kindergartners).

- Parents of young children: We have lots of babies today; we welcome you and your parents who are here to worship. We want you to know, that though we have facilities available should you need them, you are welcome among us. We will interpret the occasional cries of these children as representing the cries of the world; it is good to be reminded that there are many calling out in need for what we have here. We are glad you are among us.

- Older adults: Today we want to especially welcome our older adults. We are very blessed in this faith community to have among us many who have known God for many decades and have learned from God how to live wisely in God's world. We recognize that we need you, and we want you among us; we ask that you embed yourselves among us so that we can learn from you, and so that we can bless you also. We are glad you are among us today as we worship.

Navigate the "worship wars." For example, if we bring the generations back together for the Sunday morning worship hour, we will be required to address the issue of music styles. It seems self-evident that becoming fully and intentionally intergenerational will call for some degree of blending styles. To insist on traditional hymnody entirely, ignoring all worship music written in the last several decades, assumes an elitist historical stance that ignores the fact that God is still at work among twentieth and twenty-first century believers, pouring out new songs about old truths. However, insisting that the exclusive use of contemporary music and lyrics is necessary to keep churches vital overlooks inescapably the needs of one or two generations as well as the powerful theological and aesthetic contributions of past spiritually gifted musicians and poets. *It also unavoidably limits the worship music repertoire of future generations.*

A Chinese-German couple lives in my small town; Mei's first language is Mandarin, Kurt's is German, and they speak English as well. Their preteen children are tri-lingual, that is, fluent in all three languages. A person's first language is considered that person's "heart" language; Mei and Kurt's children have *three* heart languages—that is, languages through which they can express their deepest, most profound feelings and understandings. Perhaps it can also be said that one's first music "language" is one's heart music. What a blessing it would be if the next generation were to become "multilingual" musically from childhood—that is, they would be able to express their spiritual praise, lament, adoration, petition, and love through a wide range of musical worship styles. For this blessing to occur, it is keenly important that the worship music of our children and youth tap into the depth and breadth of theologically sound, melodically memorable, profoundly true songs, hymns, and spiritual songs not only from the ages but also from the last several decades—and last week.

Include everyone. For example, as we seek to become more intentionally intergenerational in our worship setting, we can consider every element or activity of worship as an opportunity for everyone, children through seniors, to be involved. For example:

- Recruit both older and younger greeters to welcome everyone.
- Foster cross-age drama.
- Encourage parent/child-led (or teen-led) and other cross-generationally led prayers.
- Allow gifted artists of all ages to share the work God is giving them to do.
- Look for ways the older generation in particular can share stories of their faith journey.
- Seek recent versions of older hymns—for example, the new versions of "Amazing Grace"—integrating the well-known older hymn with a newer incarnation (or vice versa—seek older hymns that reflect key theological themes in current songs and integrate the two).
- In a song such as "Be With Me, Lord" suggest that the congregants sing "us" in place of "me"; this one change can create a tangible sense of cross-age community.

Intergenerational Small Groups

For four years, my family worshiped with a church in the 1990s that promoted intergenerational small groups every Sunday evening. We met for an hour or more with adults, children, and teens together. To open the gathering each week, every person present answered an icebreaker (e.g., What is your favorite ice cream? What are you afraid of? What do you dream about?). We came to know each other quite well, old and young, in those light-hearted responses, but each week we also prayed for every family unit present (singles, couples, families). We prayed for pregnant moms, forming babies, job situations, achievement tests, bullies, fears, hopes, futures, old relational patterns, anger issues, disappointments, and losses. Also, each week we sang contemporary and traditional songs led by two different volunteers—a teen and a college student one week, a child and a mom the next, a married couple the next. We also took the Lord's Supper each week in these small groups.

What happened in those small groups over several months is that the participants entered each other's lives, the funny parts, the sad parts, the hopeful parts, and the fearful parts. Children began to see adults as whole, multi-dimensional people, and adults began to see children as complex, growing *people*. Worshiping and praying together in a close and intimate setting revealed our inner spiritual lives to our children and theirs to us. Celebrating the Lord's Supper in these close intergenerational settings provided spiritually formative opportunities for all involved. The children participated in the spiritual life of the Christians around them; they were taught; they actually served. The adults participated more interactively in this central Christian practice; they were given opportunities to express their spiritual understandings and insights, and parents and children became more comfortable discussing spiritual things.[23]

Conclusion

> *"The best way to be formed in Christ is to sit among the elders,*
> *listen to their stories, break bread with them, and drink from the*
> *same cup, observing how these earlier generations of saints ran the*
> *race, fought the fight, and survived in grace."*[24]

A biblical passage, Psalm 78 (NIV), carries a similar implication:

[1] My people, hear my teaching;
   listen to the words of my mouth.

[2] I will open my mouth with a parable;
   I will utter hidden things, things from of old—

[3] things we have heard and known,
   things our ancestors have told us.

[4] We will not hide them from their descendants;
   we will tell the next generation
   the praiseworthy deeds of the LORD,
   his power, and the wonders he has done.

⁵ He decreed statutes for Jacob
    and established the law in Israel,
    which he commanded our ancestors
    to teach their children,

⁶ so the next generation would know them,
    even the children yet to be born,
    and they in turn would tell their children.

⁷ Then they would put their trust in God
    and would not forget his deeds
    but would keep his commands.

⁸ They would not be like their ancestors—
    a stubborn and rebellious generation,
    whose hearts were not loyal to God,
    whose spirits were not faithful to him.

In order for those of the next generation to be able to place their trust in God, this psalmist says that they must hear repeatedly about this God in whom they are to trust. Whole generations are to pass to the next generations the truths of Yahweh, so that they will not forget who he is and what he has done for those he loves. In order for this progression to be possible, the generations must *be together, not just occasionally or sporadically, but often*—for important events, for rejoicing, for critical moments, for prayer, for solemn occasions, for feasts and celebrations, and for reading the word as well as for ordinary happenings.

The process of becoming Christ-like in one's attitudes, values, beliefs, and behaviors—that is, Christian formation—does not happen alone. The premise of this chapter is that intergenerational faith communities are God-designed places for Christian formation. Truly intergenerational communities welcome children, emerging adults, recovering addicts, single adults, widows, single parents, teens whose parents are not around, the elderly, those in crisis, empty nesters, and struggling parents of young children into a safe, but challenging place to be formed into the image of Christ.

Chapter 8

Communion

A Table without Boundaries

Nathan Pickard

$\mathscr{E}$ach Sunday my oldest son and I sit on the front pew. Watching my son weave between paying attention to his coloring book and participating in the rituals of worship, I wonder how and in what way the act of worship is forming him. Specifically, I wonder how the act of sharing communion is forming us. In our faith tradition, communion is shared on a weekly basis. For our congregation, communion begins with an individual welcoming us to the table of the Lord, and then speaking (sometimes way too long) about how we are called to "remember" Christ. After we listen to an admonition to remember Christ, bread and wine are passed.

My son listens and watches the ritual unfold. He watches as plates of bread are passed, but never to him. Those serving always seem to skip him; the bread and wine seem to pass over my son's head. As a result, an uneasy feeling creeps over me. Stories in the gospel reveal Jesus welcoming children into his presence; why do we not allow children to the table where Christ is host? The gospel writers show Jesus allowing the table to break down barriers and to welcome those who otherwise would not be welcomed; why have we created a barrier against children? When Jesus gathered around a table, people encountered God's love, mercy, and grace; why do we not allow the table to be a place where my child can encounter God and thus God's love, mercy and grace?

Each Sunday I want my children to be welcomed to the table of the Lord. Are there theological grounds for welcoming children? If so, what has caused us to create a barrier for children (and maybe others)? What follows is the historical account describing why Churches of Christ have traditionally not welcomed children to the table of the Lord. Following this is the exploration of a theology that will allow children to share in the table of the Lord.

1815, Ohio

In a nondescript wood-framed building, fifty saints gather to worship. They surround a table in the center that has been set with bread and wine. Against the walls, visitors sit on benches and watch worship as it unfolds.

After welcoming each other, an individual, given the title "president" and appointed by the congregation to preside over worship, calls those gathered: "Brethren, being assembled in the name and by the authority of our Lord and Savior Jesus Christ, on this day of his resurrection, let us unite in celebrating his praise." The church sings certain psalms, then a reader delivers an account of the crucifixion of the Messiah. Following the reading and a moment of silence, another leads the church in prayer.

The president of the meeting next reads from one of the epistles and calls for the congregation to sing again. At the conclusion of the song, the president rises to remind the congregation that the Lord had a table for his friends, and that he invited his disciples to sup with him there. The president speaks: "In memory of his death, this monumental table was instituted; and as the Lord ever lives in heaven, so he ever lives in the hearts of his people. As the first disciples, taught by the apostles in person, came together into one place to eat the Lord's Supper, and as they selected the first day of the week in honor of his resurrection, for this purpose; so we, having the same Lord, the same faith, the same hope with them, have vowed to do as they did. We owe as much to the Lord as they; and ought to love, honor, and obey him as much as they."

Speaking these words, the president raises a loaf of bread, breaks it, and hands the two pieces to those on either side, who in turn hand the pieces to others until all those gathered around the table share in the bread. There is no stiffness, no formality, no pageantry; all is easy, familiar, solemn, even cheerful. Following the breaking of the bread, the president takes the cup, gives thanks and hands the cup to the one sitting closest, who passes it until all share in the cup.

Following the sharing of the bread and wine, the assembly prays for the poor and destitute and takes up a collection. A general invitation is then offered to the congregation for the purpose of building up the body. Several individuals rise and read passages from the Old and New Testament. After assorted remarks and several spiritual songs, the president concludes the meeting by pronouncing a benediction.[1]

In this narrative of a nineteenth century worship service, I've summarized an account of worship from the writings of Alexander Campbell. What should be clear from this account is the centrality and importance of the Lord's table in worship for these believers. Though it may seem strange to those living in the twenty-first century, we should understand that a particular theology shaped how the church worshiped. For Campbell, the theology that governed the church involved his attempt to restore an ancient order.

Why restoration? In Campbell's time there was widespread division amongst Christians of various denominations. Campbell believed that this division hindered the kingdom of God. Campbell thought that, if Christians could be united, the millennium reign of Christ would begin. Consequently, Campbell undertook the task to unite all Christians; he did so by asserting the path to unity was in restoring primitive, first-century Christianity. To bring about this restoration, Campbell wanted everyone to read a certain section of the Bible (from Acts to Revelation) and draw careful, logical conclusions. Once Christians studied the Scriptures and reached the proper conclusions about the ancient order, they could restore the primitive church and the reign of Christ would begin.

Campbell shaped his theology with a particular reading of Scripture. He divided the Bible into three dispensations: patriarchal (Adam to Moses), the Mosaic (Moses to Peter's sermon on the Day of Pentecost—Acts 2), and Christian (Pentecost to the last judgment). For Campbell, the only dispensation providing the pattern of the primitive church was the Christian dispensation. Thus, he held to the belief that neither the Old Testament nor the Gospels were binding for Christians in his time; only the Christian dispensation mattered. Thus, Campbell read Acts 2 through Revelation 22, gathered the facts for any given topic and then drew logical conclusions based upon those facts.[2]

The 1815 worship narrative reflects more than frontier worship; it reveals a specific theology and a hermeneutic, a way of reading of Scripture guiding that congregation. Campbell, and those advocating his theology were reading Scripture with a historical and scientific lens; they were reading Scripture (Acts 2 through Revelation 22) for the purpose of discovering how the early church engaged in weekly worship practices so that they could emulate these practices. Thus, this practice of the Lord's Supper grew out of a modern reading of Scripture seeking to restore the way that the early church shared the Lord's Supper.

How has this restoration effort held up over time? To answer that question, let me describe a worship service in the late twentieth century. The same theology that governed Campbell's congregation governs this congregation, yet other factors have since changed how the community of faith shares the Lord's Supper.

1980, Ontario, Canada

In a brick building situated just on the outskirts of a Main Street meets a Church of Christ. Eighty people gather to worship. The presider and those leading in some capacity make their way from a back room and onto a raised platform, each person taking their assigned seat. The presider welcomes everyone and invites the song leader to lead a collection of songs of his choosing. After the congregational singing, the presider invites a reader to deliver a passage of Scripture and to lead a prayer on behalf of the congregation.

The presider then calls upon the song leader to lead the congregation in a song about the death of Jesus. Following this song, the presider speaks about the death of Jesus, how the death of Jesus was necessary, and how the church gathers to "remember" the death of Jesus. Four servers then pass the bread and individual cups to each baptized member of the congregation. Each takes the bread and juice in silence, remembering the death of Jesus. Following the table, the servers gather a collection for the work of the church.

During the collection, the presider makes announcements about events in the life of the church and then announces the invitational hymn to be sung after the sermon. He invites the preacher up for the proclamation of the word. The invitation follows, and finally, a concluding prayer.

This narrative describes a congregation's worship experience in an Ontario Church of Christ, and the theology governing this congregation grew out of that of Alexander Campbell. The people faithfully worshiped believing they were continuing the completely restored practices of first-century Christianity. What they failed to recognize, though, was the influence of two concepts that did not come from the early church: individualism and Anselm's sacrificial atonement theory. Thus, there were layers of a philosophy (individualism) and a theology (Anselm's) yet to be removed in restoring the primitive Christian practice of sharing of the bread and wine.

Individualism is an approach to life that is a cornerstone of modern Western thought. As a result, individualism permeates almost everything we know, do, and believe—even how we read Scripture. For example, we read the gospel story through the lens of personal atonement, thus reducing the gospel to a message focused on one's individual salvation, made evident by the question, "Are you saved?" There are at least two consequences of letting the gospel be seen through the individual lens: we unknowingly forget that salvation is a communal event, and we separate the benefits of salvation from the reason for which we are saved: to empower us as God's people to become Christ's witnesses.[3]

Anselm's sacrificial atonement theory states that Jesus suffers on the cross because God requires payment, in blood, for the guilt of humanity, and it is for this guilt that Christ substitutes himself. Christ died to avert the wrath of God. Anselm developed this theology in the European Middle Ages as a response to the anxiety of guilt and condemnation suffered by the people of that time. Anselm's theology spoke to his context.

Those attempting to restore the first-century church in the nineteenth century unwittingly left these two concepts wrapped around their theology and practice of the Lord's Supper. Thus, our current practice of sharing the Lord's Supper centers more upon the individual taking the bread and wine while allowing Anselm's theological understandings overwhelm all other theologies that might explain how the Lord's Supper functions. We have tended to carry on our founding fathers theological understanding and practices associated with the Lord's Supper without re-evaluating for ourselves whether this is a complete restoration of primitive practice.

Before I offer a third worship narrative that I believe will shed unnecessary layers of theology and restore biblical thought, I want to briefly summarize my growing uneasiness about the first two narratives and the theology giving birth to these narratives. First, while Campbell and other nineteenth century restoration leaders believed the millennial reign of Christ begins with widespread unity of all denominations—under the rubric of restoring primitive Christianity—I wonder if this is what we believe in the twenty-first century. Does the millennial reign of Christ depend upon us uniting all Christian factions through primitive Christianity? Also, Campbell's theology and his reading of Scripture were shaped by early modern, Enlightenment presuppositions; Campbell read Scripture through a scientific lens. Is this the only method of reading Scripture? Are there other methods of reading Scripture? If so, might these other methods lead us to adopt different theologies and practices?[4]

Anselm's theology of atonement developed during the Middle Ages in conjunction with its cultural context. The Middle Ages suffered from an "anxiety of guilt and condemnation." Anselm's theology allowed those living with guilt and condemnation to discover forgiveness: forgiveness based upon Christ dying to avert the wrath of God. Today, however, our culture does not suffer from having anxiety over guilt and condemnation; we suffer with meaninglessness and emptiness. Can the gospel offer a salvation that will take away our sense of meaningless and emptiness? Our theology of atonement in the twenty-first century must speak to our cultural context, not the context of the Middle Ages.[5]

Finally, and most importantly, the theology that shaped the table etiquette of Jesus and the early church—the Messianic banquet—is not given the precedence it rightly deserves. If the Messianic banquet guides the church's current practice of sharing the Lord's Supper, there will be a place of welcome for the outsider, for those who have historically been kept away from the Lord's Supper. Furthermore, the theology associated with the Messianic banquet has the ability to shape our children in ways that are unavailable if we espouse Campbell's theology of reading Scripture, the Western notion of individualism, and Anselm's theological perspective of the Lord's Supper.

With this in mind, I offer a third worship narrative. This worship centers itself in word and table, where the table welcomes all as Christ welcomes all, and that all who participate are being invited to live into the messianic era. This worship is one in which children find welcome.

In the Near Future

The church gathers and the leader of worship welcomes everyone. Following the call to worship, congregational singing engages the heart, mind and body of all. A reader delivers God's word. This particular Sunday the reading is from Isaiah 58 and Luke 4. The one who reads the word of God then calls the congregation to pray that God might strengthen and provide courage to perform the reading of God's word. Following the prayer, the congregation recites the Lord's Prayer.

The church continues in congregational singing. The song leader has a gift of moving the congregation through the songs with a tempo that carries the congregation's imagination. After congregational singing the minister brings the congregation into the narrative of Scripture. The minister preaches in such a way that the congregation discovers their story within the story of God. The final move of the sermon is a move towards the Lord's Supper.

Following a song that ties word and table together, an individual stands before the congregation and welcomes all people to the table of the Lord. This presider speaks words about how the table tells the story of God redeeming all of creation, while also painting a vision of a new heaven and a new earth. Listening, one is reminded of the narrative from Deuteronomy where the people of God gathered around the table of Passover and parents recited to the children the story of the exodus from Egypt. The children, the next generation, are caught up in the ritual of the Passover Meal, learn the story through participation so that the exodus story becomes their story, their identity. In a similar way, the children who have gathered in this worship service are the children of the next generation who are learning the story of Jesus by participation in the table and will have their identity shaped by sharing in the table.

Finally, the one leading the congregation to the table of the Lord breaks and blesses the bread. The individual says to those who are gathered, "Come to the table of mercy, each and every person, for it is Christ who meets us here and welcomes us to his table so that we might have the strength and nourishment to live the cross-shaped life in this world and to be bearers of God's in-breaking kingdom"

After everyone has feasted at the table, the one leading the congregation says, "We have come to the table to receive the gift of God and now we come to the table to bring our gifts." A collection is then taken up so that the church might minister in the name of Jesus to the surrounding neighborhood. The congregation then joins in song and goes out to live their worship in the world.

The theology behind the above worship service is "storied." Notice the phrases used to describe the "acts" of worship: "perform the reading of God's word," "the minister brings the congregation into the narrative of Scripture," and "The table tells the story of God redeeming all of creation."

Stories shape identity. We cannot understand who we are without understanding the narratives that are shaping the social world in which we find ourselves. It thus becomes very important for us to ask what stories are shaping society and individuals. What stories are shaping the world we indwell? What stories are we allowing to form our children? What stories are we embodying? Understanding that we are shaped by stories, Scripture becomes foundational to our identity because it offers up an alternative narrative within which to construe our lives, and thus to be actors in this larger story.[6]

For stories to shape the world we inhabit and to shape us as individuals, we engage rituals and rhythms, either on a subconscious level or an intentional level.[7] The act of worship is a ritual that is rooted in Scripture, with Scripture reciting the overarching story of God's redemptive activity. Thus, one function of worship is to tell the narrative of God's salvation so that we discover how to construct our lives. For those who participate in worship, we are doing what the Israelites did: allowing our worship to shape our identity.

The book of Deuteronomy is rooted within the Exodus narrative. In Deuteronomy 6–11, historical memories of the exodus are retold. These spoken memories frame and give context to the commands that are in chapters 12–25. The purpose of retelling memories that frame specific commands for the people of God is to remind God's people that they live in a covenantal relationship with God. These spoken memories are not for adults only; instead, the canonical text of Deuteronomy asserts children are very much a part of the covenantal community. Thus, children are invited to participate in the rituals and rhythms of daily life for the purpose of constructing an identity rooted in the Exodus story.[8]

Deuteronomy 6:20 reminds us that children will inquire about the meaning of the decrees, statues, and ordinances of God's people. As the children ask the parents about this lived faith, the parents recite the story of redemption:

> We were Pharaoh's slaves in Egypt, but the LORD brought us out of Egypt with a mighty hand. The LORD displayed before our eyes great and awesome signs and wonders against Egypt, against Pharaoh and all his household. He brought us out from there in order to bring us in, to give us the land that he promised on oath to our ancestors. Then the LORD commanded us to observe all these statues, to fear the LORD our God, for our lasting good, so as to keep us alive, as is now the case (Deut. 6:20–24).

Children's identity is rooted in the narrative of God's redemption. As the children receive their identity through "hearing" the narrative, they are invited to continue living in covenantal relationship with God.

One way children hear the narrative and participate in the covenantal relationship is through participation in the rituals that make up Israel's calendar. Israel's worship, shaped over time by lived circumstances and needs, finds expression in three festivals: Passover, Festival of Weeks, and Festival of Booths (see Deut. 16).[9] Israel does not reserve its worship for a select few; instead the entire community—slaves, children, widows and orphans, strangers, and Levites participate in the festivals. While participating in worship, the entire community is shaped by God's redemptive activity in their midst.[10] As a result, children are invited to embody this story and thus always be in covenantal relationship with God. The festivals do more than bring children into the community, they also teach the next generation an alternative imagination—a different way of looking at the world. By participating in the various feasts, children become part of an alternative community—an alternative to Pharaoh and slavery, Canaan and its seductions, and, as Walter Brueggemann tells us, the "deathly choices and ambiguous realities of daily life."[11]

God's people tell the story of God's redemptive activity through their worship. In their worship, the entire community, including children, is invited to participate. Through participation, worship functions to construct an identity.

The Lord's Supper Creates an Identity

Rituals shape identity. The ritual of sharing the Lord's Supper creates an identity. Just as the Passover told the story of God redeeming the people of God from slavery, so the Lord's Supper tells the story of God's redemption—this time, in and through Jesus Christ. Participation in this ritual constructs an identity—an identity shaped not through the Exodus narrative but through the narrative of Jesus Christ. The apostle Paul sums it up:

> On the night he was betrayed, Jesus took bread and when he had
> given thanks, he broke it and said, "This is my Body, which is
> for you; do this in remembrance of me." In the same way, after
> supper he took the cup, saying, "This cup is the new covenant
> in my blood; do this, whenever you drink it, in remembrance
> of me." For whenever you eat this bread and drink this cup, you
> proclaim the Lord's death until he comes (1 Cor. 11:23–26).

When Paul writes these words he is trying to correct the abusive table manners being practiced by the Corinthian church. In their worship they shared a common meal in which rich and poor and possibly children and parents joined. Unfortunately, the meal represented Roman cultural practices rather than the table manners of Jesus. Paul, to reorient the Corinthians, begins to remind them about the story that gives them their identity: the life, death and resurrection of Jesus. Beyond reorientation, Paul believes the common meal they share has eschatological overtones—eschatological, being the fullness of God's kingdom. What Paul then is asking of the Corinthian church as they share the Lord's Supper is to see their common meal as a place to embody the table etiquette of Jesus and the banquet of the last days—the Messianic banquet.

When Jesus gathered around tables of food, he was anticipating the banquet of the last days. Isaiah captures a vision of the banquet when he writes,

> On this mountain the Lord of hosts will make for all peoples a
> feast of rich food for all peoples, a banquet of aged wine—the
> best of meats and the finest of wines. On this mountain he will
> destroy the shroud that enfolds all peoples, the sheet that covers
> all nations; he will swallow up death forever (Isa. 25:6-8a).

The gospel writer Matthew links the messianic banquet, a banquet of hope, with the meals Jesus shared with tax collectors and sinners. Jesus tells a parable about dining in the kingdom of God. Those gathered at the table are tax collectors and sinners (Matt. 22:1–10). Table fellowship for Jesus was an enactment of the messianic era. The Messianic era will be a place where tax collectors, sinners, insiders and outsiders, children and parents, clean and unclean, rich and poor will find equality, forgiveness, reconciliation, abundance, and the hospitality of God.

The Lord's Supper looks backwards while also looking forward. The table looks backwards by being rooted in the death and resurrection of Jesus, while looking forward because it is a sign of the Messianic era.[12] Focusing on the forward dimension of the table, how the church engages in this ritual and the boundary markers guarding this ritual will either reflect the Messianic era or it will reflect an era other than the one ushered in by Christ. Furthermore, the Lord's Supper becomes a microcosm of the way things really ought to be. As a result, the table becomes normative; it tests our behavior and gives us hints as to how we ought to live in this world. Thus, regular participation in the ritual of the Lord's Supper helps move us from being citizens of an earthly empire to citizens of heaven. As Nora Gallagher asserts, "We are all practicing together to become more and more the makers of the kingdom."[13]

Welcoming Children

Churches of Christ have developed their worship practices based upon a modern reading of Scripture for the purpose of restoring the primitive church. The restoration of the primitive church was imperative for early leaders like Alexander Campbell, who assumed the millennial reign of Christ would begin after Christians joined one another in simple unity. However, in the quest to restore the primitive church, early leaders of the Restoration Movement unknowingly let Anselm's theological understanding of forgiveness and North America's cultural philosophical assumptions about individualism shape how congregations would share the Lord's Supper.

If, however, we move past Anselm and instead root the Lord's Supper in the Messianic banquet and in the table etiquette of Jesus, then sharing the bread and wine is not only about what God has done for us; it is also about our participation in the redemption of the world. God, through the table, is inviting us to embody the kingdom of heaven. Those who participate are invited into the story of God and invited to be performers of this story.

We are called to nurture the spirituality of the next generation, and we do so by including children into the rituals and practices of the community of faith. We invite children into the rhythms and practices so that their experience helps form their identity. Through this experience, they not only hear the story of God's salvation in and through Jesus, they begin to have their imaginations shaped by the in-breaking Messianic kingdom.

The theological trajectories we inherited for the Lord's Supper are being challenged and transformed. So, what would happen if the table we gather around on Sunday morning lost its boundary markers and altar theology, and instead, became an enactment of the Messianic era? What would happen if we welcomed our children to a table that empowered them to shape their lives by the story of Jesus? What would happen if our children saw a table without boundaries? Would it then not lead our children to be bearers of the Messianic kingdom? Would our children not be living out the story of Jesus?

Chapter 9

Baptism and Children
Finding Good Instincts

Jeff W. Childers

"My daughter wants to get baptized, but she is so young! What is the right age for baptism, anyway?"

"Our son keeps putting off baptism. At first, we weren't too worried, but now he's getting older. How can we get him to take this seriously and get baptized?"

"What if my kid gets into an accident before she's baptized? She knows the difference between right and wrong. Does that mean she could be lost?"

"Many of our youth get baptized around the ages of twelve or thirteen. But by the time they're seventeen or eighteen, some of them ask to be rebaptized. We usually do it, but we don't feel good about it."

"If one of our youth hasn't been baptized yet, what can we allow them to do? Can they pray? What should our policy be about how to deal with kids who aren't baptized yet?"

"Why don't we put more emphasis on baptism? We need to teach on it more, especially for the sake of our kids!"

"Do we have to put so much emphasis on baptism? Every time we teach on it, I feel as though we are training our kids to be sectarian!"

These are just a few of the questions parents and leaders in Churches of Christ these days have about their kids and baptism. In fact, you might hear any and all of these things at the same time in a single congregation. It is tempting to try to address them quickly, with simple answers, but that may not always be the best approach. This is not to say there are no answers to the questions we face when helping our children find their way with God. Nor do we want to over-complicate the gospel. Sometimes, insisting on the plain and simple path is a way to cut through unnecessary obstacles—but often, it can be a shortcut back into the same tangled mess we discovered when we insisted on over-simplifying things in the first place.

The reason to take a little time on the subject of children and baptism is that we need to check our instincts and deepen them in light of Scripture. It would be helpful first to get a clear sense of what Christian baptism is. We may think we know, but Scripture has a way of pushing us to refocus our ideas and traditions. Having a strong foundation for baptism will help us speak to the challenges and prescribe healthy and faithful practices. In this chapter, we will attempt to lay such a foundation for understanding the nature of Christian baptism, explore different ways in which children might legitimately come to baptism, discuss how our heritage helps and hinders us, and then think about how to address specific challenges.

Why Baptism?

Growing out of a heritage of revivalist preaching, the meaning and significance of baptism might seem plain and obvious: sinners are baptized to express their obedience to Christ, to have their sins washed away, and to become members of the Lord's church. This is good, so far as it goes. Yet when we turn to the New Testament, we discover that Jesus and the early Christian writers go much further.

For example, at one point Jesus thinks of baptism as an ordeal of sacrifice and self-denial, modeled on his own experience of the cross: "Can you be baptized with the baptism I am baptized with?" he asks his disciples, referring to his own death, clearly skeptical of their eagerness to take up their crosses and imitate him (Mark 10:38). In Jesus' conversation with Nicodemus, baptism is a sacred womb, a place of spiritual rebirth, where a person goes in order to see what the kingdom looks like (John 3:3–8). For Paul, entering the baptistery is like crossing the Red Sea, a watershed event of liberation that helps define the identity of the people and their covenant relationship with God (1 Cor. 10:1–2). As the baptized come up out of the water, they leave behind the evil powers that had enslaved them to drown under the waves. In another place, Paul takes his cue from the life, death, and resurrection of Jesus. Here he sees the baptistery as a tomb: taken under the water to join Jesus in death, the baptized person is raised up to live differently (Rom. 6:2–4). The moves of baptism are the same moves that are meant to define daily Christian life and practice.

In 1 Peter 3:20–21, baptism is the water floating Noah's boat, saving humankind. In Titus 3:4–8, it is an adoption ritual, a special venue of operation for the Holy Spirit, washing and renewing a person by God's grace so that they may become heirs of the Father, full of hope and the good deeds flowing out of it. Elsewhere, the baptistery is a place to meet the community of faith and become part of Jesus' body, as one of its many members; it is a key to congregational unity and instrumental in helping disciples find their places in the body (1 Cor. 12; Eph. 4). The baptistery is a place to change clothes, putting on Jesus, and it dismantles false distinctions between people by putting everyone on the same footing before God (Gal. 3:26–28). Baptism connects a person with the Father, Son, and Spirit, opening a door into the very life of God (Matt. 28:19). And yes—baptism cleans us, bringing forgiveness of sins.

How many different ways can we talk about the importance of baptism and its meaning? The Bible shows us how important baptism was to Jesus, the apostles, and the early church. Underemphasizing baptism is not an option. To the contrary, for these writers, baptism is an answer to many different questions. Yet the questions are not so much about qualifying for church membership or certifying eternal destiny. Most of the time, they are not even about how to "get saved." Instead, they are more about identity, the direction of a person's life, their place within the community, handling relationships, and cooperating with the activity of Father, Son, and Spirit in experiencing daily transformation of character and behavior. The New Testament is not very interested in our debates about "the essentiality" of baptism. But it is deeply interested in the essence of baptism, and it shows a profound ability to interpret just about everything in the Christian life through the waters of baptism.

What a wonderful gift we would be giving our children if we could help them see their lives through the waters of baptism into Jesus, like the early Christians did. Some people complain that they do not hear as much about baptism as they used to. But there is a big difference between hearing a lot about baptism and hearing about baptism a lot. In some churches, baptism may have been mentioned often, but only a very few things were ever said about it—usually, that you must do it, in the right way, for the right reason. Or perhaps the only slant ever given to baptism was the revivalist slant coming from the American frontier experience: that baptism is the natural and necessary climax of a dramatic experience of sudden conversion for the repentant sinner. This slant does not fit many of our children at all. Yet when we study the New Testament's full handling of baptism, we begin to see many more things that need to be said about baptism, many more aspects of what it means to practice biblical baptism. For one thing, it is obvious that baptism was not just a culminating experience of conversion. It was also something to be lived out each day, a way of seeing the Christian life and the life of the church.

The traditional emphasis on the necessity of baptism, or on revivalist conversion, turn out to be too thin to help us much when addressing many of the questions we have when it comes to baptism and children. But if we were to broaden our teaching, our practices, and our language about baptism to reflect the full picture in Scripture, baptism might become a watershed of renewal and spiritual formation, rather than a source of anxiety. In short, less preoccupation with the "essentiality of baptism" and greater study of its essence would be a welcome change, going a long way towards equipping us to address those practical matters from a solid foundation.

The Essence of Baptism

Essentially, baptism is about Jesus. That may seem obvious, but so many discussions of baptism and its place in children's ministry appear to neglect the central fact of the matter: Jesus himself. When we consider the great diversity of meanings that early Christians discovered in their baptism, as described above, it becomes apparent that what ties them all together is the person and work of Jesus Christ. In baptism, we put on Jesus; in baptism, we join Jesus; in baptism, Jesus lays a claim upon us. We are baptized in the name of Jesus.

On the day of Pentecost, Peter instructed the people to "repent and be baptized . . . in the name of Jesus Christ for the forgiveness of your sins" (Acts 2:38). But it was not baptism itself or even "forgiveness of sins" that would have surprised them. Jewish washing rituals like baptism were common; so was the idea that such washings were connected to repentance and supposed to purify people. What would have stood out to the people were two things Peter said: the promise of the "gift of the Holy Spirit" (that was new!)—and especially, that somehow this all was centered "in the name of Jesus." It was that distinctive connection to Jesus that really stood out, making Christian baptism what it was. In Ephesus, Paul made sure the believers he met were baptized specifically into "the name of Jesus" (Acts 19:1–7), because that baptism embodies the most important thing in Christianity: joining Jesus.

In fact, in baptism we are actually imitating Jesus—not just metaphorically or mystically, by emulating his death, burial, and resurrection, but literally, since Jesus himself was baptized first. The baptism of Jesus is one of the most prominent stories in the Gospels (Matt. 3:13–17; Mark 1:9–11; Luke 3:21–22; John 1:31–34). It is presented as a key to understanding Jesus' identity, which automatically makes it a key to understanding Christian identity. Early Christians commonly used the Gospel scene in the art of ancient Christian baptisteries, finding in the imagery of Jesus' baptism something meaningful for their own baptisms.

By his own admission, Jesus was baptized "to fulfill all righteousness." It was the right thing for him to do. That may surprise some of us who have traditionally approached baptism strictly as a legal maneuver by which we deal with our sins, or as the culmination of a conversion process, since those are two things that Jesus' own baptism could not mean. He needed neither conversion nor forgiveness. We may not fully understand all the reasons for Jesus' baptism, but the picture we get is unmistakable: at the Jordan we see God's fullness in acting as Father, Son, and Spirit, embracing each another in an intimate relationship. We see coming together the human and divine, the earthly and heavenly, created elements (like water) and the Creator. We see a pivotal moment in Jesus' life and ministry in which he submits to his Father, descends into the river, receives his identity as the Father's beloved, and climbs out of the water to begin pursuing his life's work of Spirit-anointed service and self-denial for the sake of the world. We see him trudge out of the mud, calling disciples to join him in the same cross-bearing daily rhythms that he practiced, the rhythms of death-to-life that baptism pictures so well (Rom. 6:2–4). Jesus does not "get saved" in the Jordan—he is fully immersed into his identity in the Father and is openly anointed for his mission. Now we are getting closer to understanding the full meaning of baptism.

In Jesus' baptism, we glimpse many reasons why Christian baptism today can be thought of as an act of joining Jesus in the river. Our baptism paints us into the central portrait of God's salvation story—the life, death, and resurrection of Jesus. It lands us squarely into the middle of the gospel action so that the Jesus-story becomes our story. The essence of baptism is about joining Jesus, about entering his story and making it our own. Since connecting with Jesus as his disciple has a variety of different aspects, it is not surprising that early Christians saw many of those aspects pictured in their practice of baptism, as the New Testament passages referred to above show us. It is not surprising that they developed the habit of seeing all sorts of things through the lens of baptism.

When we are open to the full picture of biblical baptism, we can see how much we lose if we continually stress only a few aspects of baptism's meaning, or obsess mainly over correct form. It is not that those few meanings are necessarily wrong, but they are inadequate. Being part of a heritage that emphasizes the importance of baptism is a huge blessing for children's ministry. We are not in favor of talking less about baptism, but about saying much more than we have usually said! At its core, biblical baptism is not as much about just "getting saved," or simply expressing love for Jesus, as it is about locating our *identity* and finding our life's *mission* in Jesus. Coming to that understanding would put the subject of baptism and children on an entirely new footing in many families and churches.

Salvation as Journey and Mission

One of the insights we get when we seek to appreciate baptism in the context of the life of Jesus and of the disciple is the realization that baptism is part of a journey. This is a crucial aspect of the Christian life that revivalist traditions tend to undervalue or even ignore. The reasons for that are complex, but they have to do with a particular slant on salvation and a certain way of fitting baptism into that. Understanding the problem and seeking ways to remedy it will add further solid ground to our foundation for dealing with questions about children and baptism.

American Protestant revivalism, and the popular evangelical perspectives that are shaped by it today, emphasize the importance of "getting saved" and the means of doing so. Historically, revivalism tended to summarize salvation in a simple way: it is a matter of getting right with God and having your sins forgiven, so you can qualify for entrance into heaven and enjoy eternal life with the Lord after death. This message was suited to the rough and tumble setting of the American frontier. Items such as repentance and conversion were put front and center, and the focus tended to be on the decisive and dramatic moment of salvation.

In these models of "crisis conversion," the moment of salvation was invested with great importance. Some groups looked for an irresistible emotional-spiritual experience, while others emphasized a rational moment of decision about sin or doctrine. But what they shared in common was a strong emphasis on salvation as either a *state* that the convert enters, or a *thing* that the convert possesses. In other words, salvation was *static*. The dramatic moment of entering it or getting it becomes the main thing, and that moment should be clearly marked. Marking it could happen in different ways, depending on the group: perhaps by reciting a sinner's prayer and inviting Jesus into one's heart, perhaps by an episode of testimony about the Spirit's sudden movement within, perhaps by undergoing the ritual of baptism as the culmination of conversion.

As always, history and culture have played a role in all these developments, and going into the various causes and factors would take us too far from our topic. Also, there can be no doubt that the Lord has worked through revivalism in many ways. Aspects of revivalist tendencies find their roots in certain biblical teachings and examples, and people raised in a revivalist tradition can usually recite their group's favorite Scriptures in support of their take on how one "gets saved." However, once again, we see that this narrow approach can blind us to the much larger picture in Scripture.

Revivalism focuses on how one "gets saved," but not so much on what it means to live as a saved person. It looks forward to salvation as an event of escaping the world into eternity, but can make little sense of why God would create this world in the first place, or what the purpose of our lives here in the world should be, apart from convincing others to buy into our notion of precisely how to escape it. It guarantees a resolution of a person's "legal problems" with God, i.e. forgiveness of sins for the sake of heaven, but offers very little help in discovering better ways to live in the here and now, and is often uncertain as to whether it even matters to "salvation" that you do so. This can all sit very strangely with children, and especially children raised in the church, for whom "getting in" is not really the pressing issue and "getting right" with God is an odd notion.

This picture of revivalism is probably overdrawn, but perhaps the reader will recognize many of its features in his or her own background. The point is that, in Scripture, salvation is much larger than this. Salvation is about redeeming the sinner, but it is also about the redemption of creation. It is about the age to come, but also about the ways in which God's will may be "done on earth as it is in heaven," in the here and now. It is about the individual, but also very much about the community. It is about receiving God's gracious acceptance of our unworthiness, but also about following the ways of Jesus, growing up into Jesus, and even being "perfect as your heavenly Father is perfect." It is about mountaintop episodes of amazing closeness to God, but also about the reality of spiritual life lived in the normal routines of life. In short, the testimony of Scripture is that biblical salvation entails the full will of God for creation in its entirety. It cannot be reduced to a momentary, personal transaction regarding sin and the fate of the soul in the afterlife; nor should it be boiled down to episodes of intense enthusiasm and devotion.

Salvation is a journey and a process. There may be a sense in which the Lord's salvation is a *thing* that we can possess, or a *state* that we enter at a certain crucial point in our walk, but there is also a deep sense in which "we *are being* saved," (1 Cor. 1:18). In other words, we are caught up in an ongoing process of salvation, as part of a new creation (2 Cor. 5:17). This larger, biblical view of salvation is not so easy to sum up in a few words, since it is actually about the whole experience of living with God in Jesus Christ. It is a dynamic process of transformation into the image of Jesus, the true human being and Second Adam (2 Cor. 3:18; 1 Cor. 15:45–47). In fact, that is the true endgame: that we become like Jesus (1 John 3:2), having been joined into a body with other members who are together growing up into his fullness (Eph. 4:15–16). To use Paul's language, we have been predestined for the purpose of being shaped into conformity with our Lord, and God works all things together towards that good (Rom. 8:28–29). But we also participate with him in bringing everything under Jesus' lordship in our own lives and in the world (Phil. 2:10; Eph. 1:10), as the creation strains and groans to realize its true identity in Christ—the new heavens and new earth (Rom. 8:20–22; 2 Pet. 3:13; Rev. 21:1).

"Knowing Jesus" is not just about being forgiven. To know Jesus is to be caught up in a journey of following him, becoming more like him, "pressing on" each day to embody his experience of death and resurrection more and more as part of God's mission in the world (Phil. 3:10–14). As baptism teaches us, salvation is not so much about getting something from Jesus, or even just having a personal relationship with Jesus, as it is about *joining Jesus*. The early Christians understood that Christianity really is "The Way," and that is what they called their religion (Acts 9:2; 24:14). The Way is a continuing journey of mission and purpose. Since we are the Master's students and followers, becoming like the Master (Luke 6:40), the Christian life naturally involves processes of training and growth, just like those that Jesus himself experienced (Luke 2:52; Heb. 5:8). Faith and discipleship are like organic realities, subject to growth and transformation.

These are deep subjects, but they are foundational. One of the main reasons we run into problems with practices like baptism is that we do not appreciate their deeper foundations, or we may even put them on the wrong foundations. When we understand that God's mission is much larger than the job of cleaning up disembodied spirits for the afterlife that enlarges our concept of salvation. When we remember that growth and transformation are necessary parts of the process, we can appreciate the dynamic nature of true salvation, and better understood how baptism fits into our children's own journeys. These are crucial insights if we are going to have strong biblical foundations for our baptismal practices.

Journeying into the Baptistery

What does all this have to do with children and baptism? Many of the questions we have about baptism appear in a different light when we take a second look at what baptism really is. Also, when we realize how baptism fits into a more dynamic understanding of salvation, we find important implications for our work with children. We are all on journeys, but it is especially obvious that children are on the move, because they grow and change so quickly.

Due to the influence of revivalism, so much traditional preaching focuses on salvation as primarily about fixing sin, with baptism as a response to sinfulness. The language of "conversion" implies that a person's life was moving in the wrong direction until something changed, taking a sharp turn in a different direction. Baptism marks that turn. In this way of seeing things, the very foundation of the Christian life is an acknowledgment of my utter lostness and complete depravity. A relationship with God can scarcely begin until I have come to grips with the depths of my sinful ways and repented of them. "Conversion" becomes a prerequisite to knowing Jesus.

The problem is that this does not fit the actual situations of many children, especially children raised in the church. Christian parents and leaders are trying with all their might to raise their children to love the Lord and live for God. We bring them up in a Christian environment as part of the church family. We train and help them practice the ways of Jesus for years. We witness the intensity of their devotion, and are often humbled by the depths of their faith. It makes no sense for us to assume that our kids need to get some serious sin under their belts before they can have an authentic relationship with the Lord. Yet this is precisely what our practices argue, if we handle baptism in such a way that its purpose is strictly about repentance and conversion.

For instance, churches often feel the need to create crisis conversion experiences for their children and youth. They might stage a rally or encampment, bringing in speakers skilled at stirring adolescent emotions. The aim is to get youngsters to repent in a heartfelt way and convert, or at least to have an intense burst of passionate enthusiasm for the Lord, that can be thought of as a kind of conversion. Success is measured in terms of baptisms. Another symptom of the problem is the anxiety parents commonly feel until their children have had some sort of dramatic experience of conversion that can be dated and marked on the calendar. Yet another symptom is the pervasive habit in children's ministries and youth groups to showcase the most sensational testimonies, always glorifying stories of dramatic conversion and incredible life change. We tend to connect our talk about baptism with those kinds of moments.

We recognize that all people are (or become) sinners and need forgiveness. That includes children raised in the church. Nor do we want to downplay the importance of powerful spiritual experiences in the lives of young people. But to treat those preparing for baptism as if the only way to get ready is by owning up to their sinfulness, or by having an intense experience of some kind, is to ignore the fact that *different people come to baptism in different ways*. This was as true in the first century as it is today. The Gentile idol-worshipper who was accustomed to the immoral life of his pagan culture experienced baptism in a very different way than the law-abiding Jewess who had been preparing for the Messiah's coming all her life. Their journeys into the baptistery to join Jesus were similar in some ways, but very different in others.

Similarly, for some people today, baptism represents a radical change of direction, a turning away from the past and a fresh start. But for others, baptism is the next step on a journey they have been traveling for a long time. The momentum of their whole lives has brought them to the point of immersion in the name of Jesus in the presence of their beloved church family. Most children raised in the church probably come to baptism in this way. Their baptism is just as important, but the way it connects them to the gospel story is different than for the person experiencing a complete redirection of life. Their baptism is more about claiming their full identity in Jesus, an identity that has been taking shape all along. Imitating Jesus' surrender to the will of the Father, they are joining Jesus in the water, deliberately identifying with him and his mission in a mature awareness of what that will mean for their lives.

Since people legitimately come to baptism differently, it is a mistake to force everyone into the same mold. The problem is especially obvious in the case of our children, who may find themselves at a loss to identify the sort of conversion they are expected to experience at a young age. Some adolescents legitimately have that experience; many do not. Without it, some do not know how they can conscientiously enter baptism. Others, feeling the pressure, may come to believe they are at such a point, when in fact they are not. Still others balk at the apparent inauthenticity they see in their peers or in some grown-ups, and they refuse to conform.

With a revivalistic understanding of salvation as a total package delivered all at once, it follows that everything can appear to hinge on this all-or-nothing moment of emotional conversion and baptism. If in later years a person has doubts about the way she came to baptism, as so often happens, she may question its validity. Or if she goes through a season of spiritual growth and fresh insight—as we hope she will—she may come to question her earlier conversion and baptism, since she was naturally less mature when she experienced it. She has no way to make sense of natural spiritual growth, because she has not been taught to see her spiritual life as an ongoing journey. She has not been helped to see that salvation is on the move, just like her. And she has not been shown how her baptism fits into her spiritual life as part of that journey—it is not the sum total of her salvation. The testimonies she has heard and the models she has seen may have led her to put so much emphasis on dramatic moments of conversion-like experiences, she has no other hooks on which to hang her faith. She struggles to appreciate the value of the work of God that is gradually unfolding in her life each day.

Our challenge as parents and church leaders is to change our language, teaching, and activities in order to highlight the dynamic side of the Christian life, to help our children identify how they are growing in the Lord all the time, and to help them appreciate the different ways baptism can fit into their distinctive stories.

Children in the Church

Another important implication of the insights that salvation is a dynamic process and that people come to baptism differently has to do with the place of children in the church.

We love our children. We welcome their presence in our churches as a sign of vitality and potential. However, as children's ministers know well, a revivalist heritage emphasizing baptism as a boundary marker has great difficulty knowing precisely what to do with its children. A "static" take on salvation paints the boundaries in black and white, creating harsh distinctions between the saved and the lost, the insiders and the outsiders. On one side are those who can tell the story of their dramatic conversion experience and have marked it in baptism, while those who cannot are left on the other. Yet this narrow way of constructing life with God is inadequate to make good sense out of the children among us.

Once again, Scripture helps us with a fuller and more nuanced sense of the place of children in the church. The vision of community in the Old Testament obviously includes the children, yet even in the New Testament we see God's heart for children and their place among God's people. Children raised within the church family are not mere outsiders:

> "Let the little children come to me, and do not hinder them, for the Kingdom of heaven belongs to such as these." (Matt. 19:14, NIV)

> "The promise is for you and your children . . ." (Acts 2:39, NIV)

> ". . . bring them up in the training and instruction of the Lord." (Eph. 6:4, NIV)

> "The unbelieving wife has been sanctified through her believing husband. Otherwise your children would be unclean, but as it is, they are holy." (1 Cor. 7:14, NIV)

Whatever else we may say about Paul's teaching in 1 Corinthians 7:14, he clearly believes that the children of a Christian parent enjoy the status of inclusion in God's community to some extent, even in a home where one parent is not a believer. It is worth noting that in the New Testament, the primary focus of the Holy Spirit's activity is communal, not just individual. To suggest that the Spirit is not at work in the lives of children who produce its fruit as part of the Spirit-filled community, simply because they are not yet baptized personally, does not reflect the breadth of biblical teaching. The notion that children are included in God's community fits our instincts about how relationships and community work, even if it does not always fit our artificial systems regarding how the mechanism of salvation is supposed to work.

Simply put, God wants us to see our children as belonging to the family of faith—not as outsiders. This is not to say there is no difference between the baptized and the unbaptized youngster, but the difference is not necessarily that of insider vs. outsider as the revivalist tradition presupposes. A dynamic sense of salvation teaches us to expect processes of growth, and in the case of our children, we see how their spiritual growth can begin very early, so that they function as members of our communities of faith from a young age. When we treat children raised in the church as if they are outsiders before their baptisms or conversions, we move contrary to the heart of God and against our own instincts. We let a static construction of salvation get in the way of the natural ordering of organic community.

Instead, we can favor practices that emphasize children's inclusion. This would mean striving to find ways to express their belonging in the church family, without deemphasizing the importance of believers baptism. Helping children appreciate that they fully belong does not require giving them access to everything. There is nothing wrong having children wait before they participate in certain experiences or have certain roles; it is appropriate. The wisdom of many cultures shows us the value of expectation and disciplined waiting. In cultures that have rites of passage to mark the move from childhood to adulthood, these are highly treasured and formative experiences. Youth look forward to them with great anticipation and the experiences serve as benchmarks, powerfully shaping the person's identity and providing him or her with a signpost that gives them guidance all their lives. Baptism is meant to have just such a long-term, formative impact on a person's life.

So there is no cruelty in guiding children to wait—if it is the right sort of waiting. On the one hand we can find ways of recognizing the pre-baptismal faith of children, strongly affirming their belonging in the community of faith, and speaking into their lives our expectation that they are on a journey that will take them into the river with Jesus and beyond. But we can also keep the discipleship thrust and life-shaping impact of believers baptism, by helping children prepare for that moment as a fuller and more decisive surrender to the Way of Jesus, once they are genuinely ready to commit intentionally to the death-and-life rhythms of the gospel.

Other contributions in this volume speak to the place of children in the church. Here we just want to stress the need to emphasize the place of children among us, without insisting that baptism be the only possible way for the church to recognize their belonging. Furthermore, although we would not presume to speak for God, Scripture does not support an attitude of fear and anxiety regarding the status of unbaptized children in the church, as if the ceremony of baptism were necessary to convey magical protection of our loved ones. The rush to baptism that comes out of parental anxiety, or out of a child's sense that they do not really belong unless they are baptized, or because they know no other way to express their young faith and love for the Lord, betrays poor understandings and practices on the part of church leaders and parents.

In the next chapter, we will take up some of the specific questions about children and baptism that are being asked in churches. With a foundation of good instincts, we are better able to consider the sorts of practices that make sense when working with children in this area.

Chapter 10

Baptism and Children
Finding Sound Practices

Jeff W. Childers

*M*inistry is an art. Although knowledge and technical skills are important, good ministerial leadership often relies more on other things, such as a deep sensitivity to the needs of different situations and the ability to work with whatever materials are at hand. Perhaps most important to the art of ministry are those theologically shaped instincts that help the minister imagine what it would look like for God's vision and purposes take hold and flourish in a given place. Facing the challenges of ministry, good ministers craft responses that are elegant and beautiful because they fit the situation and express the heart of God in that place. They help people catch a glimpse of that vision themselves, inviting them to lean into the picture and become part of it. This is as much about art as it is technical problem-solving,

Ministry is a craft. We have days when we wish it were more like doing math problems or repairing machines. We want definite answers that always work, and we wish we could solve serious problems by simply referring to a diagram and following plain instructions. Some aspects of ministry are like that, but often doing ministry is more like practicing a craft. Again, knowledge and technical skills matter, but there are deeper and less obvious capacities at work, and they make all the difference. Like fine woodworkers, good ministers hone their abilities over years. They use the wood that is available, and through the application of patient skill, by trial and error, they acquire the instincts they need to craft objects that are both useful and graceful, perfectly suited to the needs of particular situations. Practicing good medicine can be very similar.

Tending to the souls of others is not simply a matter of having the right answers to certain questions, or of replicating in one place what was effective in another. Good ministry depends on developing a theologically rich imagination and good biblical instincts. The preceding chapter focused on some of the deeper matters of salvation and baptism. These are difficult topics, but doing the hard work of thinking them through gives us certain instincts that can be helpful in addressing the concrete questions that surface when we are thinking about children and baptism. Church leaders often have a tendency to be reactive. But cultivating good instincts ahead of time is the best way to prepare for situations that crop up. Once the instincts are in place and have gained some momentum, we are better equipped to plan our ministries and to respond from positions of wisdom and stability when particular situations arise.

In this chapter, we give specific responses to several common questions. It will not be possible to understand the logic of these responses without first wrestling with the deeper issues we discussed in the preceding chapter.

Addressing Some Questions

We are reluctant to propose rigid policies or try to devise one-size-fits-all solutions. Circumstances vary, and people sharing the very same biblical instincts may have good reasons for adopting different approaches to certain matters. The reluctance to give "final answers" is not due to a deficiency of truth or a failure of nerve but comes from the recognition that situations can be different, sometimes greatly so. Just like a good doctor dealing with individual patients in different ways, in ministry and in parenting, we have to customize our responses to our contexts and personalize them to our kids, as they engage their faith and respond to God's call. However, the instincts we acquire will tend to lead us in some specific directions.

When Should a Young Person Be Baptized?

A static understanding of salvation, combined with a revivalist focus on crisis conversion, produces some predictable answers, depending on the situation: either a young person should be baptized once they become aware of their sin (guilt), or when they can recite a certain amount of information about the gospel (facts), or once they can attest to a dramatic overflowing of love for or faith in Jesus (love/faith). Any of these, singly or in combination, may trigger a "conversion."

Believers baptism puts a strong emphasis on the decision to follow Jesus and one's personal ownership of that decision. With that in mind, it would not be right for us to try to control all the details of when and how a person might make that decision for themselves. Furthermore, guilt, facts, faith, and love are all crucial aspects of one's relationship to the Lord and should surely enter the equation in big ways. When young people are eager to express faith and devotion, we had better be prepared to give them outlets for doing so—including public opportunities as members of the church family. The testimony of children is powerful.

However, the fuller understanding of salvation and baptism we discussed in the previous chapter leads us to look for more. When we baptize someone, the main question has to do with whether they are ready to adopt the baptized way of life, in a mature way, and commit to it. Are they ready to identify with Jesus completely, to come up out of the water on the other side of the river, and follow him in ministry—not just as an ideal, but in practice? When a person understands, in their mind and in their practices, something about what it means to do that, then they may be well prepared for baptism, and we can be more confident that they know what they are doing and will enter into it fully. Baptism will be for them what it is meant to be. Especially for children raised in the church, we would hope that the experience of joining Jesus in baptism would be less about repentance and conversion, and more about pledging oneself in a mature way to the person and mission of Jesus. Hopefully, our teaching, our mentoring, our examples, and even the ways we conduct baptisms will make it clear that an embodiment of the baptized lifestyle is expected of someone we baptize.

Of course, none of us knows everything the Lord will require of us in our life journeys, no matter how experienced we are. If a person seeks baptism in sincere faith and commitment, we do not need to be afraid that they are being baptized at the "wrong time," even if we they have much to learn. But we do need to feel a burden to equip them, after baptism, to appreciate what their baptism truly means, and how it is meant to be shaping their daily lives.

Should Someone Very Young Be Baptized?

We do not believe there is a "magic age" by which children must be baptized. The growing trend to welcome children and affirm their faith and service is good. However, the accompanying tendency to connect that with an early baptism reduces baptism's meaning and often causes problems in children's spiritual lives. Even very young children can learn the facts, grapple with guilt, and express faith and love—sometimes in ways that put the jaded faith or crusty consciences of us adult Christians to shame. Yet that does not mean they are ready to join Jesus in the river and commit to an embodiment of the death-to-life practices that believers baptism pictures.

Ideally, baptism should not just be an act of devotion, or a way to deal with a child's developing consciousness regarding guilt, or a ceremony to validate their relationship with the Lord and place in the church family. Nor should baptism be used as a way to calm the fears of parents who, when they recognize spiritual life growing in their children as part of the community, become anxious for baptism to "seal the deal" and guarantee salvation. Instead, believers baptism is a committed identification with Jesus. It is not just a means of declaring, "Jesus is my Lord" in a vague sort of way. It entails "taking up a cross and humbling myself for the sake of others;" it is a commitment to putting others first. It is a promise to practice the rhythms of death-to-life for the sake of kingdom mission in the world. In a sense, baptism is the believer's ordination to ministry, surely a more momentous decision than any future career decisions, for example. This is not to say that a child must wait until they are old enough to choose a career before choosing baptism—though thinking about the ramifications of baptism in this way puts the decision in a different light.

Baptism is a response to the invitation to leave it all, pick up a cross, and follow Jesus. Young children tend not to make such decisions, not with a deep degree of real commitment anyway. That is why believers baptism requires some maturity. It presupposes some experience with life and loss, and an ability to think realistically in terms of consequences. Its action embodies a person's joining Jesus in discipleship, and promising to spend one's life moving with the kingdom rhythms of self-denial for the sake of the world.

Churches of Christ practice believers baptism, like the early church—not infant baptism. This is not so much a matter of different opinions about the right age for baptism as it is about the nature and meaning of baptism. Infant baptism is much like circumcision was for the Jews. It presumes that everyone belongs to the community of faith, just by virtue of being born. In that sense, it presumes a "Christendom" setting for the culture in which we live. It emphasizes the faith and responsibilities of the Christian community and family rather than those of the person being baptized, since babies have no choice in the matter. Believers baptism is different. Without necessarily undervaluing the community, it presumes that a person should make and own a personal decision about their relationship to Jesus. It lays a claim on the way they shape their lives as a result of that decision. Given the instincts we have seen in Scripture about the nature of baptism, ideally it is a more weighty moment than simply a declaration of belief, an expression of love for Jesus, or a ritual conveying a sense of belonging to the group.

These instincts would lead us to be cautious rather than eager to bring very young children into the baptistery. They would lead us to teach, conduct baptisms, and use baptism language in such a way that the community understands the full meaning of the commitment. At the same time, these instincts also challenge us to do a better job of addressing the needs of the children among us. If some children are baptized very young—as is liable to happen when we practice believers baptism—the burden sits with us to be intentional about helping those young lives move into deeper levels of commitment and to meet the expectations that an "ordination to ministry" places on them. Furthermore, children need opportunities other than baptism to express faith and love publicly, and to be affirmed for doing so. They long to serve in ways that actually matter to the church. They need to be described and treated as insiders, as people already belonging to the family of faith. We bless children when we regularly draw attention to the ways they are growing in the Lord, yet they are also blessed when we speak about the future day when they commit to that life in a fuller way on their own. If we did a better job incorporating our children like this, there might be less motivation to bring them into a reduced baptism prematurely.

Should Baptisms Be Public or Private?

The theological instincts we cultivated in the previous chapter strongly favor public baptisms. Baptism may be personal, but it is not private. A great deal of baptism's meaning involves being called to something beyond oneself—beyond personal preferences, beyond a small circle of friends, beyond even one's own family—to embrace the call of Jesus. Baptism plunges a person into a distinct community. Rather than catering to the toxic individualism of our climate, we should do everything we can do to emphasize the communal dimensions of baptism that are so prominent in Scripture, including the mutual responsibilities for one another that we share because of our baptisms. Private baptisms reinforce individualist and self-focused piety, even if we do not intend them to do so.

Certainly adolescent shyness or nervousness is not a legitimate reason to plan for a private ceremony, and may be an indicator that a person is not ready for baptism, or at least they do not really understand what it is about. If I cannot surrender humbly and profess my faith in front of my Christian family, what testimony am I prepared to give in the presence of possibly hostile witnesses? In what sense am I ready to embody baptism every day as a lifestyle in the world?

Private baptisms with a small selection of friends and family convey one sense of baptism's meaning; baptisms conducted within the context of the gathered community convey another sense—one that fits our stated theological instincts much better. Parents and leaders who want to see those instincts take root and flourish will want to take advantage of every opportunity to let the event of public baptism teach and model the full meaning of baptism for the gathered community, in all its diversity.

Is It OK to Wait for Baptism?

Revivalism emphasizes dramatic moments of repentance and moments of enthusiastic faith. Either way, there is a strong impulse to get someone baptized in a hurry, once they feel either a burst of penitence or a burst of religious fervor. As it happens, bursts of fervent emotion are not uncommon with children and adolescents. At such times, we understand the wisdom of exercising caution in most areas of life and decision-making, but we tend to handle religion differently. Because of our revivalist roots—and because we do not always think through the full meaning and intended consequences of baptism—we are prone to want to move quickly towards baptism when emotions run strong, especially if a person can recite the requisite facts.

The theological instincts we have explored do not discourage prompt baptisms, but they do beg us to recognize the burden we have to help anyone who is baptized enter the full meaning of his or her baptism, which can be more challenging when someone is not well prepared before it happens. Also, those instincts caution us from acting quickly out of anxiety. Rushing to baptism out of anxiety betrays a mechanistic understanding of salvation, typically the result of either not appreciating a biblical understanding of the sanctified place of our children among us, or forgetting that salvation is dynamic and that baptism is part of a process, with crucial parts happening before and after. Finally, religious romanticism and our revivalist roots have left us with a bias for spontaneity, so that we sometimes discount the spiritual qualities of anything planned or arranged. But baptism by surprise is not the only valid form of baptism.

So when people defer baptism in order to schedule it at a particular time, to study it more, or to prepare children better and have further conversations with them about discipleship, this does not run contrary to the instincts we have been exploring. Baptism does not have to wait, but it may, and sometimes it should.

What Can Unbaptized Children Do?

One of the ways we have traditionally underscored both the importance of baptism and the distinctiveness of the church is in restricting certain activities only to the baptized. For various reasons, we have focused especially on public worship activities. This is a matter of tradition rather than clear biblical instructions, though as we have already noted, traditions that are based on a desire to respect coming-of-age and rites of passage can be beneficial and formative.

However, recognizing and affirming the full family of faith, including the children among us, is also an important formational task we have. When children are rarely seen or heard in the context of the whole church, this often happens because we do not appreciate the sanctified place of children among us, or because of a highly static understanding of salvation. When our children experience the church as though they are outsiders, we see the instincts of revivalism are strong, but biblically formed instincts about children and the community are not. For the sake of a child's faith development, parents and church leaders should strive to find more ways for children to express their faith, to serve publicly, to offer testimony, and to be welcomed and received as the community members they are. Precisely how and where to do this is a matter of creative judgment in each context. Furthermore, just as some things from which children were formerly excluded might be opened up to them, the importance of needing to wait for other things might be stressed all the more.

For some, this includes participation in the Lord's Supper. The aspects of the Lord's Supper that emphasize it as a covenant meal for those who have made a commitment favor restricting the Lord's Supper to the baptized. In that case, it is something children should be encouraged to look forward to. But the aspects of the Lord's Supper that emphasize the family setting of the Passover out of which the Supper grew, and its table hospitality, favor letting unbaptized children participate. Here we have different sets of equally biblical instincts, and it is possible to come to different appropriate decisions about whether to let children participate. Whatever churches choose to do, the Way of Jesus certainly encompasses both these instincts—the high standards of covenant commitment, and the easy welcome of open hospitality—so our practices need to attend to both as well.

What about Rebaptism?

Several things can trigger a desire for rebaptism:

- A desire to recommit one's life to God after serious sin or a season of spiritual apathy;
- The sense of having come to a strikingly new or deeper appreciation for the Lord;
- The realization that one's core beliefs have changed or deepened;
- The feeling that one's original baptism may not have been fully valid because of some perceived deficiency of understanding or intent at the time.

Those who practice believers baptism have to remain open to the possibility of rebaptism, on the basis of a person's conviction about needing it. We do not want to cast doubt on anyone's rebaptism! However, in light of the instincts we developed in the previous chapter, many of the impulses that prompt people to seek rebaptism may be in need of redirection, since they grow out of a static understanding of salvation. People often get this understanding when they are young, by watching and listening to us. Also, when children are baptized before they are well prepared for its full meaning, they are liable to seek rebaptism later.

Better teaching and modeling for our children can help reduce these problems. If they get from us a fuller understanding of what baptism is, it better prepares them to seek it when they are genuinely ready, reducing the likelihood of their questioning its validity later. If they see their spiritual lives as dynamic expressions of faith, they learn to expect change over time and will not be surprised by growth. They also learn to expect that their understandings and intentions at earlier phases in life may turn out to be inadequate for who and where they are later; this is natural, and does not mean they have to discount their past and be rebaptized. If rebaptism is a common practice, it can undermine healthy understandings of the Christian life and of baptism itself. Rebaptism typically implies that a person's previous spiritual life is invalid, when this is not in fact the case. We need to help people find other ways to embrace and mark their experiences of growth and transformation, so that rebaptism is not the common option. But first, we need to help our children understand baptism better, and show them how to lean into healthier appreciations of a dynamic and changing spiritual life.

May We Change How We Do Baptisms?

Although in many churches baptisms are conducted in much the same way, time after time, considerable variety in baptismal practice has been emerging in some places. Offering personal testimonies, building worship services around baptisms, inviting family members or others into the baptistery, and seeking verbal commitments of support from the congregation are just some of the different practices occurring in churches today.

One reason for the growing variety is that the Bible contains very little information about precisely how baptism happened in the first century. It was an immersion process, but very little can be said about the settings, who in the church would be expected to administer baptism, or what occurred before, during, and after a baptism, except for the very sketchy and diverse pictures we get in the book of Acts. As for the words we speak at a baptism, the instruction to baptize using the formula, "in the name of the Father, Son, and Holy Spirit" is strong and theologically rich (Matt. 28:19, NIV)— though merely "in the name of Jesus" occurs elsewhere too (Acts 2:38; Acts 19:5, NIV). Peter's invitation to the Jews on Pentecost to be baptized for the forgiveness of sins and to receive the gift of the Spirit helps us see what baptism means, but does not indicate that he used those words when baptizing them, nor that anyone else must do so. The common practice in Churches of Christ of using some form of those words is a fine tradition, though it stems from the desire to clarify how our doctrine of baptism differed from that of other groups. So as far as the baptism ceremony itself goes, insisting rigidly on particular forms has little biblical backing.

Repeatedly, we have stressed that our baptism practices themselves teach a great deal about the meaning and purpose of baptism. When children get to watch baptisms happen as part of the gathered community, the experiences are formative and the children probably learn as much about baptism as at any other time. As we have seen, baptismal practices that allow for only a revivalist and conversionist meaning are denying a great deal of biblical content. Instilling the fuller instincts we explored in the previous chapter will require being very intentional about the ways in which we conduct baptisms, so that all the participants—including the gathered congregation—get every opportunity to experience and be shaped by the full significance of this crucial moment. This entails being flexible with baptismal practices.

It is not spiritually healthy to seek variety merely for the sake of adding spice to a dull ceremony, or just to give someone the chance to customize their experience like they might do for a birthday party, or to accommodate someone's personal discomfort. But when we are flexible in mature ways that connect with the deep meanings of baptism, the result can be healthily transformative, both for the person being baptized and the children witnessing it. Here are some practices that we see occurring in churches that can help children appreciate and anticipate baptism:

- Having the person being baptized explain what they believe and are committing to, rather than simply answering a yes-or-no question;
- Putting on a brand new outfit after baptism, like the early Christians did, to accentuate newness and baptism's claim on a person's life;

- Having the community gather around the newly baptized person, to speak encouragement, blessing, and promises of support or service;
- Allowing the person to briefly tell the story of how they came to that point in their lives;
- Bringing the children close to the baptistery so they can experience the event more richly;
- Planning a celebration after a baptism, with the newly baptized person as the guest of honor;
- Having the person doing the baptism highlight key features of baptism's meaning in what they say;
- Designing aspects of public worship around a baptism to accentuate its meaning, perhaps with the assistance and investment of the person being baptized;
- Challenging the gathered congregation to make a verbal, corporate commitment to the person (for instance, "Will you support and pray . . . ?", followed by, "We will!")
- Inviting those who have especially impacted the person's life to play some role in the ceremony or even to join them in the water;
- Thinking globally—some evangelists in Africa hold people under the water until they feel they may drown, to impress upon them the death and resurrection occurring in baptism!

When done with intentionality and explanation, practices such as these not only have the potential to enrich baptism, but they can help children understand its full meaning better.

What Is the Best Way to Prepare Children for Baptism?

Preparing for baptism means preparing for the Christian life. That simple realization could transform the way we talk about baptism and teach our children about it. Parents and ministers ought to craft intentional plans for preparing children, with both experiential and teaching elements. Obviously, finding age appropriate ways to teach children the many facets of baptism is one important strategy for preparing them. Making sure that children regularly witness baptisms as part of the gathered community is another. The event of a baptism is a very teachable moment. After a baptism, parents and teachers can make it a point to speak with the children, giving them a chance to reflect on it, to talk about what they think it means, and to receive instruction about baptism. Teachers can invite baptized persons of various ages and spiritual journeys to visit with the children, letting the children interview them about the event and meaning of their baptism. Children should hear testimony from those whose baptism marked a moment of dramatic conversion as well as from those who may have been raised in the church, or otherwise came to baptism differently. It is important not to privilege one type of story.

Some people are very reluctant to prepare children intentionally for baptism, afraid that they are biasing children towards a religious decision they need to make on their own. While this respects certain aspects of what it means to make a personal committed to the Lord, for the most part it reveals a deeply flawed understanding of Christianity, not the instincts we discussed in the previous chapter. Again, biblical Christianity is not principally a status we get upon making a philosophical, moral, or "religious" decision in a moment of crisis, but a Way of life and set of practices. Not preparing children for that way of life makes about as much sense as not equipping them to tie their own shoes, eat healthily, or be wise about driving under the influence of alcohol—whatever decisions they may one day make about these things on their own. Training them in the Christian life is far more important than training them to play sports, for instance. The fact is, we *are* training them for their future lives, in what we do and what we neglect to do. When we speak and act as though our hope for our children is that they will enter baptism with Jesus one day, by their own choice, we are blessing them, far more than we do by any expectations we might voice regarding their success in school or a future career.

Since preparing for baptism actually means preparing for the Christian life by integrating children into the life of the church, equipping them to serve in various ministries, and guiding them into Christian practices of all sorts, we are preparing them for baptism. Children who are not regularly challenged to make sacrifices for the sake of others cannot understand the life that baptism pictures. Practicing the baptized lifestyle is the best way for children to prepare for baptism.

In order to help children capture the full breadth of Scripture's teaching about baptism, we need to use baptismal language much more often, like the New Testament does. For instance, describing someone's acts of Christian service as instances of "living out her baptism" helps children see what it is that baptism means. Lessons on creation, in the classroom or on a rafting trip, can connect the elements of key Christian rituals—like baptism—with God's creative work, the incarnation of Jesus, and the importance of water in life and the Bible. Talking about baptism as the disciple's "ordination to ministry" and about church membership more in terms of being "baptized into the body of Jesus" are just two of many ways to help children understand how it connects to the Christian life. Learning to see the Christian life "through the waters of baptism" requires creative imagination, but is a much-needed capacity among us.

There are many other ways to help prepare children for baptism, ways that fit the instincts to which we keep appealing. As we noted, "baptism by surprise" is not the only valid form of baptism. It is highly appropriate for parents, children's ministries, and youth ministries to work together in formulating intentional strategies for preparing children, without coercing them, to decide to join Jesus in the river and be baptized.

Conclusion

There are so many factors playing into the spiritual health and wellbeing of children. We have considered just a few here, as they relate to issues of baptism. In these two chapters, our discussion has ranged from the abstract, such as the totality of salvation as a dynamic experience, to the very concrete, such as using river water to help children connect baptism, creation, and the incarnation. It would be nice if we could lay all these things out sequentially, but unfortunately, they all tend to be in play at the same time. However, setting a foundation of strong biblical instincts is crucial. As parents and church leaders in different contexts try to discern where their theologically shaped instincts should lead them, the key is that they be intentional in what they teach and practice, regularly revisiting their teaching plans and practices in order to assess them again. Rather than prescribing specific narrow solutions to the questions about children and baptism that arise, we encourage parents and leaders to work on their instincts together, exercise their imaginations, and strive to find communal ways of ensuring that children are getting a powerful look into the baptistery, one that is as full and balanced and true to the gospel as possible.

There is no precise formula for calculating a person's readiness for baptism. With believers baptism, each person takes responsibility for his or her decision. However, every baptized person treads a pathway that has led them into the baptistery, and taken them on a journey beyond it. The process may not be under our control or fully predictable, but there is a process. God and the Holy Spirit are involved, as are the child's family and their church. We hope that children will make good decisions about their baptisms, but we cannot control them, nor should we try. Yet God has chosen to make us partners in the process of helping a person discover his or her salvation. If we can provide a foundation of good, biblical instincts by our teaching and examples, there is every reason to believe our children will make good decisions about baptism. We can trust that the gospel rhythms we have helped them understand and practice all along will carry them into habits of lifelong service before God.

Section Four

Our Children's Ministries

Ministry with Children
Partnerships with Purpose

Ryan Maloney

A person's a person, no matter how small.

Dr. Seuss

I'm going to stop punishing my children by saying,
"Nevermind! I'll do it myself."

Erma Bombeck

There can be no greater revelation of a society's soul
than the way in which it treats its children.

Nelson Mandela

On a cool and cloudy autumn day, my uncle takes me fishing. I excitedly put on my jacket and bucket hat and climb up into the truck. I am three at the time, but to this day, when I remember it, I still feel like I am joining him on this, my first fishing trip adventure. The destination is nothing spectacular. Looking back, we must have ventured onto a friend's back pasture. There are dirt roads and fields and a wooded area with a muddy and leaf-lined tank of water. We park the truck on one end of the pond and take our tackle boxes and poles over to a dingy and treasured couch strategically left for the comfort of future adventurers. He catches a fish and explains to me the importance of Styrofoam boxes. He teaches me how to bait the hook and shows me how to cast my line. Guiding my arm as we pull back and release the fishing rod, the hook plops into the water. I'm fascinated by the bright red bobber as it dances in the breeze. I hear the cows calling in the distance. I smell someone burning piles of oak leaves. "Hey." My uncle nudges me. "Your line is in the mud." I snap back to the purpose of this trip. My bobber is tangled in the roots of a tree. He frees me in my helplessness and guides me again out toward the middle of the water. Happy and satisfied, I nestle back into the couch and imagine catching a fish. Before long, I'm back in the mud and being rescued. We do this time and again, but I'm not disheartened. I'm enjoying every minute of it. I eventually cast the line myself, and always into the mud. But, it is *my* mud. I am doing it for myself. I am a fisherman.

When I think of this day, I ask myself: What did I experience? Was a fish given *to* me? Was fishing done *for* me while I watched and learned? Was fishing done *with* me? Actually, all three occurred, and I believe that is the reason it was such a meaningful and memorable experience.

My uncle gave me the fish he caught. I needed and enjoyed what he provided. I also learned from him. He provided guidance and tailored instruction for my specific needs. Also, he fished with me. I was a co-fisherman. He eventually left me to my own devices and allowed me the freedom to go it alone. I was given the gift of a sense of ownership and skill. By the end of the trip, despite my poor return of fish, I was fishing alongside him. It was a partnership. The experience progressed during the day. First, the object of our trip was simply provided to me. Then, tailored and specific pointers were given for my own learning. Finally, I participated in a joint partnership where we fished side-by-side. Granted, he was much more experienced and I could catch nothing on my own. However, I was fishing for myself as he sat beside and *with* me.

Defining Ministry *To, For* and *With*

What is the purpose of children's ministry? Do churches minister *to* children and their families? Do churches provide growth opportunities *for* children? Do churches minister *with* and alongside them? I believe the most robust children and family ministries include all three elements as a part of the church experience.

Ministry *to* children and families involves caring for them. Do they need help with basic necessities of food, clothing, shelter and safety? Do they know the Gospel message? In our particular tribe and movement, we place a high value on educating children so that they become fully biblically literate parts of the church family. We provide meals, clothes, Bibles, and backpacks; we support children's homes and sponsor Tuesday-Thursday schools. Focusing on the ministry of receiving is ministry *to*. Children are the objects of service and are invited to receive Christ's incarnational love.

Ministry *for* children and families involves equipping them. Are opportunities geared at their level and addressing their life stage needs? Are they receiving pastoral care? Is their spiritual diet consistent with what they require to grow through study, service and an internal life of spiritual disciplines? Many Churches of Christ equip children and families with grief therapy groups, tools and training on money management and tithing, and special needs support. All of this is informed by the Bible and equips them with tools for deepening discipleship. A ministry of equipping through strategic nurture is ministry *for*. Children and families are increasingly participants of service and included in a church's response to Christ's incarnational love through the tools given to them.

Ministry *with* children and families involves partnering with them. Churches serve and minister to others with them. We become mentors as this beautiful partnership takes root and as children begin to take ownership of the ministry in which they are involved. The discipleship cycle begins again as we walk alongside children and families and they in turn care for and minister to others. They are partners with us in service, and involved in sharing Christ's incarnational love *with* others.

All three—ministry *to*, *for* and *with*—are needed and become parts of a healthy

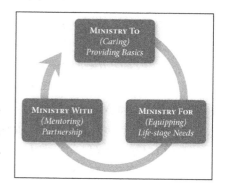

children and family ministry. It's a discipleship adventure, and we rob the church body by neglecting any one of these phases of ministry. As churches, the natural inclination lies in ministry to and for children. The most easily overlooked, most difficult, and at times the most exciting part of ministry is ministry *with* children. The remainder of this chapter will focus on this third part of the cycle.

Tenets of Ministry *With* Children

Early in its beginnings, Christianity became a relatively child-friendly religion, unique in the world, in how we relate to one another, even with the least of these.[1] Churches of Christ are already practicing ministry with children in many contexts. We encourage evangelism by providing easy ways for children and families to invite friends to church, VBS, and summer camp. We often sit alongside children and write encouragement notes to missionaries. Many of us foster a sense of belonging by giving children an opportunity to tithe and contribute monetarily. Some children's groups and parents visit shut-ins and the elderly regularly. The list goes on, depending on the context. But, do we know why we do these things? What is the purpose and theology behind promoting ministry partnerships with children? How can we be more strategic and intentional in the ways we minister with children?

The following list of tenets related to ministry with children is by no means complete or exhaustive. However, as we continue dialogue in our congregations about children and the church, these tenets may inform and support our conversations as we strive to connect our theology of children with our church practice.

Children Are the Present Church

"Our children are the future of the church." We often hear this plea in the context of advocating for children. This statement furthers the idea that children are kernels or seeds yet to germinate spiritually. They are only fragile kernels of hope that will one day sprout into abundant spirituality and usefulness in the church, not yet capable of contributing meaningfully.

Children are indeed the future of the church, but just as important, children are part of the current and active church. In a movement that believes everyone is a minister and a vital and crucial part of the body, we sometimes deny that children are a part of the body as well. Children can contribute much to the church and its mission. We sometimes discount their potential in vital roles within our faith communities. David Jensen articulates it this way:

> An ecclesiology that pays attention to childhood recognizes that children are not simply on their way to becoming members of the church and society. Instead, the church witnesses that children already are full heirs of the covenant community, who pray with desire. Childhood is not a way station on the path to human becoming; it also informs the trajectory of one's entire life. . . lived with others, dependent on others, attentive to others.[2]

Children are often valued for who they will become in the church. Instead we should spend more of our energies celebrating and encouraging who they already are, and whose they are, in and among the church body. In recognizing children as part of the present church, we begin to value what they can contribute in the here and now. Children then begin to see themselves more as partners in ministry and less as silent spectators.

Children Develop Faith Relationally

Katherine Stonehouse writes, "When we prepare to teach a value, we must begin by asking how we can lead children to experience the value."[3] During our Bible class time on Sunday, one four-year old was making use of some free-play at the end of the class period to reenact the Bible story she just experienced. We discovered a day in the lives of Mary and Martha (Luke 10). She preferred Martha's industrious nature of ministry and service to Mary's bent toward quiet contemplation. She set about the task of preparing me a scrumptious meal, as I played the part of Jesus. But "First things first," she said. "Why don't you just sit back and relax and I'll bring you something cool to drink after your long journey." A moment later, she emerged from behind the kitchen set, beaming, plopped a jug in front of me and pronounced: "Here's your beer!"

Her offering to me, though not everyone's view of appropriate Christian hospitality, touched me. She took the story she learned and related the text to her real life in a genuine and heartfelt way. She took the actions modeled in her home and expressed them in her growing faith through an act of ministry. I thanked her and joined her in her experience, as God drew her through play and through our relationship, into a deeper expression of the text and Savior.

Children develop and learn by interacting with the world around them. This is not always as tidy as many of us would like. It is much easier to guide children in a highly controlled environment where the messiness of relationship rarely clouds the facts being conveyed. However, it's the relationships, messy or not, which provide the key components of spiritual formation in the ways children can best experience them. Stonehouse describes the power of experience in learning:

> Discoveries made through direct experiences are more transformational and exciting for children than lessons in which adults tell them what they ought to know. This does not mean that adults should never pass on to children important information. It does mean, however, that we should not depend on the telling method as our main contribution to the child's development.[4]

We are teachers and guides for children on their spiritual journeys. Having any sort of relationship with them, whether as a parent, Bible class teacher, elder, group leader, greeter, requires that we are inherently teaching them spirituality through our interactions with them. In connecting and working with children, we teach them what it means to be human and how to approach life. Those of us who approach our interactions with children as a sterile process of disseminating information miss the importance of relationship. Hay and Nye assert that in the process of learning and developing faith, "spirituality cannot be nurtured where education is purveyed as just another commodity distributed at arm's length, so that the subjectivity of the of the teacher is safely concealed from the children."[5]

Not only should we avoid self-concealment, we should make intentional efforts to join with children in a special bond. More than being relational, faith is covenantal in structure. Praying for the children, living our lives alongside them, and letting them know us—these acts cultivate a covenant between the child and us. James Fowler, a faith development expert, asserts covenantal relationship requires more than just a commitment between two persons. It requires a shared trust and loyalty with a transcendent God that strengthens and deepens the covenant bond as each party actively participates in the relationship.[6] We respond to this covenant in deeper and more engaging ways than just *doing*. Instead, we respond with our whole *being*—how we are in the world. This is something even young children can embrace with joy.[7]

This type of relationship is in the intentional dedication of one soul to another. This commitment is more than an accidental acquaintance or handshake in the foyer. This involves the transforming work of our incarnational Christ, who is completely present and at work in the bond. This covenant shapes both child and adult as they take this pilgrimage together.[8]

Children Can Serve in Significant Ways

The vocation of childhood is play. It is the job of children to discover and experience the world through play. Our Creator made us for play and delights in humor. What better way for parents and church mentors to connect and partner with children than through play? Ministry fits nicely into that paradigm. Visiting the elderly, hosting a neighborhood block party and sorting cans in a food pantry all have elements of playfulness and fun. Even laborious tasks such as picking up trash and painting over graffiti can be infused with play.

Children naturally desire to contribute and be a part of something greater than themselves. However, due to their small stature and maturity we sometimes assume very few ministry tasks are suitable for them. Purposeful and playful ministry, though, is contagious for children. Coles writes, "Children very much need a sense of purpose and direction in life, a set of values grounded in moral introspection—a spiritual life that is given sanction by their parents and others in their adult world."[9] In sanctioning and blessing their efforts in ministry with us, we help to give them purpose and direction. Children begin to understand from us, through covenantal ministry relationships, what is a significant and meaningful use of our time and what blesses others. Giving cups of cold water in the name of Jesus and caring for widows are tasks that children assign significance when trusted adults model their importance in their own lives. Just as importantly, we must acknowledge those tasks as significant, overtly teaching children and guiding them through the act of ministry, reinforcing the idea they are valued partners.

If we require children to behave as adults and think like adults in order to do ministry, very few will desire ministry and service. We are communicating that ministry is meant for someone else. However, by allowing children to be children and providing guidance and service opportunities alongside us that fit their sensibilities, we kindle in them a sense of purpose and desire that continues into adulthood. Some examples might include: cooking together and taking your children with you to deliver a meal to someone, hosting a neighborhood block party where you and your children minister together to others, taking a prayer walk around your elementary school together, or interacting with others on the soccer field in meaningful and missional ways. Significant ministry can be accomplished by children, especially when guided by and alongside a nurturing adult.

Children Can Offer Spiritual Insight

It easy to fall into the trap of believing children are void of spiritual insight and that spiritual reflection is best left to the grown-ups.

David Hay conducted a study with Rebecca Nye where they found a connection between the spiritual insight of children and their participation in meaningful and relational service with adults, "out of which can arise meaningful aesthetic experience, religious experience, personal and traditional responses to mystery and being, and mystical and moral insight."[10] They add this important insight:

> Much of their [children's] interest is naturally focused on their social world. Its capacity to provide a vehicle for spirituality suggests that particular note might be taken of how children construe interpersonal relations as a means of glimpsing something in their spiritual life.[11]

Children glean spiritual insights from adults, but the relationship can be reciprocal, if we allow it. In our children's church, we discuss the Fruits of the Spirit. Toward the end of class, I ask the children what love, the first fruit, looks like. I get a lump in my throat as I listen to their answers: honest, heartfelt, and flowing out of the deep places of their souls. "Love looks like being nice to my brother even when he hits me." "Love looks like sharing my toys with kids who don't got any." "Love is giving that man on the road some food or something." "Yeah, and clothes. Sometimes they have old clothes on . . . and they are cold." In their responses, I hear echoes of Jesus' words:

> I was hungry. And you gave me something to eat. I was thirsty. And you gave me something to drink. I was a stranger. And you invited me in. I needed clothes. And you gave them to me. I was sick. And you took care of me. I was in prison. And you came to visit me (Matt. 25:35–36; NIV).

On another Sunday morning, one group of children experienced Psalm 23 through something called a "Good Shepherd box," which is a treasure chest filled with simple pieces of felt cut into shapes of different colors. The felt pieces are layered to create the psalm, and it is being experienced by the children through the telling. After the children immerse themselves in the psalm, we present wonder questions for the children to contemplate and reflect, such as: "I *wonder* where you fit into this story?" "I *wonder* what the Shepherd is feeling as he guards the entrance to the sheepfold?" "I *wonder* what the green pastures and still waters are like for the sheep?"

No answers are provided. The story is experienced and the children pray and reflect about its meaning. After some time in reflection and prayer, a seven-year-old girl walked over to me and said, "The Valley of the Shadow of Death is a scary place. Sometimes it's just a little while and sometimes it lasts a long time." She paused for a beat or two and continued. "When it lasts a long time, it can feel like it's your fault, that you caused it . . . but it's not . . . and Jesus is there with you . . . and He loves you. He helps you get through."

We would gain much in listening to children more. They desire the deep spiritual waters just as adults do. Practicing ministry with children gives the adults with them the space in our frenetic world to slow down and be witness to the still small voice we often miss from a child.

Even Young Children Are Forming a Deepening Theology

We often think that young children are not yet abstract thinkers and assume we should avoid discussing more complex notions of theology with them. In fact, even small children begin taking the tacit theology expressed by the adults around them and start to build on it. More often than not, children pick up on our theology in the ways we relate to the world, through our actions.

A two-year old gave me one of my favorite nicknames. Zane gleefully waves hello, "Hi, Church!" each time I come into view. On the way to our building, he excitedly asks his parents, "Are we going to see Church?" His parents try to explain that the church is the type of building, but also the people. It isn't really one particular person. I am "Mr. Ryan," not "Church." Church is everyone in his Bible class, all of his teachers and all the people who love him there. He wrinkles his nose and nods. The next time I see him, he busts into that contagious smile of his and exclaims: "Hello, Mr. Ryan-Church!"

It's easy to smirk and dismiss Zane as cute and ignorant of the intricacies and complexities of a well-developed ecclesiology—a theological perspective of church. Granted, much of it is lost on his developing two-year old brain. However, the idea of Church as relationship is firmly embedded into his day-to-day operating. Church is an incarnational experience. Church embodies being, rather than a place or a practice. Can he put this into words? The best he can muster is "Hello, Church!" but the beginnings of his life-long theology of ministry are being defined through his experiences with others.

Ruby Bridges, the first black child in a previously all white Louisiana elementary school, never missed a single day of her first grade class despite confronting racial slurs and angry crowds in 1960. Even more striking is that, before and after school, she would pause and say a prayer for the jeering crowds. Robert Coles, in his children's book, *The Story of Ruby Bridges*, remembers her prayer:

> Please God, try to forgive these people.
> Because even if they say those bad things,
> They don't know what they're doing.
> So You could forgive them,
> Just like you did those folks a long time ago
> When they said terrible things about You.[12]

Children can possess incredibly deep theology and even offer adults spiritual nurture. When children are relegated to another wing of the building, or not allowed to practice ministry with adults, we all miss out. By serving alongside children, we are there to shape their budding theologies "on the job," helping to make them stick.

Expanding the Family Is Just as Important as Protecting It

The world is waging war against children. Every day we hear of oppression and violence against children and families around the world. Children and families today are suffering in a world of brokenness and tragedy. It isn't difficult to understand why some Christian families feel compelled to isolate themselves in an effort to protect their children from the dangers and risks inherent to lives lived in our fallen world. Yet is safety the most important thing for parents to seek? How should the church respond? David Jenson asserts that vulnerability is part of the faithful church's response to the pain inflicted by the world.

> In the face of violence against children, the church does not resort to violence (and thus perpetuate its unending cycle), but names and claims children as heirs to the covenant. This promise is not grabbed by force, but inherited in vulnerability. By creating a space for children to be named and claimed, the church exposes the vacuous nature of power and violence, which in the end can bring only death. Here the Christian church makes a wager: that life is not found in a will to power, but in a vulnerable savior who claims our vulnerable selves.[13]

The temptation is, as a community of faith, to wage an offensive or seal ourselves off from the world in the name of protecting future generations. However, we cannot forget that Jesus' invitation is open to all, and his call for us, God's children, is to be light and salt in the world. We model our response after our loving and vulnerable Savior, expanding our family to include others who may not yet know the fullness and healing of God's love. Expanding our family is just as important as protecting it. Jesus came as one who welcomed and invited all into the family. The church offers sanctuary, even to outsiders, perhaps even to at-risk and risky outsiders, allowing for them to find spiritual nurture in the shelter of a loving congregation. The church sustains its place as spiritual harbor if it fosters children's participation in ministry.[14]

James 1:27 reminds us that genuine spirituality involves reaching out to others who need our help. Ratcliff's study of influences in developing childhood faith found that three elements were crucial: discussing faith with a parent, having a regular time of devotions with a parent, and being involved in a service project with the family.[15]

> A relationship with God should naturally move us to love those who need our help. Children need to be with us as we reach out to the unfortunate. Not only can you bring your youngsters

with you, but it is a good idea to have them participate actively in some way to help the homeless, the poor, the abused and neglected, the elderly, the infirm, or those who are wayward or lost.[16]

Valuing the gift of family requires us to both protect and expand it. We expand the family because through shared ministry experiences with children, we don't want to keep it to ourselves. We protect it because it's precious and by sharing it with others we are protecting and helping our children to grow.

What would happen if we taught children that all are welcome into the church family? How can families minister alongside children to those who look and think differently than themselves? Are our families strong enough to welcome and minister to others with whom we wouldn't ordinarily associate? How will their young and growing theologies be affected by a church and family that brings people in rather than shutting them out in the name of protection? We might be surprised.

Putting It into Practice

John H. Westerhoff III describes child faith development as a growing tree.[17] Young tree trunks possess few rings, but this changes as they grow older. Life experiences with God and people help new rings of faith to form. What better way to foster life experiences with God and people than in ministry together?

A study of congregational practices by Mercer, Matthews, and Walz revealed three common elements of vitality in church practices with children. First, all the churches in the study take into account physicality and body movement with children. Kinetic and active ministry opportunities encourage ministry partnerships with children. Second, there was a dedication of significant resources in each context so that children were given ample ability to share in ministry. Third, the churches were not always consistent across the board in providing opportunities for involvement with children in ministry, but each church provided opportunities that were strongly connected to the life of each congregation in its unique context.[18]

The easy route is to tell children to sit still and let others do ministry. In doing so, we risk raising generations ingrained with the idea that ministry is something others do while they sit nice and still. In 2 John 1:4, John said: "It has given me great joy to find some of your children walking in the truth, just as the Father commanded us." To walk in the truth and live it, our children must own it in a personal and purposeful way. By giving them a sense of mission and purpose, we combat the complacency that can creep in from an early age, instilling instead ownership and intentionality in young hearts that will grow into church leaders in the near future.

What Does This Mean for My Congregation?

Ministry with children, and the partnership that flows from it, affects how we approach many questions as we seek a more robust theology of children's ministry. Consider the following as starting points for your own conversations within your specific ministry context. Every church family will approach these questions differently. However, by exploring these ideas in community, every congregation can foster greater opportunities for children and adults in ministry together.

- Who is listening to children in our church family? What are the children saying?
- What would children bring to some of the ministries in our church?
- What will be different about our congregation when ministry partnerships with children and families take hold?
- When is ministry with children considered a burden? How do we address that?
- What is unique about our congregation and how can children become more involved with that aspect of us?
- How can our children and families partner together in ministry to our local neighborhood?

- Who would champion a shift toward ministry with children in our congregation?

Conclusion

As a movement, Churches of Christ excel at ministry to and for children. Many churches are already practicing rewarding and beneficial ministry partnerships with children. My prayer is that as we hone our theology of ministry with children and families, we will experience abundant discipleship growth and evangelism in our congregations. May we become churches that welcome the least of these into the very core of our ministry work, making them passionate fishers of people with us, among us and alongside us. The following chapters will continue this conversation as we address specifics of how to better engage in these covenant partnerships.

Chapter 12

Respect the Text and Respect the Children

Reconsidering Our Approaches to Bible School

Dana Kennamer Pemberton

The B-I-B-L-E
Yes, that's the book for me
I love to hear the stories from
The B-I-B-L-E

I learned how to teach Bible school by sitting at my mother's feet. In a small classroom off of the auditorium in my home-town church, my mom welcomed her children week after week, year after year, to a time of story, song and community. Through flip charts, flannel graph and a sand table built by my father, she engaged children in God's story. It didn't matter if others considered them "well-behaved" or not. My mom found ways to help all children be successful and, most importantly, to feel truly wanted. My mother loved all children and they knew it. There are grown children with their own children who send her Christmas cards because of the way she welcomed them. (Amazing!) My mother was very particular about the way she taught the Bible. She knew the stories well, took great care in telling them with accuracy and found age appropriate ways to help children understand how God was working through the events and the people in the Bible.

Recently, I asked my dear friend and children's minister, Suzetta Nutt, what I should tell you in this chapter about the Bible classes we provide in our children's ministries. Her answer was quick and simple, "Respect the text and respect the children." I immediately thought of my mother. That's what I learned from her in that little classroom so many years ago. It's what guides me as I join children in the word. Respect the text and respect the children.

At the risk of simply sounding nostalgic (Back to the good old days!), or worse, indicting—I worry that many of our contemporary practices don't communicate respect for children or the Biblical text. We love our children. We want them to feel welcomed. We want them to know God and be formed into God's image. Still, in our efforts to provide good programs, we have not always been discerning about what our practices truly communicate. So, please join me as we think about where we have been, where many of us are now, and what might guide us as we continue the important work of living in the word with our children. Our recollections of the past will be brief so that we can spend more time reflecting on current practices and the principles that might guide us in the future.

Where We Have Been

Like many who grew up in Churches of Christ in the 1960s and 1970s, I have strong memories of my Bible classes. I can still remember the names of most of the men and women who taught me in my small church in Hearne, Texas. They are part of my story and I am grateful.

Our tradition has a strong history of valuing Biblical knowledge. We are a "people of the Book" and believe that all Christians can study and understand God's word—and that they should. My Sunday school teachers often emphasized memorization, accuracy in the details, and knowing how to use my Bible. I remember the excitement of Bible drills—a competition to see who could be first to find a passage when the teacher called out book, chapter and verse. I think I was in my early thirties before my heart didn't race when a preacher asked the congregation to turn to a particular passage.

I still value deep and broad knowledge of God's word. This is a strength of our heritage we need not lose—something we can offer the broader family of faith. However, something happened along the way for many of us. We knew the facts of the Bible, but we didn't know God. We could name the twelve tribes, the twelve apostles and identify the kind of wood Noah used to build the ark, but we didn't know how to walk in the way of Jesus. We knew his rules, but didn't know the man. We could find book, chapter and verse, but didn't really know how to use the Bible.

To our credit, we recognized the problem. We knew something needed to change. And change we have. However, the changes made were often reactive rather than theologically informed. We didn't want meaningless facts; we sought relevance. In addition, new ideas from developmental theory became our primary lenses for our curriculum and program choices. Finally, for many reasons churches are finding it increasingly difficult to recruit volunteers who will serve in their children's classes. These changes— some from our tradition specific history and some reflecting larger cultural shifts—bring us to where we are now.

Where We Are Now

> After years of hearing Bible stories, memorizing Bible verses, and singing songs about Jesus' love for them (children), their understanding of faith, of God, and of God's plans and purposes is simplistic, individualistic, and almost secular. Yes, children's ministry in our churches is, indeed, broken.[1]

These strong words cannot be applied to all churches. However, there are several trends in many contemporary children's ministries that are cause for serious concern. Among these are the focus on entertainment, the separation of children from the broader faith community (see Chapter seven), and the trivialization and manipulation of the biblical text. We select programs on the basis of expediency. Recruiting volunteers, simplifying (or eliminating) preparation, attracting large numbers, and providing fun experiences for children often guide our decisions.

Let Me Entertain You!

Walking into the children's areas of many churches, you find an environment filled with bright images, media, and Disney-like characters. These ministries are high-energy and fast-paced. Advocates contend that to capture the attention of today's children, we must compete with television, video games and other forms of high tech entertainment. The objective is to provide a dynamic, fun, kid-friendly environment.

Entertainment approaches often utilize cartoon images and themed environments (e.g., a spaceship) to make the biblical story more interesting to children. This is problematic. First, the implicit assumption is that children will not be drawn to God's story unless it is made cute, funny, or flashy. Second, these cartoon images and themed environments can be distracting and confusing for spiritual development. Vegetables may be entertaining, but you will not find them in the biblical text.

Entertainment models are also promoted for their potential to attract young families. Contemporary parenting values activities for children—lots of activities! Since parents often choose churches for their programs for children, we better have programs that are attractive and most definitely fun! If we get the kids we get the parents—the real target. And when children have fun in class they may also invite their friends. More growth! More numbers! More energy! Everyone wins!

Rethinking the Focus on Fun

But does everyone really win? Mercer contends that it's children who lose when used in church efforts to recruit new members in a competitive market. It's dangerous to view children as a marketing tool.

> This reflects a utilitarian view of the smallest humans that reduces them to being merely the means of achieving some more desirable end. Our church leaders speak and write about the need to attract families with young children so that their congregations will have vitality. The desire for vitality is not in itself wrongheaded. But the interest in children primarily for the

purpose of getting adults onto the church rolls or making the congregation appear to have life objectifies and commodifies children . . . The theological notion of welcoming children easily slips into advertising through children.[2]

I have visited with many children's ministers whose churches use entertainment models and know their hearts. They deeply love children and are dedicated to sharing God's word with them. Still, expediency and fear can guide program choices. What if children don't like Bible class? If they like it, they'll come. They'll listen better and remember more, right? After all, they're hearing God's word. Isn't that the point? Does it really matter how we share it? Of course God can work through our flawed, imperfect attempts to share the word. Still, we must think critically about our focus on fun.

While "fun" is not an evil to be avoided, neither should it be the guiding framework for our ministry practices. Scottie May asks what might change if we replace *fun* with *meaningful* asserting that "children are eager to be involved in things that are meaningful to them, things that may not always be categorized as fun."[3] The emphasis on fun assumes that children won't engage with the biblical story without bells and whistles and gimmicks. This implies a limited view of both the power of the word and the spiritual capacities of children. There is a lack of awareness of the "children's ability to encounter God and experience God's presence and the inherent attraction that children have to awe, wonder, reverence and mystery."[4] The focus on entertainment provides little space for wonder and reverence while overshadowing the true purpose of our children's ministries—the spiritual formation of children.[5]

At a church I once visited, these words flashed on the screen to announce the time for the children to leave the communal gathering: *Children's Church! Never boring, always fun and all about Jesus!* The intent was to attract children (and their parents) by providing enjoyable programing, but I was disturbed by the underlying messages. What does this say we believe about children, worship and the word? Do we believe that the Bible is boring? Are we telling children that church must always be fun and provide what they want? The call to community is the call to service and hospitality. It includes moments of deep joy and great blessing, but it is often challenging and, at times, not at all fun. Jesus never said, "Let the little children come to me and we will have fun!"

Do we believe that children must always have fun and never be bored? Like Joyce Ann Mercer, I'm concerned that we are nurturing in our children a selfish "hunger for spectacle."[6] The need for excitement and entertainment pervades contemporary culture and has shaped many church practices, creating a consumer approach to spirituality. We also treat children as consumers, making sure to offer them fun experiences they'll like. I recently heard the phrase, "What we win them with is what we win them to." While we're always shaped by our surrounding culture, God's people must engage in continuous communal and individual discernment to determine aspects of culture not consistent with the way of Jesus. A consumerist perspective of church is clearly inconsistent.

No Preparation Needed!

Recruiting volunteers is a wide spread problem. Children's ministers spend countless hours on the phone, on email, on doorsteps, on highways and byways asking for church members to commit their time to children. Some are willing, but only for a short time—three, maybe four months or less. And the need to prepare is a definite deterrent. Busy lives, a desire to be fed themselves at church (which we taught them as children) and, at times, lack of confidence in their own biblical knowledge produce volunteers who want to simply walk in do their short term service and leave. This is a serious challenge. On the one hand, parents and church leaders demand strong programs for children. On the other, volunteers who will commit to partnering with children on the spiritual journey are rare. What are children's ministers to do? Many feel left with no real choices. Require minimal commitment. Always make volunteers feel good. And make teaching easy. No preparation needed!

Curriculum companies have responded—as have large churches that write and market their own instructional materials. Curricula are written to be easy to implement. Scripts are provided, the point of the lesson predetermined and the story often presented through video. Teacher preparation is eliminated. Just show up, be with the kids and have fun! Sold!

Asserting that a curriculum's strength is that it requires very little or no teacher preparation is frightening. First, this implies that what children can meaningfully learn from God's story is limited. Second, this suggests that characters on a screen or a prewritten script effectively nurture children's spirituality and that adult engagement with the text is needless.

It is not possible to join children meaningfully in discovering the truths of God's word with depth when the adults are not living in the story themselves. Real preparation isn't making materials and planning activities. Preparation is living in the story. As I read the text in preparation for my time with children, the story comes alive again. I often discover—or rediscover—details that capture my imagination. This preparation is critical and always spiritually formative.

However, Bible curriculum for children has already summarized and interpreted the story for the teacher. No need to read it yourself. Many provide a limited and often contrived view of the biblical story. There are at least two reasons for this: 1) the influence of cognitive developmental theories and 2) the quest for relevance.

Development as Deficit

Our practices with children are strongly influenced by developmental theorists like Piaget and Fowler.[7] These theorists helped us understand that children do not see the world as we do. Their insights about the unique qualities of children challenge us to consider developmental characteristics when providing for their education and care. These are important issues. We must not expect children to be small adults. Our interactions with them should be truly hospitable—welcoming children as children.

However, developmental theories are at the very least incomplete—and at worst, harmful—when applied to the spiritual formation of children. These theories often emphasize the limitations of children, particularly their cognitive limitations.[8] This can result in a deficit approach, focusing on the inability of children to understand the world as adults do, forgetting that Jesus said, "it is to such as these that the kingdom of heaven belongs" (Matt. 19:14, NRSV). This does not sound like a deficit.

Misapplication of developmental theories results in a dumbing down of the Bible, sacrificing the integrity of the text in an effort to make it accessible for children. When we start with what children cannot understand, we often oversimplify the story until it loses its meaning. One example is the common approach to the story of Jesus feeding the 5,000 with five loaves and two fish. Because young children are egocentric—viewing the world from their own limited perspective—and have a limited grasp of concepts of quantity (They think 5,000 is how old their grandparents are!) curriculum writers assume that they will understand and be interested in the little boy who "shared" his lunch with Jesus. The point becomes that a little boy shared so I can share. That is not the point of the story. Instead, I see a savior with compassion for people and who does not need "enough" to meet our needs. That's the point.

The Search for Relevance

Another characteristic of contemporary curricula is the focus on relevance. Each lesson must have a take-away, an immediate and clear life application from the story. This represents a misunderstanding of the Bible. The Bible is not a self-help book. Most of the individual stories don't have a "point" or simple moral lesson. The point of the Bible is to come to know God—Father, Son and Spirit—not to find quick life applications. Ivy Beckwith calls this approach the "Aesop's Fableization" of the Bible. She further adds that:

> When we use the Bible with children simply to teach doctrinal tenets, moral absolutes, tips for better living or stories of heroes to be emulated, we stunt the spiritual formation of our children and deprive them of the valuable, spiritual story of God. When we only distill the Bible into practical applications and little life lessons, we fail to teach children how to use the Bible as a means of understanding God's overarching purposes in the world.[9]

Eugene Peterson speaks more forcefully about using the Bible as a simple guide for making good and moral choices. He states that we "do violence to the biblical revelation when we **use** it for what we can get out of it or what we think will provide color and spice to our otherwise bland lives. That always results in a kind of 'decorator spirituality'– God as enhancement."[10] That is strong language. But it is important to consider, for ourselves and for our children, whether we are forcing the Bible to fit our lives rather than letting God work through the text to draw us into authentic relationship.

One common strategy for creating relevance in Bible curricula uses predetermined themes. *People Who Prayed! They Stood for God! Bible Superheroes!* "Age-appropriate" episodes are chosen to go with the theme. Writers pick and choose and sometimes manipulate the stories to make them fit. While there are certainly times to look at individual events in the Bible, I worry that children aren't seeing the text as a coherent whole. They hear bits and pieces but never see the overarching story of God's love and faithfulness.

Perhaps a better approach would be to let the theme emerge from the text in more authentic ways. When we journey with Elijah and Elisha in our Bible class, the children and I remember that these stories show us who God is. Throughout the text, the phrase "As surely as the Lord your God lives . . ." is repeated again and again. This becomes our lens for each story. What does the story of Mt. Carmel teach us about our living God? When the woman's oil and flour never run out, what do we discover about this Lord who surely lives?

We need to share the Bible with children (and adults for that matter) so that they see God's overarching story. Teaching in this way is obviously harder than providing individual lessons, clean and tidy with clear, ready-to-use-today applications. But the Bible is not clean and tidy, nor is the way of faith.

Where Do We Go from Here?

We've explored several challenges facing us as we seek to engage children with the Bible in our formal children's ministries. Some may not apply to your faith community. Still, how might those of us within Churches of Christ support and challenge each other as we seek to share God's word with children? And how might we participate in the broader conversation with other faith traditions—learning from each other—as we struggle with the same questions? What principles might guide us as we move forward?

Start with Sound Theology

We must practice greater vigilance in evaluating the theology embedded in the curricula that we use. Have other churches used it successfully? Does it work? Is it easy to use? Do the kids like it? These are the questions asked in the selection process. What often goes unasked is the question of theology.

A closer look may reveal that we're educating our children into a theology that does not fit what the rest of the church believes. Mercer cautions that because of the "structural separation between children's educational ministries and the rest of congregational life in most mainline churches, such a huge discrepancy may go unnoticed by almost everyone, including pastor(s)."[11] We need to start with our theology and ensure that we are teaching children what we truly believe.

Engage Everyone in the Conversation

We need our leaders, elders and senior ministers, to bring the conversation about children from the margins into the center. Our churches often provide special classes about children for parents. At times we have seminars for children's ministry volunteers, but I don't remember a time when the entire faith community engaged in a study of our communal responsibility to children. What might change if we did this? How might we transform our practices if we charged the entire body with the call to "let the little children come?" (Matt. 19:14) What if we believed—really believed—that children are not only recipients of God's grace, but agents of God's grace as well?

Children's ministers often try to communicate these truths. However, their words can fall on deaf ears. They're supposed to care about children. It's their job. But if elders and other ministers brought a study of children into the full congregational conversation, what might change? We might actually begin to understand what Jesus meant when he said, "the kingdom of heaven belongs" to them (Matt. 19:14, NRSV).

I recognize that our elders and ministers (even children's ministers) might not feel equipped to lead this kind of congregational study. Many children's ministers come from fields like education, with no formal training in theology or ministry. Even in seminaries and universities, most ministry majors never encounter serious study of biblical and theological perspectives on children. Perhaps this book will be a call for materials to be developed to assist churches in engaging in meaningful study about children.

Remember the Main Character

While working on my dissertation, I asked my five-year-old participants to tell me a story about God. Beyond creation, they couldn't do it. They could tell me stories about Moses, Noah and Abraham, but not about God. They could tell me stories about Jesus, but not about God. Granted, this might reflect developmental issues. God is more abstract, but Jesus has skin on just like us. Perhaps it is actually the point of the incarnation. Jesus came so that we could know God. He came so that we could see in flesh and blood what a life with God looks like. But still, it made me question my methods. I realized that I told the stories of Moses, Noah and Abraham. God had brief cameo appearances, but was definitely not the main character. That was a critical moment for me.

Now as I enter the stories with children, I am intentional about my language. For example, when we study the life of Moses, we use the framing statement "Our God Can!" that I developed from my own reading and reflection on the text. With each story, we think about what the events show that our God can do. God can see people hurting. God can use people who are not brave. God can deliver God's people. Our God can! These are messages that speak not only to the children, but to the adults in the room as well. Of course, as we journey with Moses we learn about him too—a baby rescued from a river, a murderer who flees to the desert, and a man who argues with God. Still, the focus is not on learning about Moses, but on what we learn about God through Moses' relationship **with** God. God is the main character.

The Bible is the story of how God works through, for and often in spite of God's people. When we make the story about biblical heroes we miss the point. These "heroes" were flawed folks. They made mistakes. Big mistakes! And still, our God continued to seek these broken people—to enter our mess in order to draw us into relationship. This truth about God will sustain our children far better than hero worship ever will.

Tell the Stories with Integrity

There is a strong temptation to sanitize Scripture for children—to clean up the mess we find. We want to hide the hard realities of lives in the text. Many stories are quite shocking— definitely not G rated. We need to be sensitive to children's readiness to hear some stories. However, we must not rewrite the Bible in order to make it palpable to children (or ourselves). My guiding principle is to tell the story so that I minimize the need to correct inaccuracies. As children get older (sometimes much older) we expand and deepen understanding, but children shouldn't feel they've been misled. A college student recently told me that he felt his Bible class teachers lied to him when he was little. It is important to tell children the truth about the people whose lives unfold in the Bible.

One Sunday, as my kindergarten and first grade children met Joseph's family for the first time, we re-discovered that God works through seriously messed up people. We created a family tree on the wall— Jacob, Leah, Rachel. We added children, a concubine, more children, another concubine. What a mess! Suddenly one of my first grade boys exclaimed with a bit of desperation in his voice, "But, Teacher Dana, Jesus is coming!" I said, "Yes, he is. And these people—these messed up people—are his great, great, great, great, great, great, grandparents." The children were amazed. We met again that morning a God who is not afraid of our brokenness—not a bad lesson for a Sunday morning.

From School to Journey: Live in the Questions Together

Our approach to Bible School is perhaps shaped by our use of the word school. In school, there is often one right answer. In school, we have specific and measurable objectives. In school, we have teacher and students. The teacher knows what the child needs to learn and works to present the information as effectively as possible.

If we changed our metaphor from school to journey, we could experience with children the reality that our spiritual journey is one of continual seeking and being formed more and more into the likeness of Jesus. When we apply schooling models, adults feel the need to "fill in the blanks" for children, concerned that they will be confused. But the process of spiritual formation is precisely that—a process. Caution needs to be exercised in providing quick, simple answers for children as we take this journey together.

Some of the greatest learning happens when we enter the text with children, not with ready answers, but with our hearts open for questions—ours and theirs. In the Old Testament, we read of events and symbols that God gave the people so that their children would ask questions. With the Passover (Ex. 12:25–27) and the twelve stones at the river Jordan (Josh. 4:6–7), one purpose was that the children would ask. Where in our interactions with children do we make space for questions?

In my Bible class, we often approach our unit of study with an overarching question that emerges from my reading of the text. For example, when we journey through the life of Jesus we discover that people often asked, "Who is this man?" So as the children and I learn about water turned to wine, a blind man healed, walking on water, and prayers in the garden we ask the question again. Who is this man? This calls us—me, the children and the other grown-ups in the room—to listen to the text to find answers about this man who has called all of us to follow him.

There is power in living in questions with children—wondering together as we learn about our God. The biblical narrative leaves a great deal to the imagination. Many of the details are left untold. Even adults wonder about the lives of the people described in its pages. As Peterson reminds us, "One of the characteristic marks of the biblical storytellers is a certain reticence. There is an austere, spare quality to their stories. They don't tell us too much. They leave a lot of blanks in the narration, an implicit invitation to enter the story, just as we are, and discover for ourselves how we fit into it."[12] The text compels us to wonder.

When I began exploring this idea of wondering, I was the primary person posing the wondering questions—open-ended questions inviting children to listen, reflect and respond as they made sense of God's story. I wonder what Peter was thinking when he heard the rooster crow? I wonder what Joseph felt when he saw his brothers standing before him in Egypt? I wonder what God was feeling when the people made the golden calf? As we have continued this practice, the children have begun to pose their own questions. I wonder about Dinah—what did she think about Joseph's dreams? What was Jesus like as a little boy? Did he play with friends?

We seem to fear children's questions—perhaps because we want to make sure they get things right. I also think we fear they will ask questions we can't answer. It's okay to admit that we don't have all the answers. I often acknowledge my own questions as I share confusing details of a story in the Bible. "Boys and girls, I don't understand this. I wonder." Children respect this kind of honesty. It models for them that the way of faith means trusting even when we don't understand. There is much that even the most spiritually mature adult doesn't understand. Rather than rushing to give answers, sometimes we need to take a step back, trust the children and listen. Csinos and Beckwith remark:

> Doing so shows respect for the questioner and the questions. What seems threatening at first can become an opportunity to allow children to take us on new trajectories and to learn something new. We don't need to be afraid to let a question or doubt take us off the teacher's guide track. We might just stumble into a discussion that is really meaningful for us and for the children in our midst.[13]

One Wednesday evening with about sixty Kindergarten through fifth grade children, we experienced such a moment. We had been dwelling in the parable of the Prodigal Son. A second grader volunteered to draw the story and share his thoughts. He drew the father and the son—each with one box labeled "good" and one box labeled "bad" beside them. Describing his drawing he said, "The son ran away. That was bad. But he came home and that was good. The father welcomed his son home. That was good. But he let him go. That was bad." Wait, I thought! The father was bad? Fortunately, I didn't respond immediately because then the child asked, "Why did the father let him go?" This seemingly childlike question raised some serious questions about God.

What followed was an extended conversation about free will and God's role in the world. "Why does God let people do things that are wrong?" "God should stop people from hurting other people." "But he lets us go sometimes." "But why? He should stop people. He shouldn't let people do bad things." These are profound questions with deep theological significance—questions with no easy answers that challenge adults as well. Finally, a child said, "It is hard, but God lets us choose. Sometimes he lets us go. But he always lets you come back." The children sat in silence after this final comment as if resting in that assurance, but still wrestling with the unsettling reality of choice. In the context of this quiet, respectful community, these children had the opportunity to connect personally with the biblical text, to explore important questions and to acknowledge their confusions and fears. Conversations like this prepare our children for the way of faith much better than a script with predetermined take-aways ever will.

Everyone Means Everyone!

I love Deuteronomy. It is a book that reminds people of who God is, what God has done, and who God has called them to be. The message reminds us that God's laws are not mere words; these words are life (Deut. 32:47). And Deuteronomy makes it clear that the children are to know these words as well.

Everyone must come—men, women, children, and even the foreigners who live in your towns. And each new generation will listen and learn to worship the LORD their God with fear and trembling and to do exactly what is said in God's Law. (Deut. 31:12, csv)

I am struck by the call to include children in listening to God's law. This was everyone's concern and everyone's responsibility. In these words is a clear respect for the word of the Lord and for children. And so I leave you where we began. Respect the text and respect the children. May the Lord bless you and the children as you enter the word together.

Chapter 13

Practicing Spiritual Disciplines with Children

Suzetta Nutt

"Be still and know that I am God."

Psalm 46:10, NRSV

We live in a noisy, chaotic world.

At times, it seems almost impossible these words of the psalmist can have any place in our world today. Even in our churches, we struggle with finding ways to enter the quiet, devoting time to prayer and studying God's word. So if it's hard for adults to practice these spiritual disciplines, how can children enter into God's presence and fully embrace these ancient words?

Can a wiggly, headstrong three-year-old *be still and know*?

Can a cool, tech-savvy fifth grader *be still and know*?

Asking these questions within the context of congregational life may demand a different response from our churches as they minister to children, their families, and the faith community as a whole.

Often church leaders make an assumption that because children can't fully understand the Scriptures, they need to simplify the message and tell children what to believe. Some churches decide children can't learn unless they are constantly entertained, so all their offerings for children surround a theme, with games, prizes and a party-like atmosphere. It's even becoming more common for churches to completely separate children from the congregational gathering, choosing to segregate them entirely from the adult members through children's worship or classes meeting during the adult worship time.

As a children's minister, I spend a lot of time wondering how God views the lives and hearts of children and what response must come from our faith community as we share life together. We know God values the presence of children because Jesus welcomed them (Matt. 18:5). We know God values their voices because the lips of infants and children sing God's praises and silence God's enemies (Ps. 8:2). We know Jesus cherishes the hearts of children because he says we must become like a child to enter the kingdom of heaven (Matt. 18:3).

Two important questions come as a result of these wonderings:

- What implications do these biblical truths have for our churches?
- If children are full participants in the faith community, what will our churches look like as children are welcomed and fully included in congregational life?

For the past eight years my ministry team has been on an intentional journey discovering how God works in the lives of young children, birth-fifth grade. We've been amazed, challenged and encouraged by what we've discovered.

We've learned God is at work in the hearts of children even if they don't have an adult family member who is a believer. We've listened to preschoolers ask questions worthy of the most studied theologian. We've watched elementary children confess to one another, serve the community, pray for their enemies, and gain understanding of difficult stories from God's word.

One major component in the life of a believer is the practice of spiritual disciplines. These disciplines are many and varied, and this chapter will focus on five disciplines: 1) worship, 2) study or dwelling in God's word, 3) silence or coming to the quiet, 4) prayer, and 5) confession. Each of these disciplines can bring us into God's presence. Each requires practice, training and intentionality. These disciplines are woven together, and it's often hard to tell where one ends and another begins. The practice of spiritual disciplines is transformative, as God brings us into life with God, transforming us into the image of Jesus for the sake of the world.

Richard Foster writes extensively on spiritual disciplines and says that prayer "seeks to usher us into the loving heart of God. As we pray the words, we are going beyond the words and into the reality which the words signify. Like Isaiah we are in the holy temple seeing the Lord high and lifted up. Like John we are flattened by the vision of the glorified Christ. Like the disciples in the upper room we are in intimate, life-transforming dialogue with the One who is the Way, the Truth and the Life."[1]

Can prayer change a child in this dramatic way? Can children intentionally depend on the power of God to do within them what is impossible? Can children be transformed into the image of Christ?

The answer, quite simply, is yes!

Transforming Worship

Our journey into practicing spiritual disciplines together with the children of our church began by asking a single question: can very young children worship God? This question led to many others, but every question was centered in the mystery of God and the joy of God's work in the hearts and lives of our children, no matter their age.

As we look at how children join God in worship, it's helpful to start with an understanding of how children and God interact with one another. Noted children's spirituality scholar Rebecca Nye defines children's spirituality in this way: *"God's ways of being with children and children's ways of being with God."* She continues:

> For Christians, this definition helps us to remember that children's spirituality starts with God—it is not something adults ·
> have to initiate. God and children, regardless of age or intellect, have ways of being together because this is how God created them. The difficulty comes in trying to appreciate, and support the ambiguous forms these ways can take.[2]

Recognizing that God is in charge of spiritual work in a child has been a freeing concept for our ministry team, especially in the area of children's worship. On Sunday morning we offer a children's worship time that meets during the last part of our worship service. Our preschool children, ages three–five, are dismissed from our assembly just before the sermon, which means they participate in congregational worship with their families during praise time, communion and the offering before leaving the worship center for *His Kids Worship*.

I'm privileged to serve as the worship leader for this gathering of our children, and it's not only their worship time, it's my worship time. It's my church. *His Kids Worship* is one of my favorite times of the week, but it hasn't always been so. Several years ago, as we were examining all our ministry practices and gatherings, I realized this worship time wasn't working very well. It felt chaotic and was frustrating for the children and their adult leaders. It didn't feel like a place where children were able to be with God.

During this time of ministry evaluation, my imagination was captured by the writings of several scholars including Sofia Cavalletti, Jerome Berryman, and Sonja Stewart. Each articulated a profound respect for the spiritual guidance and formation of children as well as the recognition that children have genuine, complex interactions with God through worship and the telling of the divine story.

In the book *Young Children and Worship*, Berryman and Stewart state, "The intent of worship is to experience and praise God. While the experience of God in worship leads to knowledge of God, the primary mode of knowing is by participation. God is experienced as we enter into Scripture and allow the Holy Spirit to convince us of the truth of God's Word."[3] The words of these scholars sparked within us the realization that we were taking our children out of worship, but were not replacing that time with worship. We were missing the opportunity of offering our children a time and space to experience the mystery of God. We asked another question: what should this time and space look like, and how does ordinary time and space become sacred?

Berryman and Stewart describe the mystery of helping children enter into God's presence as follows:

[we provide a] special place *apart* from the worshipping congregation so they may become able to worship meaningfully *with* the congregation. Worship transforms ordinary time and space into sacred time and space. The experience of God is one of mystery, awe and wonder. Where education attempts to explain and interpret mystery, worship allows us to experience and dwell in the presence of God as a way of knowing.[4]

We noticed the physical space of our children's worship area wasn't conducive to entering into the presence of God, so we cleared away the clutter and dimmed the lights. The impact of those two simple actions was interesting. Immediately the children realized something was different as they entered the room. You can imagine their questions, "Why are the lights off?" and "Where are the chairs and the toys?"

These changes opened up a different avenue of conversation that was completely natural and initiated by the children as we answered their questions. We began thinking critically about how we talked with our preschool children and new language began to emerge. It was a spiritual language that would become the foundation for spiritual formation.

"Today is different," I told the children. "We turned the lights off, and we changed how our room looks so we can know something special is about to happen. We are about to enter God's presence, and this is holy ground. It's God's time and God's space, and we're joining Him in worship today."

That first week, not much changed except the physical environment and how we entered our prayer time, but those small changes had a big impact. As our children responded to the improved worship space, we noticed a difference in how they behaved. They moved at a slower pace, the room was much calmer, and the children and adults were more peaceful. Sacred spaces communicate value and worth, and we discovered the children recognized the difference. Nye describes it like this, "Sacred spaces can speak their own language of meaning and help us express what we value, which can be both personal and powerful. Children are especially sensitive to the feel of a place, even as they cross the threshold. They can 'read' its language easily."[5]

I believe our new awareness of sacred space also changed our prayer time as well. Each week it was our normal practice to say a prayer after we had heard the story. This was usually a quick prayer as we dismissed the children to work at the tables, but this week we approached it differently.

As we got ready to pray, I told the children there were many ways to pray. Sometimes God's people pray with their eyes open, sometimes closed. Sometimes God's people pray out loud where others could hear their voices, other times they pray silently and in private. Sometimes God's people sit down to pray, or lie down to pray, or sometimes their whole body becomes their prayer. I told them they could pray in any way they wished as long as they weren't touching anyone else.

I will never forget what happened next.

One of our four-year-old, wiggly, active boys immediately got up, left his place in the group and laid face down on the floor with his arms out-stretched. I'm pretty sure he had never seen anyone else in that prayer posture, but he was expressing his own personal response to God's invitation to join in worship through the spiritual discipline of prayer.

This experience of watching a child express his own response to God's work within him opened our eyes to the possibility of God working in ways we had never considered. It was humbling, exciting and daunting at the same time. We wondered, "What comes next?"

Often during this time I wished for a proven resource that would lay out the next course of action. I quickly realized that even if such a resource had existed, our primary job was to ask God to give us wisdom and discernment about God's desire for our church, for our children, for this time in our city. Looking back, I don't think it would have been possible to take another church's plan and plop it into place without considering who we were and who God was calling us to become.

An observation made by Jean Vanier, founder of L'Arche, a community for mentally handicapped adults, describes how our team felt, "We can hear the wind—maybe even feel it on our faces—but we don't know where it's coming from or where it's going. So it is with things of the Spirit. You don't quite know where you are coming from or where you are going."[6]

It was clear this journey would have to be made by faith and in faith that the Holy Spirit would show us the way. We just needed to be people who were intentionally seeking relationships with the children in our church, willing to listen to them, worship and pray with them, trusting God is at work in the entire faith community, even among our youngest members.

Dwelling in the Word—Ava's Story

Several years ago our church collaborated with a group called Partnership for Missional Church led by Dr. Patrick Keifert, professor of Systematic Theology at Luther Seminary in St. Paul, Minnesota. Through that partnership our church leadership adopted the practice of *"Dwelling in the Word,"* which is the spiritual practice of listening to God's word for the purpose of transformation, rather than information. During that same time, I was researching Jerome Berryman's *Godly Play*™ curriculum of spiritual guidance. It explores the mystery of God's presence in our lives through simple, but deliberate storytelling and various ways of responding to the story.

The practice of *Dwelling in the Word* and learning about and adapting the practice of *Godly Play* prompted more questions. What if we changed the way we told God's story? What if, sometimes, we told the story as a means for transformation, rather than for information? Would that change how we listened to God? Would that change how we responded to God's word?

Where would we begin? With our preschoolers, of course!

I Wonder . . .

One primary component in *Godly Play* storytelling is allowing time for wonder and reflection through asking open-ended "I wonder . . ." questions. These questions encourage children to enter into the actual story, imagining what it would be like to be a participant in God's story. This is an interesting twist on the standard practice of asking children questions to see what information they have gained about an ancient story that is far removed from their daily life.

This practice of wondering together changed how we viewed Scripture. It provided ways to concretely link our stories together with God's big story. It personalized God's word, yet still honored Scripture, which young children can fully embrace.

Several years ago in *His Kids Worship*, I was telling the story of Mary hearing the news she would become the mother of a baby who would rescue the world. As we moved through the story, hearing God's plan for Mary, the children listened intently, getting ready for their time to offer a response.

"I wonder how Mary felt when the angel spoke to her . . . ?"

The responses from the preschoolers were as you might expect.

> *"She was surprised."*
> *"She was happy."*
> *"She was excited."*

Until four-year-old Ava responded by saying, "I think she was mad."

Her answer surprised everyone in the room, and when I asked Ava to say more about her wonder idea she said, "I think she was mad because it wasn't her plan."

Well, I don't know exactly how Mary responded to the angel Gabriel, but Ava's answer intrigued me. If a four-year-old can articulate this idea, placing herself in the story by wondering what it must have felt like to be completely vulnerable in God's hands, what are we missing with our young children? What about our older children—what are we missing with them?

Ava's wondering cautions us to resist telling children what to think, what to believe, watering down the biblical story to an object lesson or a message that doesn't maintain the integrity of God's word.

Coming to the Quiet

Ava's response also led us to examine one of our most challenging times of the week—Wednesday night gatherings with the elementary children. Wednesday nights were challenging to say the least. Children attending were tired, hungry and cranky, and the adult volunteers felt pretty much the same. We were working as hard as we could to plan meaningful experiences that were usually highly energetic requiring elaborate, time consuming preparation. In spite of all our work, it wasn't very successful.

One Wednesday night while visiting with a group of fourth and fifth graders, we had an interesting conversation. I confessed how tired I was and it had been hard for me to figure out what we should do that night in class. I even shared with them that I really would have rather been at home. You may be thinking right now, that wasn't a very smart thing for the children's minister to say, but remember, these children are my church, and my relationship with them is rooted in honesty as we are mutually share our faith journeys.

My confession opened the floodgates of conversation, and I was surprised at what they had to say.

> *"We didn't have recess today."*
> *"My class couldn't talk at lunchtime."*
> *"I haven't been home yet today."*
> *"I haven't had dinner."*
> *"I wish it was time for bed."*

We were all feeling the same thing: stressed, tired, and wishing for a better way.

Their voices touched my heart and sent me to my knees in prayer asking God to help our ministry team discern what we needed to do differently. Silence was the word that kept coming to my mind during the following week. We needed to learn how to be still and quiet together. It seemed impossible to imagine more than sixty elementary children willingly practicing the spiritual discipline of silence, or *Coming to the Quiet*, but I decided we would give it a try the following Wednesday night.

We met as usual, but before we began our story time I asked the children if we could be totally still and quiet. I'm pretty sure everyone in the room thought I had lost my mind! I honestly wasn't sure we could do it, and I was more than a little nervous, but for about thirty seconds we were able to sit in silence.

Those thirty seconds felt like an hour, and we were all a little self-conscious and uncomfortable. In spite of our discomfort, we decided to try it for a year and see how God shaped us through this practice.

It was fascinating to see how silence changed us from the inside out, which is how spiritual transformation works. We began to develop a new language of spiritual formation just from this one small change. We talked about the work of being spiritually disciplined, that it's difficult and requires regular practice. And practice, we did, every week.

Our initial thirty seconds of silence became seven minutes by the end of the year. The children were active participants in deciding how long they would practice silence, and it changed from week to week. We learned sometimes God's voice can only be heard when you're listening carefully. We also learned sometimes your neighbor has something to say that requires intentional listening.

The following year we added prayer to our quiet time. Interestingly enough, we found we didn't have to practice the discipline of complete silence every week. Instead we had a collective memory of silence within us, and we found it was easier to come to the quiet each week.

Wall of Prayer

Like in most churches, prayer has always been a part of our classroom time, but this prayer time was different and more in depth than our previous efforts. We made a "*Wall of Prayer*" by painting a large wall with chalkboard paint, where the children and adult leaders can flow to the wall, writing their prayers.

This time of prayer now serves as our call to "come to quiet." The children know what to expect, and they value this time. Each week before we begin, we talk about why we're going to spend ten minutes in prayer and how we will honor each other during this special time. Sometimes the children mention specific rules about how this practice works best, but often their conversation focuses on the importance of practicing spiritual disciplines and how God uses this time to work in our hearts. They know and understand it's sacred, holy time to be with God and God's time to be with us.

We play the same song each week as the children move to the wall. It's orderly and comforting. It's the same ritual, but is also new every week. It's a beautiful representation of the mystery of God and how God works in our lives.

It's also messy at times. Actually it is messy most of the time, but just as God's people have known through the ages, we know, and the kids know, God is in the mess.

Some nights our quiet time can be a little noisy. That concept doesn't make much sense, does it? Noisy quiet? It was a memorable conversation, initiated by a child, when we explored different kinds of quiet; a quiet gained by "shhhh," or a quietness of spirit that can actually tolerate a little bit of noise.

This regular practice of spiritual discipline began transforming us. In the beginning, our prayers were usually simple and focused inwardly, but as time passed we noticed the prayers changing. There were always names of family and friends on the wall, but we began to see more complex thoughts appear among those names.

Even though our prayer practice was collective and public, we noticed an intimacy emerging in the requests. One child began writing these two words each week—"our enemies." Clearly God was working in his mind and heart. Another child regularly wrote, "Let my hands be kind to others." Again, a glimpse into how God was changing this child's daily life.

The prayer wall created a space for us to pray for children with life-threatening illness. It's a powerful visual image to see a child's name written multiple times, and it was an encouragement to those families to know even though they were in a hospital far away, we were sharing this difficult journey with them in the only way we could, and in the best way we could.

After the death of one of those precious children, we realized practicing the discipline of coming to the quiet allowed us to have an appropriate time and space to grieve and question God together. It was natural, even comforting, although we were working through great disappointment and sadness.

A Liturgy for Children

Our Wednesday gatherings have a definite flow that we call our liturgy. After *Coming to the Quiet,* we enter God's word together using the principles of *Dwelling in the Word.* This requires us to practice listening, deep listening, for what God desires us to hear and learn on this specific day.

Like all children's ministers, I have a scope and sequence, or plan, for what we'll study each week. I've found though, that the discipline of *Dwelling in the Word,* sometimes makes changing the plan necessary as we listen and work in the word together.

One night, our lesson was from Matthew 25 where Jesus tells the parable of the sheep and goats and the least of these. Our liturgy includes children reading aloud the passage of Scripture each week, followed by simple storytelling techniques and asking "I wonder" questions. On this particular night something unusual happened.

After I asked, "I wonder who are the least of these . . . ," no one answered. That had never happened before. The room was completely silent. As I sat there with sixty pairs of eyes looking at me, I realized how our practice of silence had not only changed the kids, it had changed me as a teacher. I resisted the temptation to ask other leading questions which would give children a clue to the "right" answer, and I wasn't even tempted to tell them my thoughts. Instead, I closed my Bible and said, "It looks like God has more to say to us, so we'll dwell in this passage a little longer." And we did, for six weeks.

Sometimes it's hard to trust God's work in us.

Rebecca Nye says, "We often tell a Bible story, but rather than trusting God's word to speak for itself in God's own way, we rush to explain what is says to *us*. We miss the chance to explore how it can make meaning for the child."[7]

We've learned we're vulnerable in times of silence, and it's difficult to let silence guide us into deeper relationship with God and each other. Nye suggests "taking silence seriously. Children who choose not to speak are not spaces where 'nothing' is happening. Silence can be a way of saying something so important that it can't be put into words."[8]

Another way of saying something important without spoken words is by illustrating God's word through an art response we call "*God's Word in Color.*" It's a practice we adapted from Sybil MacBeth's book, *Praying in Color.* In this delightful, creative book, MacBeth encourages children and adults to colorfully draw their prayers in an "active, meditative, playful prayer practice."[9] She guides the reader through all types of prayer using crayons and markers instead of using spoken words.

During our Wednesday gatherings, the children use this art response to illustrate the Dwelling in the Word passage of Scripture. Children volunteer to draw while the story is being read. In preparation we ask the children to "dwell in the word," reading it at home several times, then pray asking God to reveal to them through their drawing God's truth, and what we need to know on this particular day. This practice is rooted in the ancient way of *reading* Scripture called *lectio divina,* meaning sacred, divine reading.

Interestingly enough, we've found this spiritual practice doesn't require special artistic ability. Instead, we've learned it's another way of listening, another facet of *Coming to the Quiet.*

Many of our children volunteer to lead our class in this special way, and one of our frequent volunteers, Nathan, asked his mom why she thought we asked him to draw our story. She answered him with another question: "why do you think they asked you to draw?" His answer, "Because I know how to listen." Nathan intuitively knew this practice was about listening to what God has to say.

As our children become more skilled in listening for God's voice, they become more inclined to offer a response after hearing God's word. Their response may come in the form of a question, something written, drawn or created, or it may come in the form of an action.

Confession

One response that totally surprised us was the act of confession. "Confession," Adele Calhoun writes, "may be good for the soul, but it's very hard to do."[10] This spiritual discipline is difficult for adults to practice, and it certainly isn't a discipline commonly associated with children's ministry.

As a teacher, there are times when it's appropriate to model the discipline of confession through honestly sharing your own faith journey, and recently I did just that as I was telling the story. I had no expectation our response time would turn into confession, but that's exactly what happened.

One child bravely said, "I was mean to my brother today," and other children began to share what they had done wrong that week. It was definitely holy time, and a reminder that God is at work in the lives of our children, and they need a safe space that invites them to enter the divine presence and receive God's forgiveness and mercy.

A few weeks after this night of confession a single mother of one of our neighborhood kids came to me and told me that her son, Robert, had stolen some of the missions money he had collected for our water well project. Because she was angry with him, she wanted me to tell Robert that he couldn't come to church that night. Instead, I told her he was welcome to stay and asked if she trusted me to talk with him about what he had done.

Robert and I talked privately about what he could do to make amends for taking the money. He agreed to do extra work at home and in the neighborhood to earn it back. It took him about four weeks, but he came to church excited about replacing the $10 he had originally taken. I added the money to our collection and began class thinking the matter had been settled.

But God was working in Robert's heart and soul, and something amazing was about to happen. After our prayer time, Robert came up to the front of the room and asked if he could tell the class what he had done. Even as I write this, I'm still puzzled at my initial response, at my lack of faith that God was working in powerful, meaningful ways.

My heart sank as I heard his request because I wasn't sure how the class would respond. I even went so far as to ask him if he was "sure he wanted to tell the story."

I will never forget looking into his big brown eyes as he swallowed hard and said, "I need to tell them what I did." With a prayer in my heart, I put my arms around him and invited him to begin.

As he told his story about stealing the money and lying to cover it up, I watched the children listening, trying to understand. After he was finished, the room was silent for a few minutes, and I know every adult leader was praying during that silence!

It was the silence of God at work in the lives of the people of God— a silence of something happening that can't be put into words.

A fifth grade boy who didn't know Robert very well said, "What you just did must have been very hard. I don't know if I would have had the courage." At his words, the class spontaneously burst into applause, which is not our normal practice. But the children recognized that something noteworthy had happened, and they needed to offer Robert their affirmation, grace and forgiveness in a tangible way.

Conclusion

"God and the child get along well together."[11]

These words make my heart sing every time I read them. Recognizing this truth provides the foundation of what we do as we are the church with children. Recognizing this truth is foundational to being the church with children. Our noisy, chaotic culture often sends messages about children that our churches adopt without realizing the consequences— for both the children and ultimately for the entire church.

Our children live in the same world we do. Sometimes that world is full of goodness and mercy, and sometimes it's full of heartache and pain. They need to *know* God, not just know *about* God, and in that knowing, trust God is at work in mysterious ways that cannot be explained. Children need spiritual practices and spiritual language which will give them hope, courage, gratitude and strength as they face life.

As the church, we want our children to walk in the way of Jesus, to live their entire lives for God, expressing their faith beyond the walls of the church building. Practicing spiritual disciplines with children is not the only way for our children to be transformed into the image of Jesus for the sake of the world, but it's an important avenue deserving of our attention as we discern how to best guide our children into meaningful relationship with their Creator.

It's also essential we remember we are not in charge of this relationship with God! We can create environments that encourage spiritual practices, but God alone, through the working of the Holy Spirit, will enter into intimate relationships with the children God loves.

Let's end this chapter as we began: "Be still and know that I am God."

Chapter 14

Children Serving and Proclaiming Christ

Joining the Mission of the Church

Shannon Rains

*I*n the summer of 2014, our church took about thirty men, women, and children on a disaster relief trip to Moore, Oklahoma. Severe storms, including an F5 tornado, had devastated Moore and the surrounding areas. One evening after a long workday, we took the kids to the site of Plaza Towers Elementary, the school that took a direct hit by the tornado. Early in the recovery process the school had been leveled and debris was hauled off, leaving behind a block-wide, grass covered field. Previous work crews had attached t-shirts to the chain link fence surrounding the site of the former school. These t-shirts hung as symbols of all the churches and organizations that had visited the site while serving in the surrounding area. As the t-shirts blew gently in the wind, my daughter and her best friend caught glimpses of the crosses placed there in honor of the children who died. Silence fell.

Silence often greets our children when they come face to face with suffering. Like most parents, I wanted to shield my daughter from the harsh reality that children died while a nation cried, helplessly watching the disaster unfold on live television. As the wind revealed the crosses, I was reminded that I can't hide the pain of the world from my daughter. Death, grief, and sadness are all realities of the world in which we live.

A child's innocence should be protected. At the same time, it is unwise to "bubble wrap" children and give them a disinfected view of the world.[1] Children are often moved to action when they encounter pain. They are kingdom bearers and as such must participate in God's redemptive work by sharing hope, showing compassion, and proclaiming the gospel. Not only is this kingdom work, it is essential to the spiritual formation of children.[2] This chapter will explore the call we share with children to expand the kingdom by serving the world through compassionate service and proclamation.

A Not So Perfect World

Many parents desire to raise their children in a perfect world. They limit television, buy homes in neighborhoods with great schools, and sign their kids up for all of the right enrichment experiences—soccer, piano, ballet, etc. Children of advantage often live insulated from the imperfect world in which hunger, pain, and brokenness are a normal part of life. Like other parents, I also struggle to find the right words to explain why some people are homeless or victims of war when these seem so far removed from our reality. It is important to remember that God's kingdom is not the perfect world we try to create for ourselves. It is the perfect world that God has created for us that we will inherit. While we wait, we find that the kingdom is already present and evident in so many ways. When we feel renewed hope during difficult circumstances, experience reconciliation of broken relationships, or have our deepest needs of comfort met when in pain, God's kingdom is present. We are bearers of the kingdom when we respond with Christ-like compassion to hurting people. As we serve, God's presence is made known. Our conviction is strengthened. Thinking we were bringing the kingdom to others, we find ourselves recipients of God's kingdom as well. Our children also need to be able to serve and be served in the name of Christ. They need to encounter hopelessness, so they can know the joy of receiving real hope! There is a cost to raising children in a sanitized world—hidden from the suffering and pain of the world around them—they lose the opportunity to truly see "Your kingdom come" (Matt. 6:10).

Suffering and Hope

"I consider that the sufferings of this present time are not worth comparing with the glory about to be revealed to us" (Rom. 8:18, NRSV). The comparison of suffering and glory creates a tension that gives way to hope; hope that the suffering is dim in comparison to the glory that will be received.[3] Creation, Christians, and the Spirit all bear testimony of this hope, waiting for the liberation of creation and the fulfillment of God's kingdom.[4] Suffering is a direct result of the frustration of creation in which death and decay becomes part of the human experience. Creation has now entered into a period of waiting for God to liberate all things.

In this waiting world, we all experience pain: rejection, loss, brokenness, disappointment, illness, or depression. We suffer; this is the universal human experience we all share—even children.[5] We cannot protect them from it. However, we can join children in claiming God's presence in the midst of it. Despite the pain and sorrow we all experience, believers walk in hope:

- Hope in the constant presence of the Spirit,
- Hope in the unfailing promises of the Father,
- Hope in the redemption of all creation through the Son.

This unseen hope enables us to wait, compels us to proclaim our hope to others, and allows us to share in the strength and presence of the Spirit.[6] During this time of waiting, God's people of all ages bear testimony to the salvation they have already received and the steadfast hope of the promises of God fulfilled. We bring the kingdom to a waiting world.

Children are Kingdom Bearers

Adults and children share the responsibility and opportunity to be kingdom bearers in a hurting world—serving others in the name of a savior who showed us the way of compassion. In Luke 7:18–23, Jesus has been healing the sick, restoring sight to the blind, and casting out demons, when John's disciples show up. They asked, "Are you the one?" Jesus replied, "Go back and report to John what you have seen and heard: the blind received sight, the lame walk, those who have leprosy are cleansed, the deaf hear, the dead are raised, and the good news is proclaimed to the poor" (Luke 7:18–23, NIV).

Jesus confronted disease, pain, and death with compassion and proclaimed the good news that the Kingdom was near. In the Sermon on the Plain, Jesus says, "Blessed are you who are poor, for yours is the kingdom of God" (Luke 6:20, NIV). His redeeming work began with compassion for suffering people and ended with proclamation of salvation.

As kingdom bearers, we are all—adults and children—called to emulate Jesus in every possible way. Children are aware of and can enter into the pain of the world in age appropriate ways—helping, learning, listening, giving and proclaiming God's love to others. With Christ-like compassion, children are motivated to share hope through service and proclamation.

Just a few blocks from Plaza Towers Elementary in Moore, we stepped onto the front porch of a home still standing just on the edge of the devastated neighborhood. Every house for five blocks between the school and this home had been demolished. A father of young elementary children, who were spared by the storm, watched us with wary, questioning eyes as we approached his home. My daughter, River, carried a box of supplies. We introduced ourselves, and as she gave him the supplies, he noticed the stitches just above her eye from an injury River had received at a worksite the day before. He entered into her pain by sharing his own: the terrifying day of the storm, and the continued fears of his family. River listened intently. We responded, prayed with him, and invited his family to a free concert at a local congregation. He shared that his family had not really attended church in a long time, but the kindness shown by so many Christian groups was encouraging him to rethink his faith commitment. Looking back on this encounter, I know that my daughter's willingness to serve in the name of Christ gave this hurting father hope. River brought the kingdom with her to that front porch. And in that father's gentle concern for her hurt and his willingness to invite us into his story, she too received the gift of the kingdom. This was a holy moment I will never forget.

Joining the Mission of the Church

We often associate missions with work in foreign countries for the purpose of evangelism. The call to "go" is biblical—one the church must not ignore. Still, we must not forget that every believer is called to actively live out the mission of God to bring about reconciliation through the proclamation of the gospel wherever they find themselves. Children may participate in a mission trip as part of this calling, but they also need to experience the reality that the mission of the church is not dependent upon location or on special events.

Compassionate Service

Children should be invited to partner with the church in the multifaceted, ongoing, day-to-day mission of kingdom bearing—serving others in the name of Jesus and pointing to him as the source of true hope. Their compassionate service may include food drives, fund-raising efforts, community workdays, prayer, writing cards of encouragement, joining a mission trip or simply showing kindness to a hurting friend—all things children are fully capable of doing in meaningful ways. Catherine Stonehouse and Scottie May assert that true compassion is more than empathetic concern for the feelings of others.

> A key element in compassion is empathy, the ability to imagine— enter into—what another is experiencing and how they are feeling. Without empathy there is no compassion, but to truly enter into another's suffering leads to the desire to act on the behalf of the other.[7]

True compassion is the combination of empathy plus action. Children may act in compassion when they reach out to a friend being bullied at school or join a service project filling bags of food for the homeless. In either case, they aren't doing good works simply to do something good. Nor are children oblivious to brokenness and pain. As kingdom bearers, children can connect their action of compassionate service with the proclamation of God's love, understanding that they are sharing the hope of salvation.

Proclaiming the Kingdom

Proclamation is the act of telling others about God. It is the statement that answers the question of "why" we serve. Sometimes adults with mature faith are intimidated by the idea of sharing their faith with others; they fear not knowing the right Scripture or being stumped by a challenging spiritual question. When adults feel insecure in sharing their faith, it can be difficult to for them to imagine children proclaiming God's truth to the world. Children do need to develop their own faith vocabulary that enables them to share their faith with others. We must also recognize that in the simple faith statements of children we often find the central message of the gospel. Consider the lyrics of the song "Jesus Loves Me."

> Jesus loves me, this I know,
> For the Bible tells me so.
> Little ones to him belong,
> They are weak but he is strong,
> Yes, Jesus loves me,
> Yes, Jesus loves me,
> Yes, Jesus loves me,
> The Bible tells me so.

Jesus loves me. I can be sure of this. I am his and in my weakness—my pain, my questions, my confusion and mistakes—he will be my strength. He is strong. The Bible tells me so. The child who sings this song learns and proclaims key aspects of the hope of the gospel. Apprenticed in faith by parents and a spiritual family, the child's expression of faith will deepen, building on the foundation of these simple, but profound truths. They learn to acknowledge the hurt of others, offer words of blessing, and to proclaim the good news. Jesus loves you.

Mentoring and Apprenticing: Intergenerational Influences

Children need adults to come alongside them in this kingdom journey. On our mission trip to Oklahoma, the children partnered not only with their parents, but also with other adult members of the mission team. As we worked, the adults engaged the children in spiritual discussions, wondered with them about how God was working through our offering of service, and modeled for them faith-informed responses to difficult circumstances. Allen and Ross describe service activities and mission trips as "natural means of uniting the generations, as such activities enable people of different generations to work together toward the common goal of serving others."[8] As children minister along with their parents and faith families, they are able to "test" their ideas about God, "apply" those ideas to real life, and, most importantly, "debrief the experiences with significant adults."[9] This reflection allows children to make sense of suffering and develop "spiritual awareness," strengthening their own faith.[10] Parents and significant adults must partner with children for the whole process, praying with them, serving alongside them, and encouraging them to articulate their faith.

It is important to recognize the reciprocal nature of the mentoring relationship. As adults mentor children, children also mentor adults, opening our vision to new ways to serve. Children often think outside the box of limited resources and time and encourage the church to engage in opportunities for service that may have been overlooked. In addition, we must not downplay the impact of simple child-like acts of compassion. Often a simple response can have great impact—a gentle touch, an invitation to share a meal, a kind conversation or a cup of cold water. It is children who can often lead us in following our Savior's example in these simple but powerful ways.

Recently, our children prepared care packages for military personnel serving overseas. These men and women are far away, missing their families and the comforts of home. The supply boxes included handwritten notes from the children. The service men and women frequently responded with long letters. In these letters, it was clear that while they enjoyed the treats and supplies in the care packages, what meant more was knowing that a child remembered them, prayed for them and took time to offer encouragement and hope. Through these simple child-like drawings (and reminders that "God loves you!"), these soldiers in far away and frightening places experienced the kingdom of God in meaningful ways.

Spiritual Discernment and Service

A few years ago, I had what I thought was a great idea—a children's missions committee made up third through fifth graders. This committee was charged with the task of "divvying up" the children's contribution among a variety of worthwhile service projects. I hoped that the children would see that the funds could be used in many various ways for many different people. I hoped they would wrestle with the difficult decisions of deciding what they would fund and what they would not. I anticipated that the children would need weeks to research and decide on worthwhile projects on their limited resources. But, what the children thought they needed was just more money! In a matter of minutes, they had brainstormed a long list of worthwhile projects and had moved on to fundraising ideas. They were going to need an incredible amount of money to fund their dreams. In my inexperience, I didn't know how to direct their passion, so I allowed the committee to dissolve.

This committee of children was missing a key ingredient. We missed the opportunity to mentor the children in waiting on the Lord and approaching difficult decisions with prayer and spiritual discernment. Their desire to serve got ahead of the need to take their concerns before the throne of God. If I had it to do again, I would begin by joining the children in seeking God's presence and guidance as they took on this important task—to pray and to listen. In our enthusiasm for including children in ministry, it can be easy to jump into activities and projects without nurturing in our children the discipline of spiritual reflection.

Journey Inward and Journey Outward: Connecting

Karen Marie Yust's model of spiritual reflection, Journey Inward—Journey Outward, is very helpful to understand the relationship between reflective prayer and compassionate service.[11] The Journey Inward is the "practice of living in relationship with God".[12] Since God created children with the capacity for spiritual connection, parents and spiritual mentors need to nurture this gift of connection and help children deepen their prayer relationship through spiritual reflection. "When we dwell in this space," Yust writes, "we are in listening mode, inviting the silence or the words and images of others to 'speak' a word from God"[13] (see Chapter 13 for more on silence and contemplation with children).

Through this Journey Inward, God prompts children and adults to Journey Outward, to seek "human connections" and to engage in "relationships of hospitality and justice."[14] The goal is a continuous cycle of Journey Inward—Journey Outward, each in balance with the other. Our journey outward is guided by the journey inward, and our inward relationship with God is nurtured, challenged, and shaped by our journey outward.

Most children's ministry programs include service projects. However, after years of serving in ministry, I feel confident that we do not always think about spiritual formation when offering these projects. We skip the journey inward; we offer service opportunities because good Christians help others. But what makes our service in the name of Jesus different from other organizations? Girl Scouts, Boy Scouts, and many other organizations are well known for works of service. What is different in serving through these organizations and that of a faith community?

Children are spiritually formed through service when a project is bathed in prayerful reflection. When children are able to connect the "why" of their service with the person of Jesus, they are being formed into his image. As children and adults, serving others in their hurt and pain changes us as much as it changes them. We learn to view each person with the eyes of Jesus, to step into their brokenness, and to share the hard stuff of life with them. Children discover ways to release their hurt to God, to listen to the quiet, still voice of our Savior, and to understand that suffering need not deprive us of hope. Their experience with suffering empowers them with a more intimate knowledge of a Savior who has suffered on their behalf, and to accept the ups and downs of life—joy and suffering—as part of normal life.

I know from experience that it can be difficult to think formatively about every aspect of a children's ministry program—even in the area of service. Some projects are rooted in tradition. We do them because we always have done them. Other projects are started because, "people (meaning the adults) will give more to help the kids be successful." Instead, ministers and parents should choose and construct service opportunities based on their potential for spiritual formation for the children involved. The following list provides some guiding principles for children's ministry leaders or parents to help children connect their service with their faith.

1. Prayer is the first step in preparing to serve others.
2. Listen to children articulate the call God has on their lives as kingdom bearers and imagine the possibilities with them.
3. Mentor children through intergenerational relationships that encourage reflection on spiritually formative experiences.
4. Intentionally choose service projects that invite children into the mission of the local church.
5. Tell children about the needs present in the world and help them to understand in age appropriate ways the inequity, poverty, and lack of freedom experienced by much of the world's population—including those in our own communities.
6. Encourage children to serve compassionately and to talk about God's promises as part of their daily discipleship.
7. Celebrate the feelings of accomplishment that God provides through service and encourage humility by giving the glory to God.

Conclusion

Children are full participants in the kingdom. They share in the call for all Christ followers to speak into suffering through compassionate service and proclamation. Children should be mentored as young apprentices, but they should also have a voice in our faith communities and inspire adults toward imaginative service. By taking the journey inward and journey outward with children, everyone can be convicted by God's calling and believers of all ages can be equipped for works of service for the sake of the kingdom.

Chapter 15

Holy Hospitality
Following the Call of Jesus to Welcome ALL Children

Dana Kennamer Pemberton

People were bringing little children to him in order that he might touch them; and the disciples spoke sternly to them. But when Jesus saw this, he was indignant and said to them, "Let the little children come to me; do not stop them; for it is to such as these that the kingdom of God belongs. Truly I tell you, whoever does not receive the kingdom of God as a little child will never enter it."

Mark 10:13–15, NRSV

Then little children were being brought to him in order that he might lay his hands on them and pray. The disciples spoke sternly to those who brought them; but Jesus said, "Let the little children come to me, and do not stop them; for it is to such as these that the kingdom of heaven belongs." And he laid his hands on them and went on his way.

Matthew 19:13–15, NRSV

*People were bringing even infants to him that he might touch them; and when the disciples saw it, they sternly ordered them not to do it. But Jesus called for them and said, "Let the little **children** come to me, and do not stop them; for it is to such as these that the kingdom of God belongs. Truly I tell you, whoever does not receive the kingdom of God as a little child will never enter it."*

Luke 18:15–17, NRSV

How do you picture this scene? Are the children gazing lovingly at Jesus? Are they well dressed and well behaved? Is there a holy glow about them? Are they reaching up with awe to gently touch the Savior's face? This is how artists have most often depicted Jesus and the children. We know that children are drawn to those who openly welcome them, so I can imagine that children were drawn to Jesus. But even so, children (at least those in my world) almost never look like those in the paintings. They are wiggly and messy and often unpredictable. Some wear their anger like a shield, daring me to really love them. Others are tired from the pressures the world has placed on them: testing, accountability, and the need to perform. Some have been wounded in body and in spirit in ways we cannot, or choose not to, imagine. There are those with labels that we use to sort and classify them—autistic, bipolar, ADHD, etc. Some have new clothes and smell like fresh laundry; others wear clothes that fit poorly and stink from infrequent washing. The welcoming of **all** of these children is indeed holy, but there is often no discernable glow about them.

And yet the idyllic pictures persist. We have indeed romanticized child-hood. Given the choice between the "depraved adultish" child and the "innocent childish" child, the modern western world has overwhelmingly chosen the image of the pure and innocent child.[1] "By early modernity, children were idealized as precious, delicate, and in need of vigilant and constant care."[2] This perspective on children is heard in our conversations about them: "Children are so selfless and giving. Kids are just adorable and absolutely innocent! Isn't he just the sweetest little boy! We should have pure hearts like children do. Kids are always so forgiving and loving."

All of these things are true—at times. There is a flip side as well. Anne Higonnet reminds us that children are as much about "difficulty, trouble and tension" as they are about celebration, sweetness and joy.[3]

You might be thinking, "But wait! Isn't this chapter about welcoming children? Aren't you supposed to be an advocate for kids? Someone who likes being with them?" Yes, this chapter is about welcoming children—all children. And it is my great joy to spend time with children. Like you, because of my cultural background, I am uncomfortable with leaving behind the idyllic views of childhood that we have embraced. Yet, I find that these simplified and romanticized views of children make it impossible for us to truly welcome children as Jesus did.

The Unwelcoming Ideal

There are several challenges with this pervasive idealization of children. First, while we may think these romanticized views of children communicate a high view of childhood, in fact they deny the full personhood of the child, removing opportunity to be valued participants in the body of Christ. They say and do adorable things, but not significant things. We cherish them and protect them, but do not truly include them. We provide all the right activities for them, but fail to give them opportunity to participate meaningfully in the "real" activity of the faith community.

This idealized perspective also gives us no way to respond when children are somewhat less than angelic—other than sending them to a special room down the hall or passing them off to another church. We need a more complex and nuanced notion of childhood that can stand up to the realities of the children we encounter and that fully affirms their humanity.[4] Bonnie Miller McLemore asserts that children must be "fully respected as persons, valued as gifts and viewed as agents."[5] Rather than innocent blank slates, she describes children as having a God-given capacity for "spiritual experience, moral awareness and decision making." She argues that children inhabit a state between nonagency and full responsibility. "Sometimes they are even capable of destructive or malicious behavior. They also have a desire for God and can ask profound religious questions, and anguish when they feel responsible for wrong-doing."[6]

A more complex understanding of childhood is needed if we are to welcome all children, especially those whose behavior challenges us. Joyce Ann Mercer contends that many mainline churches have come to equate faithfulness with being "happy, cooperative and nice" so that nurturing children in faith means socializing them to be smiling, happy, compliant little people.[7] Because of this we do not know what to do with the child who does not fit this happy, smiling picture. We all know children like this, and there are the children with a diagnosis that causes us to doubt our ability to serve them. You may know children who have been damaged, abused by the very ones who should have loved them the most. Children from poverty can come to us with behaviors for survival that work in their neighborhoods but not in our Bible classes. There is that kid, who for no reason we can identify, is just out of control. What about the children whose family escaped from brutality we cannot imagine in a country far away and are now "refugees" in a country they do not understand? Then there is the intellectually gifted child we feel is certainly trying to test us with questions we can't answer. Or perhaps it is the one who simply does not like to sing and draw or do any of the other great activities our curriculum provides. Our persistent view of happy innocence does not prepare us for these children.

The notion of childhood innocence is also best suited for children of privilege. The hypervigilance common among parents who have the luxury of raising their children in a sanitized world is dangerous. Welcoming children as Jesus did is lost in the focus on protecting *our own children* with the exclusion of *other people's children*. The children that Jesus blessed included poor children from the crowd, dirty children soiled from seizures, and possessed children whose bodies were not their own.[8] When we read again the passages at the beginning of this chapter, it is clear that Jesus was serious about this. He was "indignant" when the disciples shooed children away. Walter Brueggemann asserts that the "urgent issue before contemporary society concerns the connection between *our children,* to whom our devotion is limitless, and *the others,* who are at the edge of our passions".[9] This is indeed an urgent issue, one we cannot ignore. Jesus equates welcoming children with welcoming the father so our "hospitality toward children reflects one's disposition toward God"[10] (Mark 9:37).

Thomas E. Reynolds defines hospitality as "actively welcoming and befriending the stranger . . . as someone with inherent value, loved into being by God, created in the image of God, and thus having unique gifts to offer as human beings."[11] While his work explores a theology of hospitality for those with disabilities, his ideas apply as we seek to include children who do not fit our inadequate, idealized image. He reminds us that "at the heart of the Christian witness is an inclusive love of difference," challenging believers to shift from "us" and "them" thinking to true hospitality.[12] A major barrier to this call is the "cult of normalcy" that excludes those who do not measure up to the ideal.[13] Ironically, those who embody the "ideal" are small in number. And so it is with children. Those whose appearance, speech, and behavior we do not understand are labeled as "not normal." Our limited efforts of hospitality often focus on making them fit into our norms. And when they do not, we have no other response but to exclude them—an experience that for many of them is quite familiar. Csinos and Beckwith remind us that our children's ministries must be "places of radical hospitality, places where all young people are welcomed for whom they are and not whom we hope they will become, places where children who are weary from being labeled different can come and find rest."[14] Since children can teach us much about hospitality, I will share some of my experiences with children in pages that follow, changing their names to respect their privacy.

Start with the Heart

So where do we begin? What do we do? The first step must be communal commitment to biblical hospitality toward children—to welcome them even when it is inconvenient and difficult. We must examine our hearts and engage in honest conversation and spiritual discernment about our fears and our discomfort when faced with children we do not understand—children, if we are honest, we often do not like. If we believe that "walking in the way of Jesus means attending to children," we cannot pick and choose which children are included.[15]

I am asking you to be honest as we discern the condition of our hearts, so I will be honest with you. I love children. There is no place I would rather be on Sunday mornings than with my kindergarten and first grade friends. And sometimes, a child enters my world that I struggle to like. All of the things I know and believe about children fly right out the window when confronted by this child. It is rare, but it does happen. I remember one child in particular. He loved to challenge everything I said and often distracted the other children with his sarcastic comments and unruly behavior. He was highly resistant to redirection. I often work with children like this and I do not respond to them as I did this child. I am not sure why. I simply did not like him. There is no other way to say it. Other teachers didn't like him either so I was not alone in this.

Then one Wednesday evening, we were gathered for communal silence and I was sitting beside this out of control, annoying little boy. I whispered a prayer for peace and began rubbing his back in large and gentle circles. I could feel his heart beating at a furious pace, his muscles tense with anxiety. In that moment, my heart changed. He ceased to be the kid trying to make my life miserable and became a person who struggled to find peace. For the first time, I allowed myself to be fully present with him. I continued to rub his back, his breathing slowed and finally he nestled against me—a holy and convicting moment.

When I introduce our module on challenging behavior in my senior early childhood course, we begin, not with strategies, but with our hearts. I ask my students to list all of the feelings they experience when a child they are in charge of does not do what they want them to do. You can imagine what is on the list: helpless, angry, embarrassed, mad, frustrated, attacked, incompetent, impatient, disrespected, confused, and shocked. These feelings are normal. The challenge is not to respond to these feelings (which often come out as anger), but to respond to the child's needs. We must be willing to be vulnerable in this process, open to the child sitting beside us. This is true hospitality, "a gift offered without preconditions and expectations" but rather a commitment to be open and present to the other.[16] This is where we must begin, open to the other, the child we do not understand and who, we must not forget, often does not understand us.

Honor Parents

Parents of children who do not fit our notions of normal find themselves isolated and judged. They experience the embarrassment of disapproving glances when their child interrupts the serious stuff of adult worship. They hear again and again the "problems" their child caused in class, on the playground, at the birthday party, or during soccer practice. They must listen over and over to the well-meaning advice of those "just trying to help," but who have no idea what this family lives with every day. Whether the child has a diagnosis or not, these parents need our support more than our advice.

A few years ago my friend and colleague, Lesa Breeding, and I felt called to provide a place for the voices of families of children with disabilities to be heard.[17] As part of this work, Lesa spent time in conversation with the teenage siblings of children with autism and I gathered around a table for several evenings with the parents. These are conversations we will never forget. While these parents had children with a specific label, I believe their voices can guide us in our journey toward hospitality for all children.

I asked these parents what they would say to churches seeking to minister to families of children with disabilities; they all answered with the same message. They need churches to move beyond merely "finding a place" for their child. They hope for their children what we all hope—a place of belonging and welcome. Their deepest desire is that their children be wanted, not just tolerated.[18]

> Welcome them, number one. The parents need to know above all else that you love their children and not just that you love their children but that you **want** their children.

> So above all else, convey to those parents every time you see them that you are happy when their child is there and you are sad when their child is not there. And unless there is blood, don't go get those parents during worship service. Let them know you are perfectly comfortable dealing with the child. If there is a behavior problem or a meltdown, that you love them anyway. It is not a burden for you to deal with if they have a meltdown. Reassure them of that over and over and over.

One parent described the overwhelming feeling when she finally experienced this kind of welcome.

It was different with the church that John pastors. He (their son with autism) was never overlooked. He was looked for, you know? It was like, "We want this kid. We want him." They wanted him, you know. It wasn't, you know, "We can find a spot for him." It was, "We want him. If ya'll want to come too that's great, but we want him." That was different. That was really everything to us.

Parents of children with challenges of any kind are too familiar with complaints about their children's behavior. In fact, they are poised for it—shields ready for the attack. I remember a sweet little boy several years ago whose world was really difficult. His parents were having difficulties in their marriage and he was being evaluated to determine a diagnosis that could explain his extreme emotional and behavioral responses. He struggled to participate in groups. Teachers were often frustrated with him, as were the children. One Wednesday evening a missionary visited our class to share about his work for Jesus a world away. This little boy amazed me that night. He asked insightful questions and guided his peers in respectful listening. I stopped his mother after class and said, "I want to tell you about John tonight." She immediately stiffened, backed away two steps and asked, "What happened?" My heart broke. "No, this is good!" I told her about John's interest and leadership in class that night. She fell into my arms and we both cried. It was a reminder to me that parents—all parents really—need to hear good stories about their children. We must celebrate the victories (no matter how small) as much, or probably more than, identifying the problems.

Still, it is important to include parents when possible as we try to discover what the child needs in order to feel welcome and to be successful in our children's ministries. These conversations must be approached with gentleness, assuring parents that the child is wanted and loved. The child is NOT a problem. The goal is to meet the child's needs and experience together the gift of community. These parents are rarely unaware of the challenges their children bring to the church setting. When they are approached with calm openness rather than judgment or fear, they are almost always willing to help you know their child better. Listen again to the parents who gathered with me around that table.

> It is not easy to teach these children. They sometimes act out and they are aggressive and parents know that. I think they are terrified to bring their child to a new place and have him act out and kick and scream the whole time.

> You know, just be open and honest with them (the parents) and say, "You know, we're not sure how to handle this but we would like to try." They will give you some suggestions. Parents would be happy to do that and we know that our child is different.

In cases where the parent is unable to engage in these collaborative conversations with you, do not give up. We have worked with parents that were refugees struggling to feed their families and to survive in their new and sometimes frightening world, often with limited English. Others were so wounded and weary themselves that they needed their own spiritual and emotional healing before they could help us with strategies. They were simply surviving and what we needed to do was provide their child a place of hospitality so the parents could rest. It is important to walk in grace as you welcome these families. Like all families, they want their child to be safe and to be loved. In these cases, work with others in the faith community who have insights to guide you as you seek to offer hospitality in the way the child can receive it.

When the child has a diagnosis, it is critical not to reduce the child to a label as you reach out to parents. Csinos and Beckwith remind us "when we focus too much on the labels we apply to children, we can miss the uniqueness of each child, instead boiling them down to one or two ways that a particular theory or category tells us to see them."[19] Labels are often necessary because without them parents are not able to access the services the child needs. Diagnostic labels can provide needed answers for months and sometimes years of confusion and frustration. At the same time, they are often sources of grief, a confirmation of the parents' fears for their child. It is critical to remember that this is a child first—their child. Recently, I was visiting with the mother of a child with developmental disabilities. She was worried about Bible class and how her child would be welcomed. After we talked for a while, I asked her to tell me about her little girl. She began to describe her diagnosis—to list her challenges. I gently stopped her. "No, tell me about Lacey." She smiled and began with, "She is so sweet." This mom then listed details about her child's personality and interests. Parents like her are accustomed to people reducing their child to a diagnosis, and they are often still learning what this label means for them and their child. Still, the child is a person worthy of welcome and endowed with gifts to share with the community of faith. Use labels cautiously, only as needed, but respond to and talk about the child as a child.

In all of these interactions, do not forget our first principle. Ultimately, this is an issue of the heart. Are we ready to accept the call to love those who we do not understand—to extend hospitality to the stranger? Are we willing to be vulnerable in the process, honest about our limitations but committed to God's call to welcome children? The following words from one of the parents who sat with me at that table put it like this:

> Someone can teach you how to do modifications. Someone can teach you how to structure the class. Someone can teach you all of those things. If you don't have the attitude of Jesus and the heart of Jesus toward those kids then it doesn't matter. If you do, then the rest can come.

Listen to the Children

My father is a retired physician. As a family practice doctor in a small town, he actually made house calls. He was patient centered, always giving the dignity and respect deserved to people, those made in God's image. I had the chance to observe my father on many occasions listening respectfully to his patients—treating them as people, not as diseases. He often said that if doctors listen to their patients long enough, they will tell you what is wrong with them. He used the technology available to get an accurate diagnosis, but his most important tool was listening.

My father's example informs my practice with children. I believe that if we listen to children long enough and carefully enough, they too will tell us what they need. This kind of listening requires relationship. As we seek to welcome children, we cannot simply implement the right programs or find the perfect techniques. We must know children, and they must know us. Hospitality is a relational act, not a strategy. When we build trusting and respectful relationships with children, we may be surprised how insightful they can be about their own needs.

Several years ago we had a child in our children's ministry with significant challenges in social processing and high sensitivity to sensory stimulation. He was intelligent and sensitive—often worried, but with surprising insights. It became clear that the Wednesday evening gathering was not going to work for him. After a long day at school, he was unable to handle the stimulation of sixty to seventy children in one room. Suzetta sat down with him and asked what would help him. He was able to tell her exactly what he needed—a quiet room, a comfortable place to sit and soft lighting. So she created a space where he could experience calm welcome.

Some children might not be able to articulate their needs in words, but their behavior sends you a message. All behavior communicates. Ask yourself, "What is this child's behavior saying?" The following are messages I have received loud and clear from children through their behavior.

- I don't understand what you want.
- You are asking me to do something that is too hard for me.
- I need some attention.
- I want something and I want it now.
- I am feeling embarrassed.
- I am experiencing more stimulation than I can handle.
- I am tired.
- I am feeling threatened.

As I look behind the behavior to find the message, the child ceases to be a problem and becomes a person in need of understanding. Often I see that if there is a problem, it is actually with me! I have not been clear. If I am honest, I couldn't sit still that long either. I failed to be present with the child enough to see the tired eyes and shoulders weighed down with fatigue of the day. In these moments of insight I realize as the grownup in the room, I am the one who needs to change.

Be Willing to Change

Change is hard. It is easy to interpret requests that we change as an indictment of our practice, that we are doing something wrong. We must remind each other that hospitality means making adjustments. Think of all the adjustments that must be made if you are going to welcome someone into your home for an extended time. Sleep schedules change. Menus change. Room assignments change.

Adjustments can be hard, especially when our practices have worked in the past. "This is how I have always done it and I have never had a problem. Kids have always enjoyed my Bible class." It is humbling to encounter a child who does not respond to our cherished practices. Think again about the long-term houseguest. You may have a wonderful family recipe for pot roast, but your guest may be a vegetarian! There is nothing wrong with your pot roast. Your guest just needs something different. Hospitality means willingness to change.

In my role as a teacher educator, I am sometimes asked to consult with teachers who are struggling to manage their classrooms. When I make suggestions for change, I often hear, "But the other kids love the way we do this. When _____ is not here, everything goes really well." The teacher begins to hope that the "problem" child (or children) will be absent. I understand how one child can change the entire climate in a room. The danger is that we come to see that child as the problem rather than asking how we might change so that **all** children can be successful. When I make modifications, even in response to the needs of one child, the other children are fine. In fact, they are better because their friend is no longer in distress, and we can get on with the business of being God's people gathered for worship, wonder, and the word.

I had the privilege of working with my friends, Jerry Whitworth and Lesa Breeding, in writing a book to help children's ministers and volunteers in efforts to include all children—*Let All the Children Come: A Practical Guide to Including Children with Disabilities in Your Church Ministries.*[20] The book includes many simple strategies to help you include children with diverse needs. While written with children with disabilities in mind, the strategies are not specific to particular labels. Do you have children who are highly distracted or impulsive? Are there kids in your ministry who are struggling readers? What about children who are easily over stimulated? These needs are not limited to a specific diagnosis. They may be the result of family stress, limited English, or temperamental differences—to name a few. Our book is one helpful resource as you seek to welcome *all* children.

Avoid Overprotection

We began this chapter acknowledging our cultural emphasis on protecting children. In Chapter 12, we explored our belief that children's ministries should be fun so kids will want to come. Children do need to be protected; I also hope they experience joy as they participate in faith community. However, we often too quickly remove a child who does not fit. "The other kids are just not having fun! Maybe he should be somewhere else." "When she throws a fit like that, it really scares the kids. We can't have that in our Bible class." "My daughter told me what one of the kids from the neighborhood said and was really upset by it. Should we have a separate class for those kids while they learn to behave? Then they can come to class with the other kids." I want you to notice the difference between these concerns and Suzetta's response to our friend who needed a quiet place. That separate space was what *he* needed. We didn't isolate him because he was bothering the other children.

It can be a good thing for children to have the chance to work hard to welcome someone they have a hard time understanding or liking (I've already shared that it was good for me). Where in our ministry do we provide children the opportunity to do the hard work of faith community? Several years back we had a little boy in our church with significant social processing deficits. One Wednesday evening, Ryan was determined to sit by (or I should say on top of) another little boy, Blake. I watched for the entire hour as Ryan invaded Blake's personal space and Blake repeatedly, with amazing patience, reminded Ryan to "move over a little." I monitored the situation, watching for a breaking point in Blake's patience. It was clear that he was frustrated, but he never lost control. Once or twice Blake clinched his fist and I thought I might need to step in before he hit Ryan. Then he would take a deep breath and relax his hand. I chose not to intervene.

After class I pulled Blake aside. "This was a hard night for you." He responded emphatically, "Yes it was!" I continued, "Blake, you know that Ryan has a hard time knowing how to be a friend. Tonight, you were Jesus to him. You welcomed him even when it was hard—even when you wanted to hit him." He looked at me intensely and said, "I did want to hit him! But I didn't." He smiled proudly. I affirmed that it was clear that he let the Spirit help him stay calm and welcome our friend.

About a month later, I ran into Blake's mom at a party. She mentioned how much that conversation meant to Blake. Take note that I did not tell her about this. Blake told her. God gave me the courage that night to let Blake and Ryan experience the gift of faith community—messy and sometimes difficult—but absolutely holy.

As we help children extend hospitality to others who display disruptive and even disturbing behaviors, they look to us to know how to respond. The first and most important step is to become comfortable with these behaviors. I am not saying that we allow children to behave in any way they like. However, we must communicate to the child in crisis and to the other children that we are okay.

I will never forget a little girl, Tiffany, who spent a few months with us in our children's ministry. She was five years old and had been in five foster homes. Her life had been the stuff of horror stories, and she was wounded in body and spirit. At times, Tiffany's distress became so great that she would have extreme meltdowns, kicking and screaming with frightening intensity. We learned to monitor her level of distress and intervene before the meltdown, but one Sunday she became very upset with no warning. In the middle of a story, Tiffany lost it. An adult volunteer quickly helped her leave the room to calm down, but I could see that I had to talk to the other children about what they had just seen. "Boys and girls, sometimes our friend Tiffany needs to be angry. When she needs to be angry, it can be a little scary." With wide, startled eyes, the children confirmed, "Yes it is!" I smiled calmly and continued. "When she needs to be angry, you can just move away from her and a grownup will come and help her. If you can't move away, just call for a grownup and we will help you." They wondered, "Why does she need to be angry?" I explained that she had been hurt in many ways so she sometimes needed to let her anger out. I assured them that we would keep Tiffany safe and that we would keep them safe. The children relaxed and were able to welcome Tiffany back to class the following Sunday, taking their cue from me and the other adults in the room. Their calm response to Tiffany communicated, loud and clear, "We are okay."

The Church at Its Best

The church at its best is a place where "those who feel excluded in other parts of life can find a place of belonging . . . places where God's radical hospitality is extended to those who feel like they don't fit elsewhere."[21] This kind of hospitality is rare, even in our churches. Too often, children are excluded—in direct and sometimes indirect ways. We all know that being excluded is painful, causing wounds that "may take years to heal—and may never heal entirely."[22] We serve a Savior who had an obvious and often surprising preference for those the rest of the world rejected. He treated them with honor. Healed their wounds and called them friends. As we seek to follow him, we must extend the hospitality of the kingdom to all children. And in so doing, the Lord is present. May God grant us grace and wisdom as we answer the call to "let the little children come" (Matt. 19:14).

Contributor Biographies

Holly Catterton Allen [PhD—Talbot School of Theology]—Holly is a professor at Lipscomb University in Nashville, Tennessee, where she holds a dual professorship in the family life program of the College of Arts and Sciences and in the College of Bible and Ministry. She previously served as a professor of Biblical studies and the director of the Child and Family Studies program at John Brown University in Siloam Springs, Arkansas. She is co-author of *Intergenerational Christian Formation: Bringing the Whole Church Together in Ministry, Community and Worship* (2012) with Christine Ross.

Steven Bonner [DMin—Fuller Theological Seminary]—Steven is an associate professor teaching children's ministry and is the director of the Youth and Family Ministry program at Lubbock Christian University in Lubbock, Texas. He also preaches at the Tahoka Church of Christ.

Ron Bruner [DMin—Abilene Christian University]—Ron has served as the executive director of Westview Boys' Home in Hollis, Oklahoma, since 1999. He is president of the Christian Child and Family Services Association. He has practical and scholarly interests in at-risk youth, the theology of children, and intergenerational ministry. Ron worships with the Childress Church of Christ in Childress, Texas.

Jeff W. Childers [DPhil—Oxford University]—Jeff Childers is a professor in the Graduate School of Theology at Abilene Christian University. His research interests include: Oriental Christianity (especially the Syriac tradition), Church History, Biblical Text, Christian Spiritual Formation, and New Testament Textual Criticism. Jeff is active at the Highland Church of Christ in Abilene.

Samjung Kang-Hamilton [EdD—Columbia University]—Samjung is an adjunct professor in the Graduate School of Theology at Abilene Christian University, Abilene, Texas. She teaches courses in children's education and Christian education, and does research on the partnership between churches and families in the spiritual formation of children, youth, and adults. Samjung is active at the University Church of Christ in Abilene.

Ryan Maloney [MACM—Abilene Christian University]—Ryan serves as Children and Family Minister at Southern Hills Church of Christ in Abilene, Texas, and President-Elect of the Christian Education Association. Ryan is an adjunct instructor of children and family ministry at Abilene Christian University.

Suzetta Nutt—Suzetta serves as the Children's Minister at Highland Church of Christ in Abilene, Texas. She is also a Children's Ministry consultant and speaker.

Dana Kennamer Pemberton [PhD—University of Texas]—Dana is a professor and the department chair, Teacher Education, in the College of Education and Human Services, Abilene Christian University. She is a co-author of *Let All the Children Come to Me: A Practical Guide to Including Children with Disabilities in Your Church Ministries*, with MaLesa Breeding and Jerry Whitworth. (2006); and the author of *I Will Change Your Name: Messages from the Father to a Heart Broken by Divorce* (2009). She teaches children at the Highland Church of Christ in Abilene, Texas.

Nathan Pickard [DMin—Abilene Christian University]—Nathan is the preaching minister at the Newmarket Church of Christ in Newmarket, Ontario, Canada.

Shannon Rains [MS—Abilene Christian University]—Shannon has been the children and family minister at the Kingwood Church of Christ in Kingwood, Texas since 2005. Shannon is currently pursuing a Doctor of Ministry degree at Abilene Christian University.

For Further Reading

Baptism

Childers, Jeff W. "Moving to the Rhythms of Christian Life: Baptism for Children Raised in the Church," In *Like a Shepherd Lead Us: Guidance for the Gentle Art of Pastoring*, ed. David Fleer and Charles Siburt, 95–122, Abilene, TX: Leafwood, 2006.

Childers, Jeff W., and Frederick D. Aquino. *At the River's Edge: Meeting Jesus in Baptism*. Abilene, TX: ACU Press, 2004.

Ferguson, Everett. *Baptism in the Early Church: History, Theology, and Liturgy in the First Five Centuries*. Grand Rapids: Eerdmans, 2009.

Hicks, John Mark, and Greg Taylor. *Down in the River to Pray: Revisioning Baptism as God's Transforming Work*. Siloam Springs, Arkansas: Leafwood, 2004.

Hicks, John Mark. *Enter the Water, Come to the Table: Baptism and Lord's Supper in the Bible's Story of New Creation*. Abilene, TX: ACU Press, 2014.

Jeschke, Marlin. *Believers Baptism for Children of the Church*. Scottsdale, PA: Herald Press, 1983.

McNichol, Allan J. *Preparing for Baptism. Becoming Part of the Story of the People of God*. Austin: Christian Studies Press, 2001.

Children's Ministry

Beckwith, Ivy. *Postmodern Children's Ministry: Ministry to Children in the 21st Century*. El Cajon, CA: Youth Specialties, 2009.

Beckwith, Ivy. *Formational Children's Ministry: Shaping Children Using Story, Ritual, and Relationship*. Grand Rapids: Baker, 2010.

Breeding, MaLesa, Dana Kennamer Hood, and Jerry Whitworth. *Let All the Children Come to Me: A Practical Guide To Including Children with Disabilities in Your Church Ministries*. Colorado Springs: David C. Cook, 2006. Kindle edition.

Csinos, David and Ivy Beckwith. *Children's Ministry in the Way of Jesus*. Downers Grove, IL: InterVarsity Press, 2013.

Children's Spirituality

Coles, Robert. *The Spiritual Life of Children*. Boston: Houghton Mifflin Company, 1990.

Csinos, David M. *Children's Ministry That Fits: Beyond One-Size-Fits-All Approaches to Nurturing Children's Spirituality*. Eugene, OR: Wipf and Stock, 2011.

Nye, Rebecca. *Children's Spirituality: What It Is and Why It Matters*. London: Church House, 2009.

Intergenerational Ministry

Allen, Holly Catterton and Christine Lawton Ross. *Intergenerational Christian Formation: Bringing the Church Together for Ministry, Community and Worship*. Downers Grove, IL.: InterVarsity Academic, 2012.

Vanderwell, Howard, ed. *The Church of All Ages: Generations Worshiping Together*. Herndon, Va.: Alban Institute, 2008.

Westerhoff, John H., III. *Will Our Children Have Faith?* 3rd edition. Harrisburg, PA: Morehouse, 2012.

Spiritual Disciplines

Calhoun, Adele Ahlberg. *Spiritual Disciplines Handbook: Practices that Transform Us.* Downers Grove, IL: InterVarsity Press, 2009.

Foster, Richard J. *Celebration of Discipline*, rev. ed. San Francisco: Harper Collins, 1988.

MacBeth, Sybil. *Praying in Color: Kid's Edition.* Brewster, MA: Paraclete Press, 2009.

Tippens, Darryl. *Pilgrim Heart: The Way of Jesus in Everyday Life.* Abilene, TX: Leafwood, 2006.

Endnotes

Chapter 2

[1] This chapter is largely grounded in a paper I wrote in 2005. Scholars interested in more detail should consult that work. Ron Bruner, "Children and the Churches of Christ: A History of Children and the Kingdom," *Restoration Quarterly* 47,3 (2005): 143–160.

[2] Lester McAllister, *Thomas Campbell: Man of the Book* (St. Louis: Bethany Press, 1954), 98–99.

[3] Robert Richardson, *Memoirs of Alexander Campbell*, vol. 1 (Philadelphia: Lippincott, 1871; reprint ed. Indianapolis: Religious Book Service, n.d.), 345.

[4] The Campbells were married on March 12, 1811. Richardson, *Memoirs*, 363.

[5] Jane, named after Alexander's mother, arrived one day after the Campbell's first anniversary. Richardson, *Memoirs*, vol. 1, 391.

[6] Ibid., 391–405; McAllister, *Thomas Campbell*, 152–171; Douglas A. Foster, "Churches of Christ and Baptism: An Historical and Theological Overview," *Restoration Quarterly* 43,2 (2001): 79–94.

[7] Richardson, *Memoirs*, vol. 1, 395–398. Thomas and Jane Campbell, Alexander's parents; Dorothea Campbell, Alexander's sister; and James Hanen and his wife were also baptized that same day.

[8] Richardson, *Memoirs*, vol. 1, 400.

[9] Alexander Campbell, *Christian Baptism* (Bethany, VA: Alexander Campbell, 1853; reprint ed., Nashville: Gospel Advocate, 1951), 196.

[10] Ibid., 335.

[11] Royal Humbert, ed., *A Compend of Alexander Campbell's Theology, with Commentary in the Form of Critical and Historical Footnotes* (St. Louis: Bethany Press, 1961), 201.

[12] This move took place during the end of 1814; John A. Williams, *Life of Elder John Smith* (Cincinnati: R. W. Carroll, 1871), 99.

[13] Ibid., 100–103.

[14] Ibid., 105.

[15] Alexander Campbell, "To Amicus," *Christian Baptist* 3,12 (July 3, 1826): 244. Humbert notes that Campbell in some way paraphrases the Westminster Confession of 1647; Humbert, *Compend*, 81.

[16] Campbell, "Amicus," 244.

[17] Ibid.

[18] Williams, *Life of Elder John Smith*, 146–147.

[19] Alexander Campbell, *The Christian System* (Cincinnati: H. S. Bosworth, 1866; reprint ed., Nashville: Gospel Advocate, 1956), 15.

[20] Campbell, *Christian System*, 15. Edwin Groover finds "parallels" between Campbell's approach to original sin and Methodists contemporary with Campbell. Ralph Edwin Groover, *The Well Ordered Home: Alexander Campbell and the Family* (Joplin: College Press, 1988), 165.

[21] Italics by Campbell; Campbell, *Christian System*, 16.

[22] Margaret Bendroth, "Children of Adam, Children of God: Christian Nurture in Early Nineteenth-Century America," *Theology Today* 56 (2000): 496. Theologians recognize this as a tenet of Federal theology.

[23] Richardson, *Memoirs*, 80–83.

[24] Richard Hughes, *Reviving the Ancient Faith: The Story of Churches of Christ in America* (Grand Rapids: Eerdmans, 1996), 51. Richardson, *Memoirs*, 83–84.

[25] Walter Scott, *The Gospel Restored: A Discourse of the True Gospel of Jesus Christ, in Which the Facts, Principles, Duties, and Priviliges* [sic] *of Christianity Are Arranged, Defined, and Discussed, and the Gospel In Its Various Parts Shewn to Be Adapted to the Nature and Necessities of Man in His Present Condition.* (Cincinnati: O. H. Donogh, 1836; reprint ed., Kansas City, MO: Old Paths Book Club, 1949), vi.

[26] Hughes, *Reviving the Ancient Faith*, 52.

[27] J. W. McGarvey, "Religious Duties of Children," *Millennial Harbinger* (December 1864): 536–39.

[28] Ibid.

[29] Robert Milligan, *Scheme of Redemption* (St. Louis: Christian Board of Publication, 1868; reprint ed., Nashville: Gospel Advocate, 1975).

[30] M. Eugene Boring, *Disciples and the Bible: A History of Disciples Biblical Interpretation in North America* (St. Louis: Chalice, 1997), 397.

[31] T. W. Brents, *The Gospel Plan of Salvation*, 15th ed. (Cincinnati: Bosworth, Chase and Hall, 1874; reprint ed., Nashville: Gospel Advocate, 1966), 209–570.

[32] Brents, *The Gospel Plan of Salvation*, 393–394. Punctuation and italics are Brents.'

[33] Ibid., 425.

[34] Ibid., 448–449.

[35] Ibid., 189.

³⁶ Ibid., 478.

³⁷ For example, Everett Ferguson, *Baptism in the Early Church: History, Theology, and Liturgy in the First Five Centuries* (MI: Eerdmans, 2009), 377–379, 627–633. Everett Ferguson, "Inscriptions and the Origin of Infant Baptism," *Journal of Theological Studies* 30 (1979): 37–46; "Spiritual Circumcision in Early Christianity," *Scottish Journal of Theology* 41 (1988): 485–497; *Early Christians Speak* (Austin: Sweet Publishing, 1971), 53–64.

³⁸ Everett Ferguson, *The Church of Christ: A Biblical Ecclesiology for Today* (Grand Rapids: Eerdmans, 1996), 195–201.

³⁹ Ferguson, *Church of Christ*, 199.

⁴⁰ Jerry and Becky Gross, "The Age of Accountability," Audiotapes of lectures at the Abilene Christian University Bible Teachers Workshop (Abilene, TX: Abilene Christian University Tape Service, 1986): cassette tape 118, side A. This work was funded with a grant from Sweet Publishing and the Christian Education Conference.

⁴¹ Tommy W. King, *Faith Decisions: Christian Initiation for Children of the Glenwood Church of Christ* (D. Min. thesis, Abilene Christian University, 1994), 4.

⁴² King makes multiple references to Jeschke's work. Marlin Jeschke, *Believers Baptism for Children of the Church* (Scottsdale: Herald, 1983).

⁴³ King, *Faith Decisions*, 22.

⁴⁴ King, *Faith Decisions*, 6. This is in agreement with Jeschke's position; see *Believers Baptism*, 122.

Chapter 3

¹ David Csinos and Ivy Beckwith, *Children's Ministry in the Way of Jesus* (Downers Grove, IL: InterVarsity Press, 2013), 41.

² All Scripture quotations in this chapter are taken from the NET Bible.

³ Certainly more can be said about the *imago Dei*; however, my purpose is to draw the reader to the conclusion that children, too, are created in the image of God. As such, they have inherent value in and of themselves.

⁴ Dallas Willard, *The Divine Conspiracy* (San Francisco: Harper, 1998), 79.

⁵ Catherine Stonehouse, *Joining Children on the Spiritual Journey* (Grand Rapids: Baker Academic, 1998), 137.

⁶ David Csinos, *Children's Ministry that Fits: Beyond One-Size-Fits-All Approaches to Nurturing Children's Spirituality* (Eugene, OR: Wipf & Stock, 2011), 12.

⁷ Ibid., 11.

⁸ Scottie May, Beth Posterski, Catherine Stonehouse, and Linda Cannell, *Children Matter* (Grand Rapids: Eerdmans, 2005), 3.

⁹ Csinos and Beckwith, *Children's Ministry in the Way of Jesus*, 38.

¹⁰ Ibid., 57.

¹¹ Ibid., 58.

[12] Stonehouse, *Joining Children on the Spiritual Journey*, 35.

[13] Karen Crozier, "Reimagining the Spirit of Children: A Christian Pedagogical Vision," in *Nurturing Children's Spirituality*, ed. Holly Allen (Eugene, OR: Cascade Books, 2008), 350.

[14] See Mark 9:33–42 and Luke 9:46–48. I limit my scriptural study to the teachings of Jesus as they demonstrate most clearly the created intent of the kingdom of God.

[15] See Matthew 18:6, cf. Mark 9:42, Luke 17:1–2.

[16] In the Markan passage, *little ones* also refer to the marginalized, the vulnerable, and powerless, which includes adults but does not preclude children.

[17] See Matthew 19:3–5 and Luke 18:15–17.

[18] Scottie May, Beth Posterski, Catherine Stonehouse, and Linda Cannell, *Children Matter* (Grand Rapids: Eerdmans, 2005), 41.

[19] Certainly this assertion is true of the royal official from Capernaum in John 4 who, along with his entire household, believed in Jesus.

[20] Catherine Stonehouse and Scottie May, *Listening to Children on the Spiritual Journey* (Grand Rapids: Baker Academic, 2010), 14.

[21] May et al., *Children Matter*, 42.

[22] Jeff Childers, "Moving to the Rhythms of a Christian Life: Baptism for Children Raised in the Church," in *Like a Shepherd Lead Us: Guidance for the Gentle Art of Pastoring*, eds. David Fleer and Charles Siburt (Abilene: Leafwood, 2006), 110.

[23] *See* 1 Corinthians 7:14.

[24] John Mark Hicks, *Enter the Water, Come to the Table* (Abilene: ACU Press, 2014), 130.

[25] Stonehouse, *Joining Children on the Spiritual Journey*, 128.

[26] Robert Keeley, *Helping Our Children Grow in Faith* (Grand Rapids: Baker Books, 2008), 29.

[27] My conceptual thinking is informed by Urie Bronfenbrenner, *The Ecology of Human Development* (Cambridge: Harvard University Press, 1979).

[28] For her treatment of the importance of story, ritual, and relationships, see Ivy Beckwith, *Formational Children's Ministry* (Grand Rapids: Baker Books, 2010).

[29] Donald and Brenda Ratcliff, *Child Faith* (Eugene, OR: Cascade, 2010), 13.

[30] I would direct the reader to an important new book recently written by Vern Bengston, Norella Putney, and Susan Harris, *Families and Faith* (New York: Oxford University Press, 2013). In this book, the authors lay out the impressive results of 35+ year longitudinal multi-generational study of families and faith. This book confirms "When children perceive their relationships with parents as close, affirming, and accepting they are more likely to identify with their parents' religious practices and beliefs, while relationships marked by coldness, ambivalence, or preoccupation are likely to result in religious differences." 98.

[31] Csinos and Beckwith, *Children's Ministry in the Way of Jesus*, 60.

³²Ibid., 36.

³³Scottie May et al., *Children Matter*, 141.

³⁴John Westerhoff III, "The Church's Contemporary Challenge: Assisting Adults to Mature Spiritually with Their Children," in *Nurturing Children's Spirituality*, ed. Holly Allen (Eugene, OR: Cascade Books, 2008), 360.

³⁵Insight on the role of the pedagogue in the ancient world is informed by Michael Smith, "The Role of the Pedagogue in Galatians," *Bibliotheca Sacra* 163 (April-June 2006): 198.

Chapter 4

¹Bonnie J. Miller-McLemore, *In the Midst of Chaos: Caring for Children as Spiritual Practice* (San Francisco: John Wiley and Sons, 2007), 34–35.

²Adora Svitak, "What Adults Can Learn from Kids," TED Talk, February 2010, accessed at: http://www.ted.com/talks/adora_svitak on June 12, 2014.

³This literary construction of naming the end points and meaning the entirety is called a merism. Jeffrey H. Tigay, *Deuteronomy*, JPS Torah Commentary (Philadelphia: Jewish Publication Society, 1996), 78. See also: Prov. 6:21–22.

⁴Miller-McLemore, *In the Midst of Chaos*, 39–57.

⁵John H. Westerhoff, III, *Will Our Children Have Faith?* 3ʳᵈ rev. ed. (Harrisburg, PA: Morehouse, 2012), 81–88. The subsequent research of Boyatzis and Janicki confirms the co-developmental nature of faith. They characterize communication about faith as "bi-directional reciprocity in which children and parents are mutually active in their religious communication and both behave in ways that may ultimately influence the other." Thus, the new life changes the ecology by its very existence. Chris J., Boyatzis and Denise L. Janicki, "Parent-Child Communication about Religion: Survey and Diary Data on Unilateral Transmission and Bi-directional Reciprocity styles," *Review of Religious Research* 44,3 (2003): 252–270; 254. Westerhoff's assertion of learning through experiences is consistent with the assertion by Christian educators that much of faith transmission comes from informal (socialization in families, for example) and nonformal (retreats and church camp) experiences instead of formal, classroom instruction. James R. Estep, Jr., Michael J. Anthony, and Gregg R. Allison, *A Theology for Christian Education* (Nashville: B & H Publishing, 2008), 16–17.

⁶Rebecca Nye, *Children's Spirituality: What It Is and Why It Matters* (London: Church House, 2009), 6.

⁷Howard's definition reads: "Christian spiritual formation refers to the intentional and semi-intentional processes by which believers (individuals and communities) become more fully conformed and united to Christ, especially with regard to maturity of life and calling." My modification of it is more consistent with Howard's subsequent explanation of these terms elsewhere in his work. Evan B. Howard, *The Brazos Introduction to Christian Spirituality* (Grand Rapids: Brazos Press, 2008), 268.

⁸For a more complete explanation of the "image of God", see: Nonna Verna Harrison, *God's Many-Splendored Image: Theological Anthropology for Christian Formation* (Grand Rapids: Baker Academic, 2010).

[9] Social scientists have long measured the religiosity and spirituality of individuals by what they believe, how they behave, and the communities to which they belong; I have added a fourth category: becoming. See, for example, *Measures of Religiosity*, eds. Peter C. Hill and Ralph W. Hood, Jr. (Birmingham, AL: Religious Education Press, 1999). Believe, behave, belong are also terms that theologians use to discuss the entry of individuals into a community of faith. Interestingly, the communally expected order of actions described by these verbs has changed over time. Alan Kreider, *The Change of Conversion and the Origin of Christianity* (Eugene, OR: Wipf & Stock, 1999).

[10] This is a place where well-trained and insightful ministers can be of particular help to families, not by answering the questions of children for parents, but by assisting parents in finding resources to pursue their own answers to tough questions.

[11] Specifically, this is the *searching* faith to which John Westerhoff refers. Westerhoff, 96–97.

[12] Gordon Allport, *Becoming: Basic Considerations for a Psychology of Personality* (New Haven: Yale University Press, 1955), 68–74.

[13] Jean Piaget, *The Moral Judgment of the Child*, M. Gobain, trans. (New York: Free Press, 1997), 374–386.

[14] Thomas Lickona, *Raising Good Children* (New York: Bantam Books, 1983), 336–337.

[15] This concept is developed more fully in: Ron Bruner, "Through Thick and Thin: Common Ground for Ethical Conversations with At-Risk Youth," *Journal of Youth Ministry*, 12 1 (Fall 2013): 69–85.

[16] Gary Chapman and Jennifer Thomas, *The Five Languages of Apology: How to Experience Healing in All Your Relationships* (Chicago: Northfield Publishing, 2006).

[17] Robert C. Roberts, *Spiritual Emotions: A Psychology of Christian Virtues* (Grand Rapids: Eerdmans, 2007). Jerome Bruner finds that even infants act according to these concerns: "[W]e come initially equipped, if not with a 'theory' of mind, then surely with a set of predispositions to construe the social world in a particular way and to act upon our construals." Bruner, *Acts of Meaning* (Cambridge: Harvard University Press, 1990), 73.

[18] Kendra G. Hotz and Matthew T. Mathews, *Shaping the Christian Life: Worship and the Religious Affections* (Louisville: Westminster John Knox, 2006): 3–58.

[19] Jeff Childers, "Moving to the Rhythms of a Christian Life: Baptism for Children Raised in the Church," in *Like a Shepherd Lead Us: Guidance for the Gentle Art of Pastoring*, eds. David Fleer and Charles Siburt (Abilene, TX: Leafwood, 2006), 95–122.

[20] David Csinos, *Children's Ministry that Fits: Beyond One-Size-Fits-All Approaches to Nurturing Children's Spirituality* (Eugene: Wipf and Stock, 2011). His work is rooted in: Urban T. Holmes, III, *A History of Christian Spirituality: An Analytical Introduction* (New York: Seabury, 1980). Corinne Ware, *Discover Your Spiritual Type: A Guide to Individual and Congregational Growth* (Herndon, VA: Alban, 1995).

[21] This effect was observed by one of the first voices for children's spirituality, Horace Bushnell. See Horace Bushnell, *Christian Nurture*, 5th printing (New Haven: Yale University Press, 1967), 39–40.

[22] James Fowler and M. Scott Peck have worked with childhood developmental models to explain spiritual development. James Fowler, *Stages of Faith: The Psychology of*

Human Development and the Quest for Meaning, (San Francisco: Harper, 1981), 122–213. M. Scott Peck, *The Different Drum: Community Making and Peace* (New York: Simon and Schuster, 1987), 184–200. These "age and stage" models have largely failed because of their assumptions: we all start in the same place, we go through the same stages, we do so in the same order, and we never move backward. None of these ideas universally hold true. Individuality of spirituality is one of the reasons that spiritual development models fall short of reality. These models also don't take into account environment and co-developers within that environment (parents, for example).

Michael Carotta's model of spirituality doesn't assume that all humans take the same path; he suggests that we mature in three dimensions at differing rates. Those three dimensions are: spiritual faith (a combination of belief, trust, and action), moral living, and emotional intelligence. His model is more flexible, seems to better agree with our conversation in previous pages, and yet has poor predictive power. Michael Carotta, *Sometimes We Dance, Sometimes We Wrestle* (Dubuque: Harcourt Religion, 2002), 21–29.

[23] Westerhoff, 89–98.

[24] Ibid., 92.

[25] Ibid., 94.

[26] Ibid., 96–97.

[27] Ibid., 97–98.

[28] For helpful books describing individual and group spiritual disciplines, see: Richard J. Foster, *Celebration of Discipline*, rev. ed. (San Francisco: Harpers 1988); Adele Ahlberg Calhoun, *Spiritual Disciplines Handbook: Practices That Transform Us* (Downers Grove, IL: InterVarsity Press, 2009); Darryl Tippens, *Pilgrim Heart: The Way of Jesus in Everyday Life* (Abilene: Leafwood, 2006).

[29] I use the term *transformation* here, and this is consistent with the historic language for "spiritual formation" in the Stone-Campbell Movement (SCM). The broader theological term describing what I mean here, though, is *theosis*. Theosis is both becoming like God in imitating God's behavior, and in a participation with God in this life. For a description of this in historic SCM literature, see: Ron Bruner, "'A Being of Wondrous Beauty': Spiritual Formation and Theosis in the Work of J. H. Garrison," *Stone-Campbell Journal* 15,1 (Spring 2012): 3–14. For a description of theosis, see: Norman Russell, *The Doctrine of Deification in the Greek Patristic Tradition* (Oxford: Oxford University Press, 2004), 1–3.

[30] Although some rightly respond that Christians ought to seek simplicity in their lives, this advice can be somewhat naïve considering the diversity of interests experienced with parenting multiple children.

[31] Maria Lief Crabtree, "'Forbid Not the Little Ones': The Spirituality of Children in Celtic Christian Tradition," in *Nurturing Children's Spirituality: Christian Perspectives and Best Practices*, ed. Holly Catterton Allen, (Eugene: Wipf and Stock, 2008), 78–92.

[32] Joyce Denham, *A Child's Book of Celtic Prayers* (Chicago: Loyola, 1998), 2.

[33] Elaine Heath, "Disciple and Leader Formation for a Missional Church," (DMin class lectures, Abilene Christian University, Dallas, TX, June 2014).

[34] Ron Bruner and Dudley Chancey, "'Insightful and Surprising' Ideas Offered by Teens in National Survey," *Christian Chronicle* (March 2013), 13.

Chapter 5

[1] Dorothy Jean Furnish, *Living the Bible with Children* (Nashville: Abingdon, 1979), 23.

[2] J. J. Dillon, "The Spiritual Child: Appreciating Children's Transformative Effects on Adults," *Encounter* 13 (2000): 4.

[3] From Kathy Coffey, *Baptism and Beyond: Preparing for Baptism and Nurturing Your Child's Spirituality* (Harrisburg, PA: Morehouse Publishing, 2000), 115.

[4] Numerous websites, often varying in detail, cite reading level statistics of Bible translations. The numbers above give rough approximations.

[5] On Campbell's overall approach to children in ministry, see Samjung Kang-Hamilton, "The Bible and the Education of Children: Lessons from Alexander Campbell," *Restoration Quarterly* 52,3 (2010): 129–43.

[6] Walter Brueggemann, *Belonging and Growing in the Christian Community* (Atlanta: General Assembly Mission Board, 1979), 32. For a commentary on Brueggemann's insights, see Karen Marie Yust, *Real Kids, Real Faith: Practices for Nurturing Children's Spiritual Lives* (San Francisco: Jossey-Bass, 2004), 43.

[7] Diana Butler Bass, *Christianity for the Rest of Us* (New York: Harper Collins, 2006), 82.

Chapter 6

[1] Robert Coles, *The Story of Ruby Bridges,* Illustrated by George Ford (New York: Scholastic, 1995), 22.

[2] See http://www.pewresearch.org/fact-tank/2014/05/01/5-facts-about-prayer/. Accessed 20 May 2014.

[3] Dietrich Bonhoeffer, "Thy Kingdom Come! The Prayer of the Church-Community for God's Kingdom on Earth," in *The Bonhoeffer Reader*, eds. Clifford J. Green and Michael P. DeJonge (Minneapolis: Fortress, 2013), 346.

[4] Phyllis Tickle, *This Is What I Pray Today: The Divine Hours Prayer for Children*, Illustrated by Elsa Warnick (New York: Dutton Children's Books, 2007), 1.

[5] Mother Teresa, *In the Heart of the World* (Novato, Cal.: New World Library, 1997), 18–19.

[6] Adela Ahlberg Calhoun, *Spiritual Disciplines Handbook: Practices that Transform Us* (Downers Grove, IL: InterVarsity Press, 2005), 227–30.

Chapter 7

[1] Mary Pipher, "The New Generation Gap," *USA Weekend*, March 19–21, 1999, 12.

[2] Donald A. McGavran, *Understanding Church Growth* (Grand Rapids: Eerdmans, 1970).

[3] For example, Donald A. McGavran, with Win C. Arn, *How to Grow a Church* (Glendale, CA: Regal, 1973); Kennon Callahan, *Twelve Keys to an Effective Church* (New York: Harper & Row, 1983); George Barna, *Marketing the Church* (Colorado Springs: NavPress, 1988).

[4] I am not denouncing all age- or stage-defined small group gatherings; indeed they can be spiritually enriching and powerful life journey tools. However, perennially forming small groups around ages or stages promotes generational silos.

[5] William Dinges, "Faith, Hope, and (Excessive) Individualism," in *Handing on the Faith: The Church's Mission and Challenge*, ed. Robert P. Imbelli (New York: Crossroad Publishing Company, 2006), 36.

[6] For example, Carter and McGoldrick's life stages are: leaving home, the new couple, families with young children, families with adolescents, launching children, and families in later life. Elizabeth A. Carter and Monica McGoldrick, *The Changing Family Life Cycle: A Framework for Family Therapy* (New York: Allyn & Bacon, 1989), 15. Life stages are sometimes called the family career or life phases. Because of the diverse forms of families, the typical life stages don't fit the majority of families now, but churches still often form classes or ministry opportunities around these typical stages.

[7] Darwin Glassford, "Fostering an Intergenerational Culture," in *The Church of All Ages: Generations Worshiping Together*, ed. Howard Vanderwell (Herndon, VA: Alban Institute, 2008).

[8] Reggie Joiner, Chuck Bomar, and Abbie Smith, *The Slow Fade* (Colorado Springs: David C. Cook, 2010), 41.

[9] Helen Lee, "Age-Old Divide: How Do You Integrate the Generations and Life Stages at your Church? Five Church Leaders Respond," *Leadership* 27 (Autumn 2006): 43–44, 46.

[10] Chad Hall, "All in the Family Is Now Grey's Anatomy: Today's Segregation Is by Age," *Leadership* 27 (Autumn 2006): 33.

[11] Ibid., 33.

[12] Ibid., 33.

[13] Lance Armstrong, *Children in Worship: The Road to Faith* (Melbourne, AUS: Joint Board of Christian Education, 1988), 15.

[14] Ibid., 18.

[15] Jason Lanker, "The Relationship between Natural Mentoring and Spirituality in Christian Adolescents," *Journal of Youth Ministry* 9,1 (Fall 2010): 93–109; Jason Lanker, "The Family of Faith: The Place of Natural Mentoring in the Church's Christian Formation of Adolescents," *Christian Education Journal* (NS 3) 7 (Fall 2010): 267–280. Jean Rhodes, *Stand by Me: The Risks and Rewards of Mentoring Today's Youth* (Cambridge, MA: Harvard University Press, 2004); John E. Harrison, *Forming Connections: A Study of Adolescent Faith Development as Perceived by Adult Christians* (Doctoral dissertation, Princeton Theological Seminary, *Dissertation Abstracts International, 60,* 07A, 1999).

[16] Kara Powell conducted interviews and surveys among 500 graduating seniors as they moved through their first year after high school graduation. She has reported her

findings in, among other publications: "Is the Era of Age Segregation Over?" *Leadership* 30,3 (Summer 2009): 43–47; and Kara Powell, Brad M. Griffin, and Cheryl A. Crawford, *Sticky Faith: Youth Worker Edition: Practical Ideas to Nurture Long-Term Faith in Teenagers* (Grand Rapids: Zondervan, 2011).

[17] Powell et al., *Sticky Faith*, 2011, 75.

[18] Ibid.

[19] David Kinnaman, *You Lost Me: Why Young Christian Are Leaving the Church . . . and Rethinking Faith*, With Aly Hawkins (Grand Rapids: BakerBooks, 2011).

[20] Christian Smith with Patricia Snell, *Souls in Transition: The Religious and Spiritual Lives of Emerging Adults* (Oxford: Oxford University Press, 2009), 286.

[21] Ibid., 285, emphasis mine.

[22] Eddie Prest, *From One Generation to Another* (Capetown, South Africa: Training for Leadership, 1993), 20.

[23] For a fuller description of intergenerational small groups, see Holly C. Allen and Christine L. Ross, *Intergenerational Christian Formation: Bringing the Church Together for Ministry, Community and Worship* (Downers Grove, IL: InterVarsity Press, 2012). The book also offers chapters that describe intergenerational learning, intergenerational service and missions, intergenerational story-sharing, and intergenerational issues that face multicultural faith communities and megachurches.

[24] James Frazier, "All Generations of Saints at Worship," in *Across the Generations: Incorporating All Ages in Ministry: The Why and How*, eds. Vicky Goplin, Jeffrey Nelson, Mark Gardner, and Eileen Zahn (Minneapolis: Augsburg, 2001), 58.

Chapter 8

[1] Alexander Campbell, *The Christian System* (Nashville: Gospel Advocate Company), 291–94.

[2] See Richard T. Hughes, *Reviving the Ancient Faith* (Grand Rapids: Eerdmans, 1996), 21–46.

[3] See Darrell Guder, *The Continuing Conversion of the Church* (Grand Rapids: Eerdmans, 2000), 120–41.

[4] Hughes, 30–31. See also: Nathan Pickard, *Engaging Scripture through Dwelling in the Word at the Newmarket Church of Christ* (DMin Thesis, Abilene Christian University, May 2011).

[5] Douglas John Hall, *The Cross in Our Context* (Minneapolis: Fortress, 2003), 130.

[6] Joel B. Green, "The (Re-)Turn to Narrative," in *Narrative Reading, Narrative Preaching*, eds. Joel B. Green and Michael Pasquarello III (Grand Rapids: Baker Academic, 2003), 17; David M. Csinos, *Children's Ministry That Fits* (Eugene, OR: Wipf & Stock, 2011), 108–20.

[7] See James K. Smith, *Desiring the Kingdom* (Grand Rapids: Baker Academic, 2009).

[8] See Patrick Miller, "That the Children May Know: Children in Deuteronomy," in *The Child in the Bible*, eds. Marcia Bunge, Terence E. Fretheim and Beverly Roberts Gaventa (Grand Rapids: Eerdmans, 2008), 45–62.

⁹Walter Brueggemann, *Deuteronomy* (Nashville: Abingdon, 2001), 173.

¹⁰One can also read Deuteronomy 26 and the offering of firstfruits and tithes. While making the offering, the people of God recite the story of God's redemptive activity.

¹¹Bruggemann, *Deuteronomy,* 173.

¹²Jürgen Moltmann, *The Church in the Power of the Spirit* (Minneapolis: Fortress, 1993), 242–60.

¹³Nora Gallagher, *The Sacred Meal* (Nashville: Thomas Nelson, 2009), 38. For a theology rooting the Lord's Supper in the Messianic banquet, see Jürgen Moltmann, *The Church in the Power of the Spirit* (Minneapolis: Fortress, 1993), 243–50.

Chapter 11

¹O.M. Bakke, *When Children Became People: The Birth of Childhood in Early Christianity* (Minneapolis: Augsburg Fortress Press, 2005), 260.

²David H. Jensen, *Graced Vulnerability: A Theology of Childhood* (Cleveland: The Pilgrim Press, 2005), 120.

³Catherine Stonehouse, *Joining Children on the Spiritual Journey: Nurturing a Life of Faith* (Grand Rapids: Baker Academic, 1998), 88.

⁴Ibid., 87.

⁵David Hay, *The Spirit of the Child,* With Rebecca Nye, rev. ed. (London: Jessica Kingsley, 2006), 148.

⁶James W. Fowler, Karl Ernst Nipkow, and Friedrich Schweitzer, *Stages of Faith and Religious Development: Implications for Church, Education and Society.* (New York: Crossroad, 1991), 23.

⁷Sofia Cavaletti, *The Religious Potential of the Child: 6-12 Years Old* (Chicago: Catechesis of the Good Shepherd Publications, 2002), 9.

⁸Robert Coles, *The Spiritual Life of Children* (Boston: Houghton Mifflin Company, 1990), 322, 350.

⁹Robert Coles, *The Moral Intelligence of Children* (New York: Random House, 1997), 177.

¹⁰Hay, *The Spirit of the Child,* 109.

¹¹Ibid., 116.

¹²Robert Coles, *The Story of Ruby Bridges,* Illustrated by George Ford (New York: Scholastic, 1995).

¹³Jensen, *Graced Vulnerability,* 107.

¹⁴Ibid., 113.

¹⁵Donald and Brenda Ratcliff, *Child Faith: Experiencing God and Spiritual Growth with Your Children* (Eugene, OR: Cascade Books, 2010), 81.

¹⁶Ibid.

¹⁷John H. Westerhoff, III, *Will Our Children Have Faith?* 3ʳᵈ rev. ed. (Harrisburg, PA: Morehouse Publishing, 2012), 90–91.

[18] Joyce Ann Mercer, Deborah L. Matthews and Scott Walz, "Children in Congregations: Congregations as Contexts for Children's Spiritual Growth," in Donald Ratcliff, ed., *Children's Spirituality: Christian Perspectives, Research and Applications* (Eugene, OR: Cascade Books, 2004), 262–263.

Chapter 12

[1] Ivy Beckwith, *Formational Children's Ministry: Shaping Children Using Story, Ritual, and Relationship* (Grand Rapids, MI: Baker Books, 2010), 13.

[2] Joyce Mercer, *Welcoming Children: A Practical Theology of Childhood* (St. Louis, MO: Chalice Press, 2005), 34.

[3] Scottie May, "The Contemplative-Reflective Model," in *Perspectives on Children's Spiritual Formation: Four Views,* ed., M. J. Anthony (Nashville: Broadman & Holman Publishers, 2006), 209.

[4] Ibid., 252.

[5] Ivy Beckwith, *Postmodern Children's Ministry: Ministry to Children in the 21st Century* (Grand Rapids: Zondervan, 2004), 10.

[6] Mercer, *Welcoming Children*, 91.

[7] Jean Piaget, *The Child and Reality* (New York: Grossman Publishers, 1974); J. W. Fowler, *Stages of Faith: The Psychology of Human Development and the Quest for Meaning* (New York: Harper & Row, 1981).

[8] K. Tamminen, R. Vianello, J. Jaspard, & D. Ratcliff, "The Religious Concepts of Preschoolers," in *Handbook of Preschool Religious Education,* ed., Donald Ratcliff (Birmingham: Religious Education Press, 1988).

[9] Beckwith, *Postmodern Children's Ministry*, 126.

[10] Eugene Peterson, *Eat This Book: A Conversation in the Art of Spiritual Reading* (Grand Rapids, MI: Eerdmans, 2006), 44, emphasis mine.

[11] Mercer, *Welcoming Children*, 149.

[12] Peterson, *Eat This Book*, 42.

[13] David Csinos and Ivy Beckwith, *Children's Ministry in the Way of Jesus* (Downers Grove, IL: InterVarsity Press, 2013) 107.

Chapter 13

[1] Richard J. Foster, *Prayers from the Heart* (New York: Harper Collins, 1994), xiii.

[2] Rebecca Nye, *Children's Spirituality: What It Is and Why It Matters* (Norwich: Church House Publishing, 2009), 5.

[3] Sonja M. Stewart and Jerome W. Berryman, *Young Children and Worship* (Louisville: Westminster John Knox Press, 1989), 13.

[4] Ibid., 13–14.

[5] Nye, 42.

⁶Jean Vanier, "The Fragility of L'Arche and the Friendship of God," in *Living Gently in a Violent World: The Prophetic Witness of Weakness,* eds. Stanley Hauerwaus and Jean Vanier (Downers Grove, IL: InterVarsity Press, 2008), 22–23.

⁷Nye, 34.

⁸Ibid., 45.

⁹Sybil MacBeth, *Praying in Color, Drawing a New Path to God* (Brewster, MA: Paraclete Press, 2007), 5.

¹⁰Adele Ahlberg Calhoun, *Spiritual Disciplines Handbook, Practices That Transform Us* (Downers Grove, IL: InterVarsity Press, 2005), 91.

¹¹Sofia Cavalletti, *The Religious Potential of the Child* (Chicago: Liturgy Training Publications, 1992), 44.

Chapter 14

¹David Csinos and Ivy Beckwith, *Children's Ministry in the Way of Jesus* (Downers Grove, IL: InterVarsity Press, 2013), 169.

²Ibid.

³Joseph A. Fitzmyer, *Romans* (New York: Doubleday, 1993), 505.

⁴Ibid.

⁵Peter Kreeft, *Making Sense Out Of Suffering* (Ann Arbor, MI: Servant Books, 1986), 10.

⁶Fitzmyer, 514–515.

⁷Catherine Stonehouse and Scottie May, *Listening to Children on the Spiritual Journey* (Grand Rapids: Baker Academic, 2010), 112.

⁸Holly Allen and Christine Ross, *Intergenerational Christian Formation* (Downers Grove, IL: InterVarsity Press, 2012), 229.

⁹Jane Carr, "Equipping Children for Ministry," in *Nurturing Children's Spirituality,* ed. Holly Allen (Eugene, OR: Cascade Books, 2008), 206.

¹⁰Karen Marie Yust, *Real Kids, Real Faith* (San Francisco, CA: Jossey-Bass, 2004), 122.

¹¹Ibid, 144.

¹²Ibid, 145.

¹³Ibid., 145.

¹⁴Ibid.

Chapter 15

¹Bonnie J. Miller-McLemore, *Let the Children Come: Reimagining Childhood from a Christian Perspective* (San Francisco: Jossey Bass,2003), 22.

²Ibid., 7.

³Ann Higonnet, *Pictures of Innocence: The History and Crisis of Ideal Childhood* (New York: Thames and Hudson, 1998), 224.

4 Joyce Ann Mercer, *Welcoming Children: A Practical Theology of Childhood* (St. Louis: Chalice Press, 2005), 127.

5 Miller-McLemore, xii.

6 Ibid., xiii.

7 Mercer, 120.

8 Ibid., 63.

9 Walter Brueggemann, "Vulnerable Children, Divine Passion, and Human Obligation," in *The Child in the Bible,* ed. Marcia J. Bunge (Grand Rapids: Eerdmans, 2008), 419.

10 John T. Carroll, "'What Then Will This Child Become?' Perspectives on Children in the Gospel of Luke," in *The Child in the Bible,* ed. Marcia J. Bunge (Grand Rapids: Eerdmans, 2008), 177.

11 Thomas E. Reynolds, *Vulnerable Communion: A Theology of Disability and Hospitality* (Grand Rapids: Brazos Press, 2008), 14.

12 Ibid., 20.

13 Ibid., 60.

14 David M. Csinos and Ivy Beckwith, *Children's Ministry in the Way of Jesus* (Downers Grove, IL: InterVarsity Press, 2013), 127.

15 Mercer, 73.

16 Reynolds, 20.

17 Lesa Breeding and Dana Hood, "Voices Unheard: Exploring the Spiritual Needs of Families of Children with Disabilities," *Childhood Education Journal* 4,2 (2008): 279–292.

18 Ibid., 290.

19 Csinos and Beckwith, 135.

20 MaLesa Breeding, Dana Kennamer Hood, and Jerry Whitworth, *Let All the Children Come to Me: A Practical Guide To Including Children with Disabilities in Your Church Ministries* (Colorado Springs: David C. Cook, 2006). Kindle edition.

21 Csinos and Beckwith, 139.

22 Ibid., 127.